"*The River Road* is an evocative nov... the start of the original running boom. Set in 1972, Dan... would go on to become a top U.S. running coach, weaves together hints of his own running journey with the American running success of that summer and a bit of the social change happening in the world at the time. A classic coming-of-age story, it's a compelling read that will appeal to longtime runners, fans of the sport and anyone who appreciates how running can change a life forever."

- *Competitor Magazine*

Dennis Barker's *The River Road* is one of the finest coming-of-age stories I have read. Lenny, a young distance runner, evolves from the uncertainty of adolescence into young adulthood before us. Evoking memories of a simpler time where hopes and dreams lived in anonymity, *The River Road* is both Cormac McCarthy and Jon Krakauer - beautifully descriptive with characters we all possess within us. Barker's novel should be on every nightstand."

- Pete Rea, ZAP Fitness

"You've read all the books about fictional Olympic heroes, high school four-minute milers, and marathoners who have succeeded against impossible odds. Now read something real - something more like your own running experience. Dennis Barker's *The River Road* explores - hill workout by long run by conference cross country meet - how running can add insight, character, growth and self-knowledge to a teenager's life."

- Amby Burfoot, *Runner's World* Editor-At-Large
& 1968 Boston Marathon Champion

"*The River Road* is not just a colorful and nostalgic tale of the sport in the 1960s and 70s, but more importantly, it is a clear and accurate portrayal of every runner's own realization of the value of the sport - development of self, self-confidence and personal growth through individual achievement. It defines why we love running and why we believe that running changes lives, regardless of the age one takes it up."

- Scott Simmons, Coach of the American Distance Project

# THE RIVER ROAD

## Dennis Barker

This book is dedicated to Minnesota Olympic distance runners past and future, and all those who have run on the River Road that winds between Minneapolis and St. Paul. While some names of places in St. Paul have been used, others have been invented, and the geography has been altered somewhat. However, descriptions of places along the river are an accurate representation of real places along both the Minneapolis and St. Paul shores. While I have used some names of past teammates and coaches, it is only to honor them. No character portrayed, nor event depicted, with the exception of the historical figures and events recounted, is real. They are an amalgam of the many runners, teammates, coaches and people I have come in contact with over many years in the wonderful sport of running.

Grateful acknowledgement is made to Frank Murphy for his wonderful book on Buddy Edelen, *A Cold Clear Day,* the late Ron Daws for his book *The Self-Made Olympian,* and to Van Nelson for his generous time.

# 1

# Death of an Old Friend

Len runs along the Mississippi River, the warm Indian Summer sun penetrating a thin layer of cloth down into his skin. The narrow, dirt path angles gently down the bluff into the river valley, beneath massive cottonwood and oak trees, around ash and box elder, the venous roots mapping the ancient bank. The air is musty with the smell of decaying leaves, dry grass and mud. He comes into a small clearing where the sun is bright and the sweet smell of overripe fruit rises as he passes a small, gnarled tree. The clearing commands an expansive view of the river. Pin pricks of glittering sunlight bounce across the brown water like jacks across a table. The surface is littered with the last refuse of autumn, the current clearing it away before winter's icy table is set upon the river.

Whenever Len felt the need for a respite or calming pause in his life, he came to run on this old, unkempt path. He couldn't quite put his finger on what he was feeling today, but it was closer to loneliness than sadness, to longing than grief. He had taken a couple of days off of work to arrange his old friend's funeral and settle his affairs, but after securing a funeral home to begin the arrangements, he put on his running clothes and drove through his old St. Paul neighborhood to the river.

He slowed the car as he passed the Corner Market a few blocks from the house where his parents still lived. It was a small grocery store that had once been owned by an effeminate old bachelor named Lawrence. It had been a friendly little hangout for the neighborhood kids when Len was growing up. The sign had read Lawrence's Market until Lawrence retired and the store was sold a few years after Len moved out of the house. Lawrence ran the place by himself and had no hires. He was open Monday through Saturday from nine to six and closed on Sundays. He could often be found standing behind a refrigerated display case cutting meat or cheese on a machine. Occasionally, when he thought no one was looking, he slipped a thin slice of whatever was on the machine into his mouth and chewed discreetly. He was soft and slightly overweight, and kind to every living thing. Len had seen him set out food scraps or milk for stray cats or dogs beneath the loading dock behind the store. He also gently chided older kids if he saw or heard them picking on someone smaller in the store, and they respected him enough to stop, at least in his presence. The market smelled of produce, meat, fish, cheese and the cardboard boxes he had broken up and stacked in the back once they had been emptied. His other station was behind the cash register near the front of the store, surrounded by candy and cigarettes of all sorts.

The only time Lawrence wasn't in the store for more than a day or so was once a year for one week during the Minnesota State Fair in late August. Lawrence's sister, Alice, who lived with him and who looked very much like him, took over the store so he could enter his flower arrangements at the fair. Her friend, Beryl, often helped out in the store during this week. Lawrence didn't sell flowers in the store but Len had heard him talking about his garden and the beautiful flowers it produced with different women who came into the store. Many of the women asked him questions about flowers and how to grow them and usually finished by saying they could never grow anything as beautiful as he did. Alice said everything he touched loved him back with all its beauty.

It was in front of Lawrence's Market in the summer of 1969 that Len began his paper route. He inherited the route from a neighbor kid who had moved away at the end of the school year. At twelve years old, Len's parents deemed him old enough, and he was looking forward to having his own money. The papers were dropped in front of the market every day at four in the afternoon and Len had them delivered by six. A St. Paul Dispatch truck rumbled up to the curb, its brakes squealing as it slowed, and jerked to a stop. The driver's door flew open and a rough-looking man jumped out of the truck, ran around to the back, opened two big double doors, grabbed a large bundle of papers and heaved the bundle onto the sidewalk. Then he slammed and latched the doors, ran around to the front, jumped back into the truck and gunned the engine. The truck leapt away from the curb and careened out of sight around the next corner, the whole episode taking mere seconds. Len took a small wire cutter out of his canvas bag, snipped the wires holding the bundle together, folded the papers into the bag and walked out into the neighborhood.

It was a pleasant job during the soft days of summer when it wasn't too hot. Len enjoyed walking leisurely through the neighborhood throwing the papers as he went. He was rarely in a hurry for anything at that age, so became a keen observer of life in the neighborhood during that time of day. People were arriving home from work, preparing dinner, settling in to watch the evening news. He finished the route a block away from his house, then walked in to the kitchen to the reassuring smell of whatever his mother was preparing for dinner that evening.

Len turned his car into the neighborhood a block past the Corner Market and drove under a canopy of large, bare elm and maple branches that stretched out over the street from both sides. Most of the leaves had been cleaned away but a few stray brown and yellow leaves still littered the streets or had blown back into the yards. It was a peaceful neighborhood of modest but well-kept two and three bedroom homes. He drove slowly past his old house. It seemed to have grown smaller and more decrepit along with his aging parents. Maybe it was because the maple trees that lined one border of the property had been allowed to grow unpruned in recent years and now dwarfed the house. The branches reached out over the top of the roof, blocking out the sunlight so that most of the grass on that side of the house had died. He looked up at the window of his old room and remembered breezy nights when the rustling of those maples had been his lullaby.

He continued to drive slowly along his old mile-long running route to the Mississippi River. He glanced at the sidewalk intermittently for the spots raised by the roots of large trees he had tripped on and the low spots where he had jumped puddles when it rained. The route was largely unchanged and the familiarity made his feeling of longing even stronger. At a stop sign, he remained still for a long moment, taking in a panorama of the intersection he had run through so often. It was not a busy intersection and no other cars were there now. He rolled the window down and breathed in the redolent fall air. An overwhelming feeling of nostalgia rushed in with the air, replacing the melancholy that had gripped him the last few days. It was only now that he noticed the anxiety that seemed to have collected in his shoulders as he slowly exhaled.

Some days as a high school runner, he had flown through this intersection, barely looking for cars, as he kicked in the last mile home. Other times, when he was more tired, he was thankful to have to stop and wait for a car to cross before finishing out the run. Most days this mile was his warm-up on the way out and sprint on the way back. The river had been like a loyal training companion and he rarely ran elsewhere except when he ran from school with the team. He drove through the intersection and on to the river.

He turned onto the River Road, parked and sat in the car for a minute looking down along the road's gently curving contours. He thought back to how it had looked when he had first run here. The old dirt path between the road and the river bluff was now paved. A few wooden benches and scenic overlooks, aimed out at the river, had also been installed along the path. There were bald eagles here now as well. It had taken many years for them to return to this part of the river after the DDT ban was enacted in 1972. But the essence of the River Road had remained the same. Old, gnarly oak trees with branches twisting out over the path were interspersed with juniper and sumac. Towering cottonwood, ash and box elder trees rose up from further down the bluff. Large homes, with well-tended yards, were set back from the road opposite the river. This is what the River

Road had always been for the Minnesotans who had run, raced and become Olympians here.

Len got out of the car, stepped up onto the curb and did a few light stretches before crossing over to the path and working his legs up into a jog. The November air was reminiscent and warm. Breathing it, running here again, seemed to disperse old, familiar feelings out from his lungs into his veins and throughout his entire body. After several minutes of running, he came to the smaller path down to the water, the one he called his path. It looked now like a thin, rocky gully eroding down from the pavement rather than a trail. He stepped down onto it, placing his feet carefully among the rocks and tree roots protruding from the dirt. The path disappeared into a cluster of low shrubs a few feet away, his legs brushing against the scratchy shrub ends as he went. As the path dropped slowly toward the river, the shrubs gave way to a more open path that was covered by a thick layer of fallen leaves. The path was hardly distinguishable from the rest of the leaf-covered forest floor. Farther down the bluff, where all traces of the city disappeared, the immutable souls of the river, land and forest that conjoined here and that he had always felt here, were more extant than ever. He came into a clearing, that he also called his, and stopped just past the weathered old crab apple tree, which had dropped its fruit another year. He breathed in deeply and looked out over the river. The air here always seemed fresher, more incipient, than the air at the top of the bluff. It was here, when he had been a runner for just a short time and was only beginning to identify himself as a runner, that his desire to run and knowledge of running were nurtured. A world of running lore that he never knew existed was opened to him and helped him begin to explore and realize his own ability to run.

# 2

# A Step Into Manhood

Len first began to run in the eighth grade on the junior high cross country team. He had been on the seventh grade football team the previous year but even before the season was over, he knew he would not play again. It was at the pre-seventh grade sports physical that he first began to have doubts about playing football. The physicals were given free at the junior high school the last two Saturday mornings of August to boys going out for sports in the coming year. Len asked his older brother Del to drive him to the junior high for the physical. Len knew that if he wasn't occupied, Del would jump at the chance to get out of the house and drive. Any time he and Del were alone in the car, Len felt they were doing something together, even though Del was often distracted looking for any of his friends that might be about. If he saw one, he pulled over to talk, most often without having anything real to talk about. Len didn't mind. He liked hearing some occasional detail of Del's life away from home that he had not previously known. Sometimes Del took Len into his confidence by saying, "Don't say anything to mom or dad about that," and Len never did.

Anyone looking at the two brothers would have picked Del for the athlete. He was from the taller, more slender side of the family. His lanky body moved deliberately with assurance. He had a large Adam's apple that moved smoothly under his skin like a muscle when he swallowed, and long, thin mantis-like fingers that appeared good for gripping. He had tried a few sports when he was younger and had displayed some talent, but his interests lay elsewhere. Len's genes were of a smaller, more blunt sort. At one time, he thought he would grow to look like Del, but approaching junior high, as those around him seemed to sometimes grow inches overnight, he remained small for his age and in his class.

Len had never had a physical or been to see a doctor and didn't know what happened at a physical. Del said it was no big deal.

"You just pee in a cup and turn your head and cough," he said.

Del could see that Len was confused by his description, so he added, "Just do what they tell you to do. But don't pee before you go because if you can't go, you'll have to sit there until you can."

Del pulled the brown Rambler station wagon up to Ramsey Junior High and said, "I'll be back in half-an-hour."

"Okay," said Len and got out. He looked at the huge, old brick building that he had only been in once. Some other boys were going in. He followed them and walked a short distance down a hallway suffused in a smell he had only smelled in schools. It was a stale blend of cleaning fluid, floor polish and paint, that had been trapped inside in the summer heat. A sign for the physicals with an arrow pointing down a poorly lit stairwell stood in the hall. He followed the others down the stairs and made his way to the locker room through winding cement hallways in the bowels of the ancient building. Walking into the locker room, he saw a ragged line of ungainly, angular boys in their white underwear and t-shirts waiting to enter, one by one, the PE office to receive their physical. Some were joking and poking those around them. Others watched in amusement, hoping to be included. Still others watched with dread, hoping not to be included. He saw clothes draped, scattered across wooden benches fixed to the floor in front of rows of half-sized lockers. He went to a bench, took off his clothes and went to the back of the line. It was cool in the dingy basement locker room and he began to shiver. His bladder was already uncomfortable. He received a few side-glances from other boys but no one took any more notice of him than that. There were groups of boys that knew each other. They were already talking about what positions they would play on the football team. Len didn't know anyone in the line. He lived on the outer fringe of the school zone so the kids in his neighborhood went to two different junior high schools. Most went to the other junior high. Others went to a Catholic school.

The line had been moving Len gradually closer to the office. Yet when the door opened, dispensing his predecessor and Mr. Moore, the PE teacher, stepped into the doorway and barked "Next!" Len's pulse spiked and he felt a slight wave of nausea as he forced his legs forward. He had become less nervous as he had seen others come out of the office after only a few minutes and smile at their friends. Some had come out grimacing, holding their sides in pain, only to have their friends crack up and then crack up themselves. Len walked into the office.

Mr Moore closed the door behind him. The doctor was sitting in a chair next to a desk and motioned Len over. Len walked to the desk and stopped in front of the doctor. The doctor brought a stethoscope up to Len's slender chest. He moved it to a couple more spots and told him to breathe deep. Then he said, "Drop your shorts." Len wasn't sure what he meant by this so he started pulling them down and would have taken them completely off if the doctor hadn't said, "That's good," when he got the top band below his genitals. A large finger immediately pushed up below Len's left side and the doctor told him to look to the side and cough. Len could hardly help but do it. Then the doctor did the same on Len's right side, and once again his cough came as a nearly involuntarily reaction to the probing finger.

Mr. Moore then handed Len a Dixie cup. The doctor pointed to a small bathroom attached to the office and said, "Go in there and get a sample." Len looked into the bathroom. There was a wastebasket overflowing with empty Dixie cups. He went into the bathroom and filled the Dixie cup close enough to the top that he had to walk slowly and carefully back into the office to avoid spilling. "Hold it still," the doctor said with some irritation as he dipped what looked like a small thermometer into the yellow fluid. He drew the strip out and looked at it like Len's mom looked at a thermometer when checking for fever, then said, "Pour it out." Len turned and walked it tremulously back into the bathroom, poured it out and dropped the

Dixie cup on the pile. By the time he got back into the office, the door was open and Mr. Moore was calling, "Next!" Len walked out, passing the next white-clad boy in the doorway. The line was the same as it had been when he arrived, with new kids coming in steadily. Len got dressed, went into the bathroom to finish peeing, then walked outside.

When Len came out of the junior high, the Rambler was sitting at the curb, with Del slumped in the driver's seat reading *Slaughterhouse-Five* by Kurt Vonnegut. Len got in. Del closed the book and dropped it on the seat between them but didn't say anything. He put his hands on the steering wheel but his face looked like he was finishing a thought he didn't want to lose. Len was okay not talking about the physical. In his observance, he knew that men didn't always have to talk about things that were understood by other men. It was part of their bond. The physical seemed to Len like a step into manhood that Del and others had taken before him, and now he had taken. It was something he and Del would share independent of their parents. Len felt close to Del in that moment. He looked at the book on the seat between them and asked, "Is that a good book?"

"Yeah, it's got some crazy stuff in it," said Del. "Vonnegut's cool." Len smiled as Del pulled away from the curb. When they got home, Len went to his room, looked at the green and gray plastic soldiers he had lined up in opposition to each other the night before, and felt bored.

# 3

# Intentional Running

The first week of football practice was called conditioning. But for the coaches it was more about identifying the best athletes and dividing the team into groups. At the end of the week, a list of player positions was tacked up next to the PE office door. Len was listed as a halfback. He was excited all weekend and envisioned himself slicing through the line, breaking tackles and winning an open field sprint to the end zone. At practice the following Monday, the team was separated into groups and taken to different parts of the field. As the practice wore on, Len realized the other groups were in formations and going through plays. His group was running through tires and doing calisthenics. It dawned on him, as he surveyed his group, that all of the smallest kids were in his group, but also bigger kids who lacked coordination. They were the scrubs. He had worked hard during the conditioning week and even though he was small, didn't understand why he had been placed in this group. Maybe he had just been overlooked. In his mind, he had the speed and maneuverability to be a halfback. He was determined to try to demonstrate these qualities during practice, certain that once the coaches noticed him, he would be brought up to a higher group, one that actually got to play football.

The day before the first game, during practice, there was a run-through of a kick off return. The scrubs were called in to be the defense. Len must not have heard the instructions clearly through his daydream of finally getting a chance to show, in front of the head coach, of what he was capable. The ball was kicked and it seemed as though he was the fastest player on the field. He threaded his way nimbly through the oncoming players toward the ball carrier and threw his weight at him with the force of a charging rhino. He brought the bigger boy down like a bag of cement, then jumped up to receive congratulations and his new assignment. Instead, the coach yelled, "Take it easy! This is just a run-through, we don't need the starters getting hurt today!" There were no pats on the back from his teammates. Instead of congratulations, he received insolent stares. There was no new assignment. He remained a scrub.

Len began and ended each football game that season on the bench. He didn't get in for a single play. There were a couple of games when the team had a good lead late in the fourth quarter. Len got up off the bench, positioned himself in the sight lines of the coach and cheered enthusiastically, hoping to be rewarded with a few meager minutes of playing time. Once, he thought it had worked. He was standing along the sideline in a small cluster of players when the coach turned abruptly and strode their way. He stopped in front of the group and looked right at Len. Len looked up at him expectantly. Then the coached barked, "Sit down! Everybody sit down! This one's almost in the bag." Len went to the bench and sat down like a scolded dog.

As the season progressed, it was hard for Len to stay motivated practicing with the scrubs because they had a scrub coach. He was one of the science teachers who was in it for the few measly dollars earned by an assistant coach. It was clear that he knew little about the game and bumbled through practice every day doing, more or less, what he had been told to do, which was to keep his group busy and out of the way. But he affected the harsh exterior of a hard driving, battle tested, veteran football coach with his yelling. He prescribed a lot of calisthenics and running through tires, a routine that changed little from week to week. His continuous refrain throughout practice was for one of the players to, "Give me twenty!" pushups or, "Take a lap!" around the outside of the practice field for some lack of enthusiasm during an exercise or drill.

It was on one of these punishment runs along the far fence that Len first noticed the cross country team. They were a small band of kids who seemed mostly to lie around on the grass or play loosely organized games of touch football. They wore baggy gray sweatpants and hooded sweatshirts on cool days, shorts and t-shirts on warm days, and ran every day out past the football practice field to a park adjoining the school property. Often, they tossed a football between them as they trotted along. Once there, they flopped onto the ground, apparently to stretch. It was not the rigorous, bouncy stretching the football team did to their leader's call of "One, two, three, four! Two, two, three, four! Three, two, three, four!" It was a languid reaching type of stretching that took little effort or coordination and sometimes looked more like preparing for bed than stretching. After a bit, they would get up and run around the perimeter of the park or begin a casual game of touch football. Then, usually a couple of minutes before football practice ended, they jogged back past the practice field, to the junior high. They always seemed to be enjoying themselves, Len thought, and never seemed to get punished. Their running was intentional.

# 4

# Boom Boom Brown

At the beginning of the year, Len had thought he would go out for basketball during the winter. But when the time came to sign up, he didn't. He didn't want to sit on anymore benches. He opted for last period study hall. He usually got a little homework done without putting too much effort into it or was pulled into a small group of boys that were allowed to play chess quietly in the corner. He knew how the chess pieces moved but little else. He was valuable to the group as a playing partner any day there was an odd number of them. He never won a game but gradually stayed in them longer and began to see patterns in how the games developed.

Each day after study hall he went home, changed his clothes and delivered his papers. It was dark now by the time he unbundled and folded the papers, and soon, it was snowy as well. His pace was quicker, his imagination more vivid, walking along the shadowy snowdrift-lined sidewalks. Sometimes his fingers and toes lost feeling from the cold by the end of the route and tingled as they warmed while he ate his supper. He felt even more like an observer, while he walked, as lights went on in the houses but shades had not yet been drawn. But he was an unseen observer in the dark street looking into the domestic scenes unfolding in the warm glow of each house. The occupants knew he had been there only by the presence of the paper on their step.

As the winter progressed, the mounds of snow between the houses grew larger as people shoveled their walks after each storm. To Len, the mounds became embattled lines of scrimmage, his paper bag, a football. He became Bill "Boom Boom" Brown of the Vikings, called in to grind out the last three yards of a touchdown drive or get a crucial first down. When he had delivered enough papers and the bag became light enough, he pulled it up under his arm and drove into the snow piles, legs churning behind his blockers as they pushed against the opposing line. When the snow stopped his momentum or he fell, the play ended. He imagined the officials sorting through a pile of bodies to discern if he had made it to the goal line or attained the necessary yardage. As the battered bodies peeled off the pile one by one, the crowd roared to see the ball sitting on the goal line or, after a tense measurement, that the ball was placed just far enough to make the first down. Sometimes, despite his heroic effort, the defense had held him infinitesimally short. The crowd gasped as the decision was made to go for it on fourth and inches, and Len eyed the snow pile at the next house. The defense knew what was coming but couldn't stop it. The announcers effused over his bruising style of running. As he came to the end of his route, his toes numb from the snow that had filtered into his boots and down to his feet, Len had once again carried the team on his back to victory.

# 5

# The Man in the Uniform

By spring, Len was eager to be outside more. He learned that everyone got to participate in the junior high track meets, so he signed up for the team. Practice was fun. They changed into their gym clothes and jogged out to the track on fragrant spring days. Len knew there were a lot of different events in track but was unsure what they all were. He chose the sprints and threw in the hurdles and long jump. The coaches were spread thin so there were times when a coach wasn't watching that some small group could goof around, doing things like wrestle on the high jump mat, use the shot to pound a large hole into the ground or put sand from the long jump pit down the back of someone's shorts. Len looked forward to this enjoyable, occasionally hilarious, part of the day.

He was missing the day equipment was issued so he had to settle for what was left. He liked the thick, cotton sweat suit but it was huge and the crotch hung down to his knees. The uniform was also huge. The straps of the singlet would not stay on his narrow shoulders, even just standing still. If both straps slipped off at the same time the singlet was wide enough to fall all the way to the floor. The elastic of the shorts had been exhausted seasons ago and they would not stay up either. The bottom of the shorts came to the same spot just below his kneecaps as the singlet. At the first meet, when one of the coaches overheard Len complaining about his uniform, the coach looked at him and in a strong, firm voice said, "It's not the uniform that counts, it's the man in the uniform." But Len didn't feel like a man in that uniform. He felt like what he was - a small boy with a lot of cloth draped and pinned over him.

Before the uniforms were issued, Len had envisioned himself speeding down the track in the school colors as the crowd cheered, flying over the hurdles, launching himself in the long jump. But as he jogged out to the track with a handful of material bunched and pinned behind him, he began to have doubts. He was not sure why this vision had entered his brain in the first place. The reality of his practices was much different. He was not fast compared to the other sprinters and hurdlers, and had no form whatsoever. It took a lot of effort for him to run and jump over a single hurdle. The race had ten of them. He had not yet run over ten hurdles in a row, and as he stood behind his starting block for the first time, waiting for the race to begin, he wondered why he had not. Maybe at that age, some important connection in his brain was not yet complete. A correlation between what he did at practice and his meet performance had not even occurred to him. He finished each hurdle race that season significantly behind the rest of the field, bent over and trembling from the effort. The one hundred yard dash and long jump were not much better. At least the track coaches didn't yell at kids who finished behind, as long as they kept trying. They said, "Good job" to everyone, but in varying tones of enthusiasm it seemed to Len.

Len entered the last week of seventh grade subdued and was glad that the school year was coming to an end. The only event of mild interest to him that week was the President's Physical Fitness Test scheduled in PE class. The test was split into two days. His first day results in the shuttle run, push-ups, pull-ups and sit-ups were unremarkably within the class range. The test finished the second day with a timed 660 yard run, one-and-a-half times around the track. Len had never run even one lap around the track.

The morning of the run was cool and dewy as the class walked outside in their gym clothes. They lined up on the black cinder track. There were too many to fit on one line so Len moved to the back. He generally tried to stay out of the way of the top athletes in the class. They were competitive in every activity and causing one of them to be at a disadvantage could invite ridicule or getting your jockstrap pulled up over your head. Len had seen kids on the receiving end of both of these punishments and didn't want to chance it. Once you became a target, it was hard to shake the bull's eye off your back.

Mr. Moore strode onto the infield next to the track in the same outfit he wore every day of the year. He seemed to have an endless supply of high-waisted, polyester gym shorts, loose-fitting, open-collar polyester shirts and over-the-calf tube socks to go with his black, rubber-cleated shoes. "Set!" he yelled, then blew the whistle that hung perpetually around his neck. All of the top athletes sprang off the line and down the track. Len ran in the middle of the pack, nearer the back than the front. He felt like he was running faster than he should. His breathing was already ragged from the sudden start. He labored around the first turn and doubted his ability to finish without slowing significantly. But on the backstretch, to his surprise, his fatigue was no worse and his breathing evened out. The class was already stringing out in mostly single file. As runners in front of Len began to slow, he moved to pass them without any increase in effort. He ran in lane two, his spirits buoyed, his confidence growing as he went by the string of runners in the inside lane. Into the next turn, half-way through the run, the line had thinned, with more space between each runner. Len continued to pass but moved into lane one to save distance when he could. Onto the penultimate straight, approaching the 440 yard mark, he passed guys every few yards. Fatigue was now spreading out from his lungs into his extremities. His arms began to ride higher as his shoulders tightened. There were fewer runners in front of him now, but they were still coming back to him. He pushed around the turn into the final straight with just three runners still ahead of him. Two of them, he had been reeling in and passed at the top of the straight. The third, who had shot out to the lead at the whistle, and had remained in front the entire way, was another ten yards up. Len had been gaining on him but not quick enough to overtake him. Len was resigned, but ecstatic, with second place. He put his head down and drove for the finish to preserve his spot. When he looked up, twenty yards from the finish, he was up on the faltering leader's shoulder. Len's legs felt like cement blocks. His head tilted back. He began to wheeze. A spot below his sternum felt as it did only in the seconds before vomiting when he had the flu. He was slowing, but still inching his way into the lead. The leader tried to summon something more as Len pulled even but when nothing came, he broke, and Len struggled to the finish first in the final yards.

Across the line, Len bent over tenuously, hands on his knees supporting his trembling legs, gasping, incapacitated. Out of the corner of his eye, he saw his final rival step off the track and collapse onto the infield grass. Other runners came in now, clumsily sidestepping Len, some bumping against him or touching his back to keep their balance. Len moved slowly onto the infield to where the second place runner lay. The boy glanced up, a surprised, almost confused look on his face in recognition that it was Len who had bested him. The entire class now wallowed in their fatigue, used up, prostrate on the infield grass.

After several minutes of scribbling on his clipboard, Mr. Moore told the class to shower up. They struggled to overcome gravity, pushed themselves up off the ground and began to shuffle toward the school. He gave his usual call of "Jog it in!" but the class made no attempt to jog and Mr. Moore ignored their disobedience. The year was over.

On the way in, Len found himself next to Mike, one of the top athletes in the class, and casually asked how he had done.

"I finished," said Mike, "I'm glad I don't have to do that again until next year." He paused, then asked how Len did.

"I won," said Len.

"You're a better man than me," Mike said offhandedly.

Len lingered in the locker room hoping someone, anyone, would acknowledge his feat. Starting the conversation himself would sound too eager or cocky. Nothing was said, so Len slowly left the locker room and moved onto his final classes of the school year. For the rest of the day, in the aftermath of the 660 yard run, he was flushed with a feeling he had never experienced. It had come unexpectedly and suddenly, and ignited something inside of him that he did not know he was missing until he felt it. It was a good feeling, but also tinged with some inexplicable sadness. The small ember now burning inside of him had replaced the discomfiture that had been with him all year. He went into the summer feeling better about himself than he had just a week earlier or for the whole year.

# 6

# Blisters

The world outside of Len's sphere seemed to change that summer, or maybe he just became more aware of it. His window to the world was the front page of the newspaper he delivered, and for the first time, he took notice of what was happening as he folded the papers. There were huge protests against the Vietnam War in Washington, D.C. and other U.S. cities, resulting in thousands of arrests. There was another Apollo moon landing, which seemed to have become almost routine. This was the first landing that the astronauts had the lunar rover to drive, and there were pictures of them bumping along on the moon's surface. Two huge towers, the tallest in the world, were nearing completion in New York City. An amendment to the U.S. constitution lowering the voting age from twenty-one to eighteen was passed. Del would turn twenty that year and was looking forward to voting against Nixon in the next presidential election. To Len it felt like the future had arrived all at once.

As the fulgent days of July became the amber afternoons of August, Len began to anticipate the coming school year. While some apprehension about the academic and social aspects weighed on him, he felt anticipation about his decision to join the cross country team. There would be no more sitting on a bench in a clunky uniform trying to please an overzealous coach. He would get to stretch in the grass and play touch football in his thick, baggy cotton sweat suit.

At the end of the first day of class, Len strode eagerly to the locker room. A dozen members of the nascent cross country team had already gathered. Most knew each other. Len knew several of them from the track team. Mr. Adams, the coach, stood next to the equipment manager with a clipboard.

"You get one pair of sweats and one uniform," he said, "line up and make sure Roland gets the numbers on the front written down." He handed the clipboard to Roland then sat down in a chair he had pulled out of the PE office, opened a book and began to read.

Mr. Adams looked up from his book occasionally, and as the last man recorded his equipment with Roland said, "Ok, change and jog out to the park," and headed for the door. The team dispersed to their lockers, changed into the gym shorts and shirts they had already purchased for PE class and stepped out into a warm, beautiful fall day. Len broke a sweat before even clearing the parking lot in the heavy, reversible PE shirt. By the second week of school, a rank aroma began to pervade the locker room, PE classes and athletic teams. The teachers and coaches had to remind the boys that the reversibility of the shirts didn't mean they could be worn twice as long without washing. Mr. Adams remarked that the team didn't need to hang up their clothes, they could stand up on their own.

Each year Len got a new pair of gym shoes before school. They were always canvas court shoes that came in black or white. He alternated between the colors from year to year depending on his mood the day of the purchase. This year he had noticed a pair of shoes that had Bart Starr LaCrosse stamped across the back. They were black canvas but were made to wear on an outside field rather than a court. They also had three white stripes on each side. They looked faster than other gym shoes and Len liked Bart Starr, the quarterback for the Green Bay Packers. They were the same price as the court shoes and to his mom there was no difference. But to Len, as he carried them out of the store, he held a new shoe for a new sport. These were his first running shoes.

As Len jogged out to the park the first day, his new shoes bending reluctantly, a hot spot was already developing on his heel. Mr. Adams was already there when the team arrived.

"Form a circle," he called, "Gary, get in the middle and lead the stretches."

The team settled onto the grass and gently went through the stretches while Mr. Adams ambled around the perimeter looking them over. There were always a lot of changes to the team each year, he thought. Kids sometimes grew half-a-foot over the summer or slimmed out as they grew up. The team's hair was longer this year. Then there were the new faces. Would any of these have the desire or ability to become good cross country runners?

"Ok, that's it," said Gary, after guiding the team through half-a-dozen stretches.

"Take three laps around the park," said Mr. Adams.

"Alright, a mile-and-a-half," said Gary to the group.

There was a sound of indistinct murmuring as the team trotted off.

Len ran in the middle of the pack, the hot spot on his heel growing hotter. Now he had one on the other heel as well, but kept running. The pace was slow but steady. The team finished and flopped down on the grass where they had started. The raw flesh on Len's heels throbbed. This had been his longest run ever, but still a half-mile short of the race distance.

"Stretch out," said Mr. Adams.

After a few minutes, Mr. Adams told the team to jog back to the school. Pain stabbed into Len's heels as he stood up. He tried to jog but could only hobble a couple of steps. He sat down and took off his shoes. He looked back at his heels as the team jogged away. Bright crimson eyes stared back at him through his white socks. He took off the socks, stuffed them into his shoes and walked gingerly back to the school.

By second hour the next day, the bandaids Len had put on that morning had quit sticking to his skin and were rolled up in his socks. He hobbled painfully through the day. He could barely walk, let alone run. He wobbled erratically past a group of girls standing in the hall and heard the word, "Spaz." He couldn't tell for sure, but he thought it was Randi's voice. He didn't need to look to know that her eyes had rolled up into her head as she spoke. Len thought she was maybe the coolest girl in his class. She had a cool name, wore cool clothes, sang the words to the coolest songs and had long, straight hair parted in the middle like Cher, except that it was honey-colored.

She had only spoken to him once but it had been humiliating. One day in seventh grade biology, the class had gotten out of their desks to look at displays along the wall showing the difference between gymnosperms and angiosperms. She appeared to be looking at the displays but was quietly singing, "Yummy, yummy, yummy, I've got love in my tummy." Len glanced furtively over at her. She looked at him and snapped, "It's a song you know!"

"I know!" he blurted.

She rolled her eyes, exhaled loudly and turned away. He looked after her in anguish, his chest thumping, hot perspiration surfacing from every pore. He was wrecked for the rest of the day and avoided her the rest of the year whenever he could.

By practice time, the ooze on Len's heels was sticking to his socks. Mr. Adams said he should take the day off and get better bandaids. That night, Len's mom filled a large bowl with warm water, poured in epsom salt and told Len to stick his heels in it to prevent infection. He gently lowered his heels into the water and was greeted with the most searing pain he had ever experienced. He didn't hear her say it would get better in a few seconds. He was focused on grinding his clenched fists into his temples. The blisters were left to air out over night, then covered with larger, gauzy bandaids in the morning.

Len dressed for practice that day and hobbled delicately out to the field. He stretched with the team but didn't run anymore until they jogged back to the school. The next day was a speed day, which meant touch football. Mondays, Wednesdays and Fridays were designated distance days, when the team ran laps around the park. Tuesdays and Thursdays were speed days when the team played touch football. It was mainly a passing game, with team members rotating as the passer so everyone got a chance to sprint out for passes. Over the course of an hour-long game each runner got in fifteen or twenty sprints. Len remained the stationary passer for his team that day.

The football accompanied the team on most days, even when a game wasn't on the schedule, crisscrossing between them as they jogged. There were occasional close calls with cars as they cut across the school parking lot. They spread out as they jogged, so were easy to spot as a group. It was a missed or dropped ball, a carom off a parked car, a bounce into a driveway outside the perimeter of the group that caused the occasional slamming of breaks or honking of horns.

# 7

# Chess

Len usually sat on a bench outside of Lawrence's Market while he folded his papers. But in bad weather, and when the store wasn't busy, Lawrence let him come into the market to fold them. Len always gave Lawrence his paper right away off the top of the bundle. Lawrence invariably asked, "What's happening today, Lenny?" as Len handed him the paper. If there were no customers in the store, Lawrence spread his paper on the counter and began to read while Len folded. Lawrence often commented on articles as he read and followed up his comment by asking Len, "What do you think of that?"

"I don't know," said Len.

"Me neither," said Lawrence, sometimes shaking his head.

One day Lawrence said, "This Bobby Fischer seems like quite a character."

Len perked up at the mention of Bobby Fischer. It was a name he had heard his chess group talk about with reverence. He had noticed that Fischer's name or photo had begun popping up on the front page recently, and he had been drawn into his story. Fischer had beaten most of the top chess players in the world that year, and had earned a chance to play for the World Chess Championship the following summer against Boris Spassky of the Soviet Union. But what interested Len was that the stories about Fischer were written as if he were a street tough as much as a chess phenom. Most of the best chess players in the world were Soviets. It had long been their national game. Now a lone American threatened to shake up the status quo and wrest the championship from its rightful owners.

There had not been an American to lay claim to the title in nearly a century. But Fischer was different. He was a tough New York City kid who talked tough and was a ruthless competitor. He was brilliant and unorthodox. In the media, and in Washington, D.C. and Moscow, the match had also set up as a front line in the Cold War. It pitted American individualism and exceptionalism against Soviet communism and conformity. As with everything else playing out around the globe in the Cold War, the winner would be held up as a product of a superior political system.

Len also noticed that Del now sometimes carried a small, portable chess set with him. Del was back at the University of Minnesota but came by the house occasionally for a meal or a night's sleep. One day Len saw him looking over his chess board while reading a book on strategy and moving the pieces as he read. After awhile, he exclaimed "Brilliant!" and shook his head. "Fischer can think farther ahead than anybody," he said. "He knows what they're going to do and traps them, and they don't even know they're being trapped until it's too late." He set up the pieces for he and Len to play and explained things as the game progressed. A couple of times after Len moved, Del asked, "Are you sure you want to do that?"

"I think so," said Len, then looking at Del said, "No, I guess not." Then, "I don't know."

They began to play more often when Del was home. It was the only time that Len played anymore, but he knew that Del was playing a lot at the university. Del had become a quick, efficient player. He gave Len suggestions while they played to make the game more challenging, but the outcome was never in doubt. That was fine with Len. He didn't care so much about winning the game as just spending time with Del.

# 8

# Unfettered Running

The skin on Len's heels gradually healed and calloused. His shoes became more pliable. The laps around the field became easier, and as the temperature cooled the team ran them quicker. At first Len ran in the middle of the pack, but soon ran easily near the front. He never went ahead but increasingly felt that he could. The returners were still teaching the new runners the ropes, offering advice now and then such as, "Speed up before a turn so you can get the inside" and, "Let the other guy break the wind." These were things that had not occurred to Len but seemed wise. They demonstrated their expertise at these strategies at every turn and in every wind, sprinting ahead to the turns and falling behind into the wind. Soon the entire team raced to be first to the turns and jostled to get behind going into the wind. Len enjoyed this free-spirited, unfettered running. He looked forward to practice. He liked the team and started to hang out with a few of the guys outside of practice.

Mr. Adams seemed an atypical coach to Len. He was easy going, friendly and didn't waste a lot of words, especially on motivational cliches. His philosophy was that running came naturally to kids. They did not need to be taught to do it, just given the opportunity. If they enjoyed it, they would want to do more and, as a result, would become better runners. Usually he strolled among the team during their pre-workout stretching, asking how classes had gone that day. He then wandered over to a nearby bench with a book as the team ran laps or played touch football. Sometimes he sat on the ground under a tree. He looked up when the team ran near and called out encouragement as they ran by. He always seemed to be in a good mood and looked content to be there and satisfied with what the team was doing. He didn't volunteer a lot of running information, but when asked, offered what the team thought to be sound advice. Some of the guys had been in his class. They thought he was probably pretty smart because he told jokes that nobody got. In the classroom, as on the field, he was amiable and seemed to enjoy being around the kids.

The first junior high meet was a dual against Wilson Junior High. It would be four laps around the perimeter of the park for a distance of two miles. The night before the race, Len tried on his uniform in his bedroom. An extra small would have fit best, but small was as low as they went. Still it felt sleek to Len, lighter and better fitting than the previous spring and, he felt, made a difference to the man inside the uniform. Later, as he lay in bed, he pondered the race. He was unfamiliar with cross country racing and couldn't visualize it. Yet his heart rate quickened, his muscles tensed, not unlike what occurred in one of his chance encounters with Randi. His reaction to these two dissimilar events was curious to him and he thought about that for awhile before his mind gently wandered away from the race to Randi's honey colored hair. Soon, he fell into a deep sleep.

The next morning in class, the race insinuated itself into Len's thoughts and he felt a sudden pang in his chest. He calmed himself. He had realized, gradually over the first weeks of practice, that he had a talent for long distance running. He saw that it came more easily to him than to others. As his body became more physically fit to the task, the psychological and emotional part of him ignited. For the first time in his life he felt invested in something. He felt the pang several more times during the day and his anticipation soon occupied the major portion of his attention.

In the locker room, he could tell that others were experiencing the same agitation. The usual facetious atmosphere was more restrained. The team jogged to the park, where there were now chalk lines and flags around the corners of the course and at the start and finish lines. Even the park looked anomalous. They took one lap of the perimeter then plopped down at their usual stretching spot. They removed their shoes and sweats. One of the strategic gems imparted by the returners was to train in shoes but race barefoot so their feet would feel lighter during the race.

They stood up and jogged out onto the course. Len felt fast and light. His confidence grew. The team opened their strides and sprinted a few times over the final yards of the course, practicing crossing the finish line. When Mr. Adams had first talked about these sprints the day before, Len had thought he was saying, "win" sprints, and thought this was a good name for sprints you did into the finish. He learned later that Mr. Adams was saying, "wind" sprints and he did not think that was as good a name. But after doing them, Len felt ready to race. The Wilson team was walking to the starting line. Len felt the pang in his chest one last time.

The team stepped up to the white chalk line in the thick, green grass. The same old guy who had started the track races the previous spring emerged on the side of the course, gave a few final instructions to the runners and raised a starter's pistol in the air. He fired the gun and both teams took off in a loosely knit formation, soon merging into one larger, amorphous herd. After just a few seconds, three Wilson runners strode out to the front. By the end of the first lap they had opened a small gap on the rest of the field. Len waited for Gary to lead the charge after them. Gary was the top returner and led most workouts. But Gary was letting them go. "Let's go!" said Len. "Go ahead," said Gary, with a slight, but unmistakable, snarl. Maybe Gary thought the Wilson runners had gone out too fast and would come back later, thought Len, so he stayed behind. But the gap kept growing until, at the end of the second lap, it was clear Gary was laboring and there would be no charge. Len went by and struck out on his own. "Go get 'em," said Gary in a tone that was now sincere. Len was relieved at Gary's approval and moved away.

This was the first time Len had run in front of his teammates, setting his own pace. It felt good - he felt good! He was moving faster now than in the first mile, pulling away from Gary quickly, running as if he had been wearing an overcoat that had now been thrown off. He felt the exhilaration of the hounds as he stretched out his stride and gave chase. On the far side of the park the course went through a small, silent clump of trees where there were no spectators. Len had always been in a group running through here, but now he ran through alone. The stark sound of his own breathing and footfalls in this quiet grove affirmed the simple, inherent nature of cross country running for him.

He came to the end of the third lap, where most of the parents and spectators stood. For the first time in his running career he heard, "Way to go Lenny!" and, "Go get 'em Lenny!" Up ahead he saw that the three Wilson runners were no longer in a pack but a line, with several yards between them. He thought of the 660 yard run the previous spring and gradually began reeling them in. He moved into third shortly into the final lap, then second with half-a-lap to go.

The effort had become uncomfortable but Len maintained his pace. He didn't know if he had enough to overtake the leader. He looked behind him around a turn. He had gapped the other runners. He looked back to the leader and knew that his race was in front of him. He pushed harder. He was gaining on the leader, but was still twenty yards back rounding an enormous elm tree one hundred yards from the finish. The leader knew Len was there and pumped his arms harder coming out of the turn. Len did the same.

Into the last fifty yards, Len sprinted after the leader, closing with every furious stride, his head tilting back, his eyes narrowing to watery slits. He ran out of room, finishing a step behind, his momentum carrying him past the leader in the finishing chute. An official rearranged the two as they walked unsteadily to the back. Len turned to see other runners nearing the finish. A girl he recognized from his grade but didn't know, stood at the end of the chute. She thrust a small card with the number two on it in front of him. He took it and glanced quickly at her face. She had large, inviting, brown eyes with long lashes and was smiling brightly. He straightened up, his recovery quickened. As he walked away, he glanced back. She was still smiling as she handed cards to the other runners, but not as brightly as she had smiled at him he thought.

Len sat down and examined the soles of his feet. He had felt a few quick stings during the race in some dry spots on the course, but there were no cuts or blood on the roughened skin. They were dirty and smelled like new-mown grass. His teammates began to wander back.

"I saw you up there. Did you get 'em?" asked one.

"All but one," said Len.

Gary was back but hadn't said anything.

"Good job," Len said to him. Gary snorted and shook his head no.

"I felt like crap," he said, "I should have been up there with you."

But they both knew that time had passed. Sometime in the previous weeks, without either of them knowing it, Len had surpassed Gary as the top runner. It had taken the race to discover it. Len knew that if he had moved out even a few yards earlier, he could have won. Next time, he would have the confidence to do it.

# 9

## Squirrels and a Shark

There were two weeks before the next meet so the team settled back into their running and touch football routine. The leaves were changing and some days were cool enough that they kept their sweats on through the entire practice. Len still ran alongside or behind Gary on their distance days. These were not hard runs for him but running out in front would have changed the team dynamic and challenged Gary's leadership. As it was, Gary was less assertive than he had been, while being almost too complimentary of Len's assent. But any tension was slight and Len enjoyed, and looked forward to, this part of his day. Sometimes he looked over at Mr. Adams as they ran by or while they played football, and saw a happy look on his face, especially when the team was engaged in lively banter.

The second meet was another dual on the same course, this time with Monroe Junior High. The day of the race, as Len walked past Mr. Adams's room between classes, he saw the girl with the beautiful brown eyes who had given him the finishing card at the end of the first race. He didn't see her very often but had learned that her name was Jan. She was surprised to see him.

"Hi!" she blurted.

"Hi," said Len.

"I'm helping out at the cross country meet today," she said brightly, "are you running?"

"Yeah."

"After getting second last time, maybe you'll win this time!"

"I don't know. Are you handing out cards at the finish again?"

"Yep, that's my job!" she said proudly.

"You're good at it."

She blushed a little, and beautifully, Len thought.

"Well, I'll see you out there then," she said.

"See ya," he said.

The locker room atmosphere was more loose for this meet. The team had grown used to each other and had gained confidence from winning the first meet. There were also a few squirrelly seventh graders on the team, who had become bolder in being themselves since the first meet. The team jogged out to the park and around the perimeter. The seventh graders jogged along at the back, goofing off and gradually falling further behind. The team finished their jog and sat down to stretch. As the seventh graders finally approached, a squirrel popped out from behind a nearby tree. One of the seventh graders sprinted toward it, attracting a couple of his friends, who joined the chase. The three seventh graders converged at the bottom of the tree, bumping into each other and causing two of them to fall down, as the squirrel scurried up the tree. Their still-standing friend gleefully took the opportunity to pounce on them and begin a wrestling match. The squirrel had since climbed high into the branches and was out of the picture, but the three seventh graders were now wrestling and laughing playfully on the ground where they had fallen. Mr. Adams walked up and called, "Listen up!" The team, excluding the wrestlers, assembled around him. He looked over at the pile-up by the tree and called louder, "Hey you knuckleheads, get over here." They looked up, surprised, then got up and walked over, smirking.

Mr. Adams reminded the team to bring their finishing cards back to the camp right away so he could get them all to the scorer. Gary grabbed one of the small seventh graders by the front of his shirt with both hands and pulled him close.

"Did you hear that!" he said with mock aggression, "Get your card back here right away!" then gave him a little shove. The serious faces around Mr. Adams turned to smiles and the seventh grader laughed as his friends poked him and said "Yeah, get your card back here!"

"Alright," interrupted Mr. Adams, "Get your wind sprints in. We'll start in ten minutes."

The team finished their sprints and assembled on the starting line next to the Monroe team. The seventh graders wandered over slowly, some of the shoulder straps of their singlets slipping off as they walked. Mr. Adams looked over at them.

"Ready to go men!" he said firmly.

They looked at each other, unsure if Mr. Adams had been talking to them.

"Yeah," they mumbled quietly.

"Good," he said pointing at the assemblage, "Hurry up and get in behind there."

They shuffled over to the starting line smiling at each other.

"He called us men," one of them laughed.

"I'm a man," another one said.

"No you're not," said the first one, laughing.

"You're not either!" countered the other as they fell in at the back of the pack.

"I'm a little girl," said the first one in a high voice.

There were snickers as the starter called "Runners set!"

The teams leaned forward then held still. The gun fired and they sprinted off the line. A couple of Monroe runners sprinted out to the front in the first 100 yards as if they were on fire. Len went out quicker than he had in the first meet, but knew that trying to go out with the Monroe runners was not smart. By the quarter mile, it was clear that it had not been smart for them either. They began to fade quickly. Len moved into the lead and set a strong pace. By the end of the first lap he had opened up a gap.

"Good job Lenny," he heard Mr. Adams say as he finished the first lap.

"Way to go Lenny!" someone yelled from the crowd.

"Go Lenny!" he heard Jan call as he headed out onto the second lap.

He ran alone and felt alone with his own thoughts the rest of the race. After the opening strides, he was clear of the field, running freely, flowing with the contours of the course. He ran hard and even, and in the final strides, savored the affirmation of a winning race. He looked back as he walked into the finish chute and saw the next runner just rounding the big elm tree.

"You did it!" Jan exclaimed as he got to the end of the chute.

She handed a card with the number one on it to him. He smiled and took the card.

"Yeah," said Len. "I heard you cheer."

She smiled.

He walked out of the chute and around toward the finish line. Gary was sprinting across the line in second. A Monroe runner followed him in third. A stream of runners was now sprinting in from the giant elm tree. Two of Len's best friends on the team and in his class, Russell and Steve came in fifth and sixth. They had been improving steadily along with Len since the beginning of the year. The other member of Len's inner circle, Paul, enjoyed being out of study hall and being on the team, but he had little desire to excel as a runner. At practice and in races, he ran comfortably, and happily, near the back of the pack. But he had good speed and had learned to exploit it to great effect by delivering a flashy finishing sprint. Now, as Len looked out onto the course, he saw that Paul was getting ready to unleash it.

As the stream of runners into the finishing chute slowed and the crowd's attention began to wane, Paul rounded the big elm. There were a handful of runners strung out in front of him within striking distance. Suddenly and without warning, as if a high voltage switch had been flipped, Paul's arms and legs churned into a furious blur. "Look at that!" exclaimed someone in the crowd. Other heads turned. There were more exclamations. Those who had begun to wander off, stopped and looked back to see what the excitement was about. Now their eyes widened, their jaws dropped. Paul was flying by his marks as if they were standing still. His face grimaced, his lips pulled back wide so that his large, white teeth, clenched and protruding, made him look like an attacking shark.

Twenty yards from the finish, a Monroe runner who couldn't help but hear from the sideline whoops, that someone behind was making a play for him, suddenly found new life. Paul's momentum had carried him up to his opponent's side, but now the Monroe runner lowered his head, pumped his arms and matched Paul's stride. Shrieks erupted from the crowd as the two barreled toward the finish like a couple of out-of-control locomotives. Both runners strained every sinew to get to the line first. They leaned in tandem, but the Monroe runner held his spot by the slimmest of margins. They staggered through the chute congratulating each other. Only a few runners had come in behind them, but their twenty yard battle had electrified the crowd like none other this day.

Back with the team, Paul basked in as much adulation and received as many pats on the back as if he had won the race.

"You were truckin'!" someone exclaimed.

"You flew past those guys," another bellowed.

"I shifted gears after the elm tree," said Paul to his assemblage.

"I thought you were going to get that last guy," yapped one of the seventh graders, smiling up at him adoringly.

"You left a little too much in the tank today," said Mr. Adams, but this didn't dampen the mood.

Paul's kick became legendary as he repeated the performance in his remaining junior high meets and throughout his high school cross country years.

The third, and last meet, of the season was the championship of the city junior high schools at Mounds Park. Len finished third, running his fastest time of the season but getting beat by two kids from Johnson, who led from the start and never slowed down. He pushed hard the entire time but could not close the gap. The Wilson runner who had beaten him in the first meet, finished fourth, staying with Len until just past halfway before dropping off.

# 10

## The Mile

That winter Len chose wrestling over study hall. He was now committed to the individual sports where sitting on a bench was not part of the program. He tried unsuccessfully to talk some of his cross country buddies into wrestling. But he quickly made some new wrestling friends. The competitions were all invitationals where everyone got to wrestle two or three matches. All of the wrestlers in each weight class on every team were thrown into the brackets, so sometimes guys wrestled their own teammates. Len enjoyed working on moves with the other guys at his weight class, rolling around on the warm, soft mats and slacking off when the coach wasn't watching.

In the first invitational, he drew a Wilson Junior High kid for his first match. The boy collapsed like a Slinky when Len went for his leg. Once on the mat, his opponent attempted a maneuver that caused him to essentially roll onto his own back and inadvertently pull Len on top of him. Len would have had to try hard not to pin him, but he was stuck on top of him and couldn't help it. The match was over in less than a minute.

His second match was against one of his own teammates, a training partner who he worked out with most often. They smiled at each other as they stood on opposite sides of the center circle, waiting for the starting whistle. They wrestled like they did in practice, half-hearted. Len went for a takedown and his partner let him get it. Later, Len let him get a reversal. After that, they were careful not to score any points so that they ended in a tie.

Len only lost a couple of matches during the season and finished with a winning record. He had fun in wrestling but didn't feel the same passion for it as he had for cross country running. By late February, with wrestling winding down, he began looking forward to track and getting outside again. This year he would not be a sprinter, hurdler and jumper. He would be a long distance runner.

The football coach, Mr. Shipp, had taken over the head track job. Mr. Adams still worked with the distance runners as an assistant coach. The practices became more regimented, like a football practice. "I'm going to make this outfit ship-shape!" Mr. Shipp exclaimed the first day of practice as he lined the team up for calisthenics in the gym. He had used this same line in football. There was still snow melting on the track in mid-March so there was a week of "conditioning" with calisthenics in the gym and some running in the school parking lot. He had selected a couple of football players, who were also in track, to lead the calisthenics to the brisk count of "One, two, three, four! Two, two, three, four! Three, two, three, four!"

Once the snow was gone, the calisthenics were moved onto the football field before the team broke up each day into their event groups. Most days the distance runners jogged off the track over to the park and ran a couple of miles on the grass. Twice a week there was a speed workout on the track, usually consisting of eight 220s or 440s, or four 880s. On those days, as the distance runners ran by Mr. Shipp, he barked things like, "Make it hurt!" and, "No pain, no gain!" at them. He would have been happy for them to do this type of work every day, believing the more pain that was experienced, the more puke that was spewed, the more runners who fell to the ground in exhaustion, the better.

Len ran the mile in the first two meets. These were dual meets with little competition. He won the races easily, with opponents clinging to him for a lap or so before dropping back. The final track meet was the city junior high championship, where he faced the two Johnson runners who had beaten him in the city cross country championship. Again, beginning the night before and getting more

44

frequent until race time, was the feeling below his sternum of impending challenge. Over the years, he would come to know this feeling acutely when the stakes were high. Where in his background the ability to drive himself and compete intensely derived was unclear. He had not been a particularly competitive child nor did he have an intense or combative personality. Quite the opposite. But increasingly, when Len stood at a starting line looking out onto his arena, it was with the cold, clear eyes of intent.

Though he had not run over the winter, except for the few laps around the gym the wrestling team did prior to practice, Len took up where he left off at the end of cross country. He started out with the team on runs around the park but there were days now when his mind drifted to another place, his pace increasing effortlessly until he was alone in front, moving quickly, smoothly over the terrain, more content and comfortable than at any other time during his day. Sometimes he ran by rote in this private realm, his imagination feeding his body's instinct to run. There was no more intimate time for him than when he was running. He let his body run the way it felt, sometimes feeling so facile that practice ended without inducing fatigue, no matter what the pace.

At home at night, he was hungry and fell asleep easily. It was the first time he had a conscious thought that his body felt good. His muscles stretched and strengthened, beginning to work smoothly together rather than in opposition, coordinating movements as never before. The team had become his center, but it was some more personal aspect of running that drove and intrigued him. He had a vague sense of some internal impulse that had been sparked, that he knew could just as easily have been channelled in a different direction, but he was glad it had been channelled into running.

He had run the mile in 5:21 in the second meet, but in the city championship, time was secondary. He decided that his race would be with the two runners from Johnson. He would go out with them, stay with them as long as possible, and win if he could. He knew he could run a faster time than he had if there were faster guys in front of him to chase. The five-minute mile loomed in his mind.

One day in late winter, when he was eager for track to start, he had been dawdling in the school library, lacking motivation on an assignment. He decided to see if there were any books about runners or running. He discovered *The Jim Ryun Story*. It was the only running book in the library. He took it home and read late into that night about the first sub-four-minute high school miler. He forsook some of his school work over the next week while he read the book. The five minute mile that year became to him what the four minute mile was to Ryun. But the early spring in Minnesota is frequently wet, windy and cold, and that is what the conditions had been for the first two meets.

The day of the city meet, Len sat on the cool grass of the infield of the St. Paul Central High School track and took off his sweats under a low, gray sky. Wisps of analgesic from the infield, cigar smoke from the bleachers, hotdogs and popcorn from the concession stand flitted about in a lightly swirling breeze. He pulled his spikes on and did a couple of final wind sprints on the grass. Other milers were doing the same. The Johnson runners blazed across the field a final time, looking fit and fast.

"Final call, mile run!" yelled the starter.

A dozen milers coalesced at the starting line. Len stepped out onto the track, his spikes crunching down into the black cinders. The runners were sorted into their assigned starting positions and stood, fidgeting, at the white chalk line in front of them.

"Runners set!" called the starter, as he raised his pistol.

The runners tensed themselves and waited for the gun to fire. At the report, the two Johnson runners shot to the front. Len shot out after them, but another runner, who he had beaten earlier in the season, stepped in front of him and tucked in behind them. Len knew the other runner would not last and it irritated him that he had made such an effort to get in front of him. He was an annoyance, inconsequential to Len's race, except that now he might become a hinderance. Len didn't want to waste energy that he would need later, battling to get around this pest so early in the race. He stayed in fourth down the backstretch of the first lap and into the second curve.

The third place runner began to slow and a gap opened between him and the two leaders. Len didn't want to pass on the turn but he didn't want to lose more ground either. The gap grew to three yards, then five. Len moved out into lane two to pass. The other runner sped up just enough to hold Len off until the straight before ceding third place. Infuriated, Len snarled an internal curse as he passed. He was seven yards behind the leaders and running hard just to maintain that distance. During the second lap he felt like he was running on the edge of his ability. He began to have doubts that he could continue to chase the leaders. Maybe he had gone out too fast and would get passed by runners behind him that he knew were inferior. He hit the half mile in 2:29, sub-five minute mile pace, but was now ten yards back. Still, he was buoyed by the thought of the five minute mile. He pressed on, but now too, he heard footsteps at his heels.

Len heard the gun fire as the leaders entered the final lap. A slight gap had opened between the two Johnson runners. It gave him heart that he might be able to nab the second place runner if he faltered. He put his head down and tried to summon more going into the final lap. His upper body muscles strained as his legs became heavier. Down the final backstretch he remained ten yards out of second, with first being a few more yards further on. But his attention was on the runner he now glimpsed in the corner of his eye making a move to pass him. He pushed harder to hold him off before the final turn. Len had used nearly everything up but held his place into the final straight. He glared at the back of the second place runner the entire way in to the finish line without getting any closer. His challenger stayed two steps off his shoulder all the way to the line. Len finished third in 5:02 and stumbled onto the infield.

Russell ran up and grabbed his arm. "You got the school record!" he exclaimed. After Len's race the previous week, Mr. Adams said he thought he could break the school record of 5:12. Len thought he could do it too, but now having done it by so much, yet come so close to breaking five minutes, he felt both exhilarated and disappointed. The time had been in his mind during the race, but his main focus had been on the Johnson runners. They had pulled him along like a magnet.

As Len sat on the infield putting his sweats back on, a man dressed like a teacher walked up and stood next to him.

"That was a nice run," he said, looking down at Len.

"Thanks," said Len.

"I'm Mr. Renner, the coach at Central. You'll be in ninth grade next year, won't you?" he asked.

"Yeah," answered Len.

"You'll be eligible to run on the varsity cross country team as a freshman," he said. "I think you could help us out."

Len didn't know what to say. It seemed a little weird to think of running with guys who drove cars and dated girls. He liked the junior high team, jogging out to the park and touch football games. He didn't say anything so Mr. Renner said, "Practice starts two weeks before school. I'll talk to Mr. Adams."

Len felt a slight panic at the mention of Mr. Adams. He didn't want Mr. Adams to think he didn't like being on the junior high team or that he was abandoning them. But Mr. Renner was already moving away. Len looked after him until his line of sight was crossed by the two Johnson runners jogging on the grass. His gaze followed them and he thought "Next year, I want to run up with those guys."

# 11

# Our Man in the Long Distances

When Len got home that day, Del was there with a large bandage on his head. There had been a huge, raucous anti-war protest at the university that day and Del had been right in the middle of it. Neither Del nor his parents brought the subject up at dinner. Len knew they had already been through it. In the next day's paper there were photos of police in riot gear, burning cars, tear gas, broken windows and a large barricade protesters had erected on Washington Avenue to block traffic. Bottles had been thrown and dozens of people had been injured and arrested. One of the photos showed two policemen dragging a protester away to be arrested. It was Del, and his head was bleeding.

Del stayed home for a few days as his head healed before going back to school. Len noticed that with increasing frequency there was a strange aroma that accompanied Del. Sometimes after Del left, Len went into his room to smell the not-unpleasant odor. From bits of arguments he had heard between his parents and Del, he guessed it was marijuana. Del didn't smoke it in the house but the scent on his clothes was enough to fill the room when he closed his door to listen to Led Zeppelin, the Grateful Dead or Jimi Hendrix.

Len had seen stories and photos of Vietnam War protests on college campuses and Washington, D.C. in the newspaper from time to time, but this was the first he had seen in Minnesota. What had started as a small dot in southeast Asia had gradually spread like a growing stain across the U.S. and finally to Minnesota. It was confusing to Len how the country that had won World War II was losing a war to a tiny country of rice farmers. But the body counts kept getting higher and what the American people now saw daily in their newspapers and on the evening news repelled them.

The last week of school brought the 660 yard run again. Len ran twelve seconds faster than the previous year and had a gap behind him. His prowess as a distance runner had become a curiosity to many of the top athletes in the other sports, who were a head or two taller and more muscular. But there was an acknowledgement that he possessed an inscrutable kind of athleticism unlike their own.

There was one person Len looked up to and whose opinion he valued above all others. Mike was one of the best athletes in his class in football, basketball and baseball. Len didn't think that Mike remembered their first encounter, which had come just a couple of weeks into the seventh grade. As the football team walked back to the locker room after practice, Mike came up beside Len and said, "Keep working hard and you might make it into the starting line up" and patted his shoulder. Len thought he must have looked discouraged as he walked into the building for Mike to do that. But he could have just as easily been tired or bored. Mike had moved past him before he could say anything. But this small, encouraging gesture to a scrub he didn't even know caused Len to respect and look up to him. It made Len want to work hard and, for awhile at least, hope that he could make it into the starting line up. Even after Len realized that he would never make the starting line up, he worked hard whenever he thought Mike might be watching. Later, Len heard him make similar comments to others and realized that, although he was encouraging to all his teammates, Mike went out of his way to encourage those who needed it most. This didn't diminish the effect. The other players responded as Len had. Mike energized those around him and made them want to work harder for him and the team.

As the class neared the locker room after the 660 yard run, Mike was beside Len again. They were acquaintances now, though they moved in different circles. "Man, you're getting good!" said Mike, "You're our man in the long distances." Len was caught by surprise, had no response, but finally blurted, "You should come out for track, I bet you would be really good."

"I don't think I could do this every day," he said. Len realized much later, that the few encouraging words Mike had spoken to him in those two formative years, had as much impact on him, had inspired him more, than just about anything anyone else had said to him during that time.

Len finished the eighth grade with burgeoning confidence that extended to his life outside of running as well. His attention and interest had roused in a few of his classes. Socially, he still flew under the radar of most of his classmates, but he had a small group of good and loyal friends, mainly from the cross country team. For the first time, he was already looking forward to the next year. But for the time being, he was glad for the summer.

# 12

# An Empty Chair

As spring warmed into summer, Len noticed more people carrying portable chess sets. Games were being played outside on picnic tables, benches and cross-legged on the grass. In the lead up to the World Chess Championship, Bobby Fischer had ignited a chessmania across the U.S. He had seized America's attention as much with his outlandish behavior as with his prodigious chess genius. His ascension to within one step of chess's pinnacle had captured the country's imagination, but his mental state seemed to be more like a precipice on which he teetered precariously. Every part of his story seemed more fantastic than the last to Len. His brilliance was matched by his audacity. He was an enigma the media strived to understand, or at least chronicle. He was temperamental, eccentric, reclusive. Len picked up a magazine that Del had brought home and became absorbed reading a long story about Fischer.

Fischer had become the U.S. Chess Champion at fourteen, the same age Len was now. At fifteen, he became the youngest International Grand Master in history and the youngest challenger ever for the World Chess Championship. At sixteen, bored with high school, he dropped out to focus on chess. His distraught mother, who he argued with constantly, moved out of their Brooklyn, New York apartment. His father, who was speculated to be either a German biophysicist or a Hungarian physicist, had never been around.

At sixteen, Fischer was on his own. That year he finished fifth out of the eight qualifiers in the Candidates Tournament, the winner of which earned the right to play for the world championship. That was also the year that he published his first book on chess. This seemed like an unreal world to Len, so far removed from his own reality, like some kind of teen fantasy; living alone in a tough New York City neighborhood, focused not on his own needs for survival, but solely on chess, spawned by a brilliant but unknown father, so profound and accomplished at the age of sixteen that others clamored for his knowledge. But even as Fischer's story stirred Len's imagination, it was becoming a dark comedy with Fischer's sanity at the center.

Though his formal education was done at sixteen, Fischer taught himself several languages so that he could read foreign chess journals. By the time he was eighteen, he had won two more U.S. Chess Championships. But as his chess acumen increased, so did his erratic, sometimes boorish behavior. He refused to play, or withdrew from matches that didn't meet his peculiar demands.

In 1962, Fischer became the first non-Soviet Union winner of the Interzonal Tournament, the qualifier for the Candidates Tournament, in fourteen years. Of the eight competitors in that year's Candidates Tournament, five were from the Soviet Union. Fischer finished fourth, publicly accusing the top three, all Soviets, of collusion in order to prevent him from winning. The three had tied all twelve games against each other in an average of just nineteen moves, but had played long, hard games against him. As a result of his complaint, the World Chess Federation changed the format for future Candidates Tournaments to prevent collusion. But this wasn't enough for Fischer. He boycotted major international chess competitions for the next three years.

At home, Fischer produced the greatest exhibition ever seen at the U.S. Chess Championships of 1963-64. He recorded the first and only perfect score in history. His celebrity grew to unprecedented levels for a chess player. *Sports Illustrated* diagrammed each of his eleven championship games. Soon, he would appear on the cover of *LIFE Magazine*. Still, he refused to play the Interzonal Tournament for a shot at the world championship.

In 1967, he won his eighth U.S. championship. This time he entered the Interzonal Tournament and blitzed through the field in his first ten games. Then abruptly, while leading the tournament, he walked out. He would not play if the tournament format, prize money, lighting, color of the board, noise level, spectator proximity or journalist's behavior didn't meet his strict conditions. Boris Spassky of the Soviet Union won the tournament and went on to win the world championship.

The next world championship cycle began in 1969 with the U.S. championship. Fischer refused to play because of disagreements with the organizers. This meant he was ineligible for the 1970 Interzonal Tournament. The only way he could compete in the Interzonal was if another U.S. player gave up his spot. His friend, Pal Benko, recognizing that Fischer was at the top of his game, gave up his spot to Fischer and convinced him to play.

Fischer rolled through the Interzonal Tournament with victory after victory, winning by a record amount. He began the 1971 Candidates Tournament by crushing one of the top Soviet grandmasters in six straight games. He continued to steamroll his way through the tournament, earning the right to play Spassky in 1972 for the World Chess Championship in Reykjavik, Iceland. The championship would be played as a best of twenty-four game match, with one point given for each win, and a half-point for each draw. The match would end when one player reached twelve-and-a-half points.

A couple of days later, Len unbundled his papers to see a photo of the opening ceremony of the World Chess Championship. The ceremony was held at the Reykjavik National Theater. The President of Iceland presided. Many dignitaries were in attendance. The photo showed a packed theater, with every seat filled, except for one - Fischer's awkwardly empty chair next to Boris Spassky.

Len eagerly read the article below the photo. Fischer had hired an attorney to negotiate the conditions under which he would play the championship. But even after his conditions had been met, Fischer balked. He was scheduled to arrive in Reykjavik on June twenty-fifth, with the match beginning July second. But on June twenty-seventh he was still in New York. On June twenty-eighth, Fischer's attorney drove with him to the airport, but when Fischer saw a crowd of reporters and photographers waiting for him, he turned around and left the airport. A new list of demands, however, had been delivered to the match organizers, igniting a furor from New York to Moscow.

Lawrence was reading the same article.

"I wonder if he'll even go to Iceland?" he said.

"Why did they have the opening ceremony without him?" asked Len.

"I don't know," said Lawrence. "It's very strange."

# 13

## The Mayor's Son

School had been out for only a couple of weeks when Len saw a TV commercial for the upcoming U.S. Olympic Track and Field Trials. He vaguely knew what the Olympics were, though he had never seen them. Two of the runners shown in the commercial were Jim Ryun and Steve Prefontaine. He didn't know as much about Prefontaine as he knew about Ryun. He had never seen a track meet on TV, but the short video clips he saw in the commercial were enough to excite him about watching two of America's greatest distance runners race.

The preliminaries for the trials started in late June and as he perused the newspaper each day looking for stories or photos, a brief item in the sports section about Jim Ryun caught his attention. Ryun had qualified for the final in the 800 meters, which would be run the following Saturday and would be on television.

That Saturday Len plopped down in front of the family's wood-encased Philco TV as the Olympic Trials 800-meter finalists jogged out onto the track of Hayward Field at the University of Oregon. The stands, with a huge roof hanging farther out over the seats than seemed possible, looked like the gaping mouth of a giant, green serpent, the crowd's roar as loud as any monster. Len was amazed at the size and enthusiasm of the crowd. He knew that this was Prefontaine's home track and that the fans would cheer for him, but Prefontaine was not in this race and the stands were full and the crowd was exuberant.

Jim McKay, who Len would come to know over the next three months as a knowledgeable and passionate announcer, introduced a pre-recorded story about Jim Ryun. It began with the gangly prodigy running the first ever sub-four minute mile by a high schooler, then sprinting his way onto the 1964 U.S. Olympic team in the 1500 meters. Len was transfixed watching the last 100 meters of the Olympic Trials race where Ryun, still with his senior year at Wichita East High School ahead of him, came off the final turn in fifth place.

"And here comes Ryun!" exclaimed Jim McKay as Ryun moved into fourth. "Here they come to the finish line, ten yards to go! Burleson, O'Hara and Ryun! I think Ryun beat Grelle at the tape!"

The story then showed Ryun as a more muscular collegian at the University of Kansas in 1967, setting world records in the half-mile, 1500 meters and the mile. He had won over forty straight 1500 meter and mile races going into the 1968 Olympics as a twenty-one-year-old. But Kenya's Kip Keino ran a stunning Olympic 1500 meter record of 3:34.91, just 1.81 seconds off of Ryun's sea level world record, in the high altitude of Mexico City to win the gold medal by three seconds over Ryun. The silver medal was considered a defeat, a failure by Ryun and others, particularly the media. He had always handled Keino. But in Mexico City he came up short, blaming an illness earlier in the year that had cut into his training, the altitude and the Kenyan racing tactics. He had placed as high or higher than any other non-altitude raised runner in the distance races at those Olympics, but even his anguished explanations came off as awkward excuses.

Now as Ryun walked onto the track in Eugene for the 1972 Olympic Trials 800 meter final, his own expectations and those of others, had accompanied him for nearly a decade. At the age of twenty-five, after a career of prodigious highs and a devastating Olympic low, he was talked about as a seasoned veteran trying to regain past glory. He still owned the world records in the 1500 and mile, that he had set in 1967, as he stood on the line of the 800 meter final. His toughest competition would be from the slight Rick Wohlhuter and the fast closing Dave Wottle.

The race started fast, with Ryun and Wohlhuter in the middle of the pack and the golf cap wearing Wottle near the back. The tight pack went through 400 meters in fifty-two seconds. With 300 meters to go, Ryun shot to the front with Wottle chasing and the rest of the field stringing out behind. Ryun was eating up huge chunks of the track with each powerful stride, his head rolling from side to side.

"Ryun is now making his move," exclaimed Jim McKay, "Ryun is looking terrific at this point!"

This was the great Ryun kick Len had read about! Ryun led coming off the final turn. Wottle's stride quickened coming onto the straight. He passed Ryun in the middle of the final straight. Then Wohlhuter, with longer, more powerful strides than seemed natural for a person of his size, went by the faltering Ryun. Finally, Ken Swenson caught Ryun at the line to take the third, and final, Olympic spot. Len cringed.

"I don't think Jim Ryun made it!" declared McKay. His announcing partner, Marty Liquori said, "I think he just missed it by an inch."

Ryun had made his move too early. He had still run fast, finishing less than one second behind Wottle, who had equaled the world record of 1:44.3. Len was electrified by this race! Ryun looked in pain on the infield. His next, and last, chance to make the Olympic team would be in the 1500 meters. He had several days to regroup before the 1500 prelim, which would be the same day as Prefontaine's 5,000 meter prelim.

The next day, Len was looking forward to the final of the 10,000 meter run. The only runner in the field he had heard of was Frank Shorter. Jim McKay said Shorter was an Olympic favorite in the marathon, but was also the top American at 10,000 meters, and would run both in Munich if he qualified.

But the first event to be run that day was the 3,000 meter steeplechase, an event Len didn't even know existed. McKay explained that runners jumped over or stepped on wooden barriers placed on the track, and ran inside the track each lap to go over a barrier with a small pool of water on the other side, splashing through the shallow outer edge of the pool, back out onto the track again. It sounded crazy to Len, but held the promise of good entertainment.

Despite its novelty, the first few laps of the steeplechase were somewhat of a disappointment to Len. The field stayed in a close pack, and the barriers didn't provide any additional drama or seem to put the runners in any more distress. Then McKay said that the temperature was ninety-five degrees and Len understood the pack's caution. The pace didn't prevent the Eugene crowd from clapping in unison as the runners passed, increasing their noise level as the race progressed. Len thought how great it would be to run on this track in front of this crowd.

With three laps to go, the steeplechase began to fulfill its promise. Teeth were gritted, faces grimaced, with the effort of lifting heavy legs over the barriers. Runners staggered to exit the water jump that they had smoothly traversed only a lap earlier. Despite the quickening egress of their balance and coordination, the runners lowered their heads and drove onto the next barrier.

Going into the last lap, the loud Oregon crowd was in a frenzy as two local guys from the Oregon Track Club pulled away and battled for the lead. Mike Manley and Steve Savage looked to be clear of the field. Behind them, Doug Brown and Jim Dare contended desperately for the third Olympic spot. Suddenly, Brown clipped a barrier and went down! Dare was alone in third. But the crisis had ignited Brown. He sprang up and chased after Dare. He flew into the final turn, passing Dare and closing furiously on Savage. He passed Savage just before the finish line to take second in 8:31.8. Mike Manley held form for the win in 8:29.8. Dare was the odd man out as Ryun had been in the 800. The barriers had indeed taken a toll on the runners in the final three laps.

After the steeplechase, Len thought the 10,000 meter run would seem slow. But despite the heat, Frank Shorter set a fast pace through the first two miles, hitting the first mile in 4:25 and two miles in 8:58. Shorter kept the pressure on and a few laps later was running all alone. The camera panned back to the rest of the field, where Shorter's Florida Track Club teammates Jeff Galloway and the towering Jack Bacheler had pulled out of the pack into second and third. The three tan runners with Florida oranges on their shirts appeared poised to sweep the 10,000 meters.

With a lap-and-a-half to go, Galloway had pulled clear of Bacheler into second, with Jon Anderson sixty yards behind Bacheler in fourth. But now a clamorous din rose from the crowd, surging from the gaping maw of the huge wooden stands, rolling across Hayward Field as Anderson, a hometown boy, the Eugene mayor's son, who had grown up just blocks from where he now faced his ultimate challenge, started a long, furious drive for the finish. He looked too far back to catch Bacheler, yet he was flying and Bacheler had begun to struggle. If Bacheler had any sprint left in him at all, Anderson's valiant effort would secure him only fourth.

The grimacing Bacheler seemed to be living the runner's nightmare. The more he strained, the farther the finish line receded. He ran as if on a long, thin rug being reeled in by Anderson, taking two steps backward for every step forward. With each turn and each straightaway, Anderson drew closer, and in the final meters, to the delight of the astonished, wild crowd, pulled even with Bacheler. If Bacheler was living the runner's nightmare, Anderson was living a dream he must have had as a young runner growing up in the shadow of the immense wooden stands of Hayward Field.

Approaching the finish, as Anderson moved to pass Bacheler, the anguished Bacheler reached out and grabbed at him. Or did he? Len was not sure. The contact between the two happened so unexpectedly and quickly that Len wondered at what he had seen. But in the final strides as Anderson drove for the finish, his momentum carried him clear of the distraught Bacheler into the third Olympic spot, and Bacheler was disqualified from the race.

Later in life, as Len witnessed similar moments of human endeavor, in both triumph and failure, he wondered about the ascendancy of the subconscious, where our most fervent passions exist in uneasy accord, our conscious and outward probity quelling our darker impulses, except when our passions become too intense. Had all of Bacheler's training, anticipation and passion reached an unbearable crescendo with the finish line nearly in reach, and had a dark impulse, that was almost instantly suppressed and regretted, burst forth? Or had the great depth of his fatigue caused the contact as he tried desperately to respond as Anderson went by?

McKay said that Bacheler had been on the 1968 Olympic team in the 5,000 meters, and was the only U.S. runner to make it into the Mexico City final. The day before the final, however, he was attacked by dysentery and, after a night of vomiting and diarrhea, went to the stadium seven pounds lighter, unable to compete. In Eugene, Bacheler had held an Olympic berth nearly the entire race, the familiarity of his training partners bolstering his confidence, only to have it wrenched away in the raucous final strides. He had been denied a chance for Olympic redemption. His emotion had to be raw.

Shorter won the 10,000 in 28:35, with Galloway running 28:48 and Anderson 29:08. Len's appetite was whetted, but he had to wait until the following weekend for the rematch between Ryun and Wottle in the 1500, and Prefontaine's 5,000 meter run.

# 14

# A Contradictory Personality

It was raining the next day so Len took his papers into Lawrence's Market to fold.

"What's happening today, Lenny?" asked Lawrence.

"The Olympic Trials," said Len. "I watched them yesterday."

"Oh, are the Olympics this year?"

"Yeah, they're having the trials now to see who gets on the team."

"I don't follow sports," said Lawrence as he spread his paper on the counter and began to read, then added, "There's Bobby Fischer again."

Len looked at the front page. Like millions of people in the U.S. and around the world, he had been incredulously following Fischer's antics, and the machinations of the organizers to get the World Chess Championship underway. Now a British millionaire and chess enthusiast, James Slater, had heard that Bobby Fischer had not shown up in Iceland. He contacted the World Chess Championship organizers and doubled the prize purse for the championship out of his own pocket. One of Fischer's complaints had been that the prize purse was too small. In the article, Slater goaded Fischer, saying that now that money was not an obstacle, Fischer would play, unless he was afraid of Spassky.

The article concluded by reporting that Henry Kissinger, President Nixon's national security advisor, who Nixon moved all over the globe as his own personal chess piece in the Cold War, had also taken an interest in Bobby Fischer and the World Chess Championship. There was a picture of Kissinger calling Fischer on the phone, appealing to his patriotism, urging him to go to Iceland.

Fischer, piqued at the suggestion that he was a coward, and flattered by Kissinger's entreaty, decided he would go to Reykjavik, not only for himself, but for his country.

There were two photos of Fischer within the article. In one, Fischer looked arrogant and dismissive, like some dictator ruling over a cowed populous. In the other, he looked disconcerted and afraid, like a cornered animal ready to strike out. The photos captured Fischer's contradictory personality, which had become a world-wide fascination. On the one hand, was his single-minded devotion to a game that required order and precision, and his imperious confidence that he was the best at it. On the other, was paranoia and suspicion that simultaneously created turmoil within him and chaos wherever he went. In the balance, was his ability to play with such acuity in the midst of such anarchy.

A couple of days later, a photo of Fischer arriving in Reykjavik appeared on the front page. It was very early in the morning there, but a line of dignitaries had assembled to greet him, and a large group of reporters and photographers were standing by. Fischer rushed past the dignitaries as if they weren't there, pushed his way through the reporters and photographers to his waiting car, and sped away from the airport. What was being called the Chess Match of the Century was on the verge of beginning.

Len struggled to understand everything going on around and within Bobby Fischer. He had never thought about the psychological aspects of competition. Though he would not have been able to articulate it, running, to him, seemed a purely physical act, born of talent, opportunity and inclination. But Fischer's talent, opportunity and inclination was of an intellectual, not physical, nature. His all-consuming psychological approach to competition was enigmatic, but seemed, by design or accident, to bring out the best of his intellectual abilities. In the coming years, Len discovered that only by honing his own psychological approach could he bring out the best of his physical abilities. The times that he failed in this area were the most disappointing of his career, because it was his mind, not his body, that had failed. But it was those psychological low points that taught him what he needed to know to become successful, and motivated him to his best races more deeply than any physical failure could have.

# 15

# Pre's People

The next Saturday, Len watched as the Olympic Trials 1500 meter finalists were introduced. Jim McKay thought the 1500 meters was Ryun's best chance to make the team. In the 1968 Olympic Trials, Ryun had also failed to make the team in the 800, only to come back and win the 1500. The strain was clear on Ryun's face. The crowd seemed to be on his side. But even his most ardent fans must have had doubts. He had been great, could he still be? His running career presented everything necessary to be called great, except for an Olympic gold medal.

The runners came off the line quickly, but the pace slowed after the first 100 meters, no one wanting to be in the vulnerable front. The nervous pack jostled and jockeyed its way cautiously through the race to the bell beginning the final lap. As in the 800, Ryun moved with 300 meters to go. But this time it wasn't the huge burst down the back stretch that had been too much too soon in the 800. This was a controlled acceleration that propelled him to the front going into the final curve, with Wottle again giving chase and the field stringing out behind.

This time Ryun had saved enough to hold his form to the finish, his rangy, powerful strides driving him down the long straight in front of a loud, adoring crowd. He had run his last lap in fifty-one seconds to finish in 3:41.5. Wottle followed but could not run down Ryun this time. Ryun looked relieved as he breasted the tape, his sinewy arms wide as if preparing to embrace those who called out encouragement to him from the stands, who wanted so badly for him to succeed, and who were now so effusive in his moment of victory.

"Fifty-one seconds!" thought Len. He had tried to identify with Ryun since reading *The Jim Ryun Story* but a fifty-one second last lap seemed other-worldly to him. He tried to imagine himself winning races with a massive kick, but when the races came he had to run hard all the way and was barely able to keep the same pace at the end, let alone kick. Plus Ryun was close to a foot taller than him. But even though he could not emulate Ryun, he could be amazed by him, and he was.

The next day's Olympic Trials coverage started with a story about Prefontaine and "his" people at Hayward Field. It was of a confident kid growing up in the blue-collar coastal city of Coos Bay, Oregon and becoming the national high school record holder in the two mile run. He had joined his brawn to the iconic Bill Bowerman's brains at the home state University of Oregon. His races drove the Hayward faithful to a furor of clapping, shouting and foot stomping as he burst out the front of races like a stricken match and burned the last laps as brightly, of what were as much exhibitions as races. He was unbeatable in Eugene.

Pre's people anticipated a victory sendoff of their native son in pursuit of running's top prize. None of them could know that the 1972 Olympic Trials 5,000 meter final would perhaps be Pre's and their greatest Hayward moment. There would be a few more races for Prefontaine at Hayward before his tragic death less than three years from now, but there would not be another Olympic Trials - nothing to match the exhilaration of witnessing their home-grown son become an Olympian, pulling away from America's best distance runners as they wildly cheered and stamped their feet, setting an American record on their track. Both Pre and his people were at their best on this day.

Prefontaine's main competition would be the veteran George Young, one of America's greatest distance runners, who was attempting to make his fourth Olympic team. He was a three-time Olympian in the steeplechase, winning the bronze medal in the 1968 games in the thin air of Mexico City. In the twilight of his career, he still was regarded as a tough, gutsy competitor.

Pre's people began the rhythmic clapping from the start, getting louder and more insistent with each lap, the indigenous wooden stands clamoring under their feet, eager for Pre's head-cocked surge to the front. They could hardly wait! Prefontaine ran near the front of the pack but let others lead through the first mile in 4:22. He stayed in the pack for two more laps then discharged out the front with a sixty-four second lap, then a sixty-five. His people came to their feet. Just two runners clung to him, Young and Len Hilton. He turned the screws tighter with laps of sixty-four and sixty-three seconds, his people's current flowing freely through him. Hilton came off the back.

The race was down to one of America's great veterans and one of its great hopes, the torch being visibly passed. The moment had arrived for Pre and his people. A gap opened behind Pre as he churned laps of sixty-one and fifty-eight seconds.

Alone now, with the race won, Prefontaine eased up in the last few meters of the home stretch, acknowledging his people, prolonging their frenzy. Even so, he ran an American record of 13:22.8, the fourth fastest time ever in the world, six seconds off of the world record. He grabbed the finish line tape triumphantly with both hands as he crossed, then turned around to see by how far he had won. Young was seven seconds back, struggling to get to the finish line.

Pre's people urged him onto a victory lap; a slower, still raucous but more intimate interaction between Pre and his people. As he began the lap, a fan leaned over the railing of the stands above him and unrolled a white t-shirt with a bright red stop sign on the front and the words "Stop Pre" printed on it. "Go Pre" shirts were a common sight in the stands, but a handful of "Stop Pre" shirts had appeared just this day. Prefontaine grabbed the shirt, put it on and took off happily on his victory lap, to the delight of the crowd.

At the end of the lap, Prefontaine stopped on the infield for a brief TV interview. "If I can run like this in Munich, I think I'm going to be pretty hard to stop," he said.

While Len had not been able to identify with Jim Ryun's kick, he latched onto the idea of Prefontaine's long, hard drive over the last mile. He had run in the front and already had a sense that is how he would be most successful. In the story about Pre, he said he could push harder and take more pain than anyone, and Len thought that was the key to being a frontrunner. Plus, Pre was more his size and Len could see himself running and looking like Pre.

Jim McKay then introduced a short pre-recorded video of the Olympic Trials Marathon, which had been run earlier on that warm Eugene day. Five days after winning the 10,000 meters, Frank Shorter crossed the finish line in the marathon alongside Kenny Moore, both satisfied with defeating the distance rather than each other on this day. Once they were clear of the field and their Olympic berth secured, they had run together to the finish in 2:15:57.

Jeff Galloway and Jack Bacheler crossed the line together in third and fourth in 2:20:29. They had not raced to the finish either. Galloway had already announced that he would not run the Olympic Marathon if he made the team. He had run to help Bacheler. While Shorter and Moore had run from the front, burning off the other competitors one by one, Galloway and Bacheler ran from behind, moving through the field until they reached the third and fourth spots. Their positions secure, the two Olympians, teammates and friends continued running side by side to the end.

Len couldn't wait for the Olympics! This was running as he had never seen it, and it was going to get even better. Jim McKay said the United States would be competing for gold in most of the distance events: Dave Wottle in the 800, Jim Ryun in the 1500, Steve Prefontaine in the 5,000, Frank Shorter in the 10,000 and the marathon.

# 16

# A Beginner's Blunder

Len had not seen a lot of Del since school let out. Del had gotten a job with the St. Paul Parks Department and spent his days mowing, trimming and painting wherever he was told to go. He spent his evenings out with his friends, and when he was home, he mostly slept. He carried his portable chess set with him most every time he left the house and continued to smell of marijuana. Every once in awhile, when his friends stopped by the house to pick him up, there was a girl too. Del's summer of chess, marijuana, girls and music seemed magical and elusively cool to Len. Not that he desired it. Nothing had ever excited him as much as the Olympic Trials, which also seemed magical and elusive, but to which he did aspire.

But one Saturday, after sleeping until nearly noon, Del came down to the kitchen to find Len eating a peanut butter and jelly sandwich with a glass of milk. "I guess that's lunch," said Del as he foraged a bowl, spoon, milk and box of cereal. "I'm still on breakfast," he said as he sat down at the table across from Len.

"Who do you think will win the World Chess Championship?" asked Len. He had read updates on the match during the previous week, but had not had a chance to talk with Del. The organizers had delayed the start of the match until July eleventh to allow Fischer time to get settled in Reykjavik. During Fischer's settling-in time, he demanded that the chess board to be played on be remade to his specifications. He also wanted the hotel kitchen staff to be available twenty-four hours a day, and a bowling alley, tennis court, ping pong table and swimming pool, along with playing partners, all available twenty-four hours a day, ready for his use at a moment's notice.

Spassky had come to Reykjavik with a team of chess grandmasters to analyze every move, study for weaknesses in Fischer's game, and plot game-to-game strategy. Fischer came with two lawyers, who were already wearing out the organizers, and his welcome, by issuing demand after demand almost daily.

The media had played up the Cold War angle of the match. Many of the conflicts between the two protagonists took place around the globe by proxy. But this was a head-to-head battle between the ideologies, systems of government, the Soviet chess machine and a lone symbol of freedom as iconic as the American cowboy. The U.S. population, who previously had little knowledge or appreciation of chess, rallied around Fischer. The Vietnam War and debasing Paris peace talks continued to drag on unresolved. The U.S. wanted a win in the global game. To beat the Soviet Union at its own national game would be even sweeter.

"That's a good question," said Del. "I think it's going to be a tough battle. This guy at work was telling me about chess in the Soviet Union, how it's so important and Spassky is such a big celebrity. Right from the beginning the Bolsheviks made chess part of their political plan to control the people. They thought it would improve discipline and make the people smarter. They sent chess experts all over the country to teach chess. They made millions of farmers and factory workers start playing and had tournaments with thousands of just regular people playing. That's why they have dominated world chess for so long. But Fischer hates the Soviets. He thinks they cheated him when he first tried to win the championship. But everybody says he's at the top of his game, and so is Spassky, so it should be good."

"Yeah," said Len. "Do you want to play after you eat?"

Del smiled at him. "Sure, Squirt," he said.

A couple of days later, Len gave Lawrence his paper then sat down outside to fold the rest. Lawrence came out a few minutes later with his paper spread in his hands, walking and reading at the same time.

"That chess match is finally starting," he said, "It seems like they've been talking about it for months already. It says that Lenin said, 'Chess is the high expression of the socialist mind,' but Bobby Fischer says 'Chess is war.' Hmm."

Len smiled. Lawrence always seemed to pick out the most provocative part of an article on which to comment, but then never really commented on it. But it always condensed the essence of the article into one thought that Len mulled over as he began his route.

The next day Len read about the first game of the match with amazement. With the game ready to start and the Reykjavik auditorium filled to capacity, Spassky sat on his side of the table, but Fischer was not there. The referee began the playing clock. Spassky made his opening move, then sat back. Six minutes later, Fischer walked onto the stage to the applause of the audience, shook Spassky's hand and sat down. The two played a game that appeared to be headed toward a draw, when on the twenty-ninth move, Fischer moved cursorily, and it cost him the game. Chess experts called Fischer's move "inexplicable," a "beginner's blunder." There was speculation that now that the match had actually begun and Fischer sat facing the world champion, with the eyes of the world on him, his nerves had gotten the best of him.

The article showed New Yorkers standing in crowds on the sidewalk looking into shop windows at TVs reporting on the match. All three U.S. television networks had sent crews to Reykjavik. The New York City public TV channel, which broadcast the games live through a special telegraph hookup, had its highest ratings ever. It was reported later that in New York City during one of the games, more bars had their TV tuned to the chess match than to a concurrent New York Mets game.

There was an article next to the game report about the chess craze that had overtaken the world and the Twin Cities. There was a photo of two men in business suits playing chess on the Nicollet Mall during their lunch hour, next to an advertisement for chess sets at Dayton's department store. Even global chaos and violence from Northern Ireland to Chile to Vietnam could not push the match off of the front pages. Thousands of people across the U.S. were bent over their own chess boards, sometimes with a small crowd looking over their shoulders, in parks and on the streets in the American summer.

# 17

## Summer Running

The Olympic Trials races played over in Len's mind for days. He felt eager for the cross country season to begin. It had never occurred to him, nor been expected, advocated or even mentioned by Mr. Adams or any of Len's teammates, to run outside of the season. But he wanted to run. His imagination was brimming with Ryun, Prefontaine, Shorter, Wottle, Anderson, Bacheler and Galloway. In their interviews they talked about training on the roads around Gainesville, Eugene and Wichita. Len had never run from home before, always from the school and always in the park or on the track. He pulled out his gym clothes. They were the only clothes in which he had ever run. Holding them up here, in his room, seemed out of place, like a costume from a different play. He put them on, then pulled on his well-worn Bart Starr LaCrosse shoes.

He stepped out the door into a warm summer afternoon and ran toward the Mississippi River. He jogged self-consciously along the sidewalk glancing at houses where he delivered newspapers to see if anyone was watching. He got to the River Road and crossed to the dirt path that ran alongside the road on top of the bluff overlooking the river. He remembered seeing a man running on it once a couple of years ago as they drove by. The man was older and Len wondered why he was running.

There was no one else on the path, though it was worn, with rocks and tree roots protruding from the compressed dirt. Low, craggy oak branches hung out over it. Len ran on the path for only a few minutes before turning back, estimating the distance to be close to what he had run on distance days during the track season. He made his way back to the sidewalk and turned for home, his shirt clinging to his back under a cloak of thick humidity. It was an uneasy yet invigorating run, up and down sidewalk curbs, stopping and starting at traffic lights, tap dancing around rocks and roots on the path. But as Len stood by the kitchen sink drinking a glass of water, he felt more like a runner than he ever had.

He did not run the next two days, giving the pleasant soreness in his legs from his first run a chance to subside. The next morning, he decided to run before it got too hot. He woke up in the middle of the morning, put on his gym clothes and went downstairs. His mother was there and asked why he had on his gym clothes. A quizzical look appeared on her face when he told her he was going to run to the river.

"How come?" she asked.

"To get in shape for cross country," said Len.

She studied him, realized he was earnest, then said, "Watch out for cars."

Like his previous run, he stopped at the red lights even if there were no cars coming. After the first two lights, he just slowed and continued when the coast was clear, without waiting for the light to change. His legs felt good. He felt more fit from having done just that one run. At the River Road he crossed to the dirt path and ran farther out this time before turning back.

During the rest of July, Len ran a few days a week, three or four miles on the same out-and-back route. As he grew more fit, he began to run faster on the return trip on some days. He didn't always know when those days would be, sometimes even surprising himself when he took off, as if his muscles ran before his brain decided to. On those days, he almost couldn't run fast enough to tire, reaching home knowing he still had more, running unconstrained by feel, without timing or measurement, inherently understanding his affinity for it.

Some days he imagined himself as Jim Ryun or Dave Wottle, emerging out of a pack of runners with jaw dropping speed in the last block to his house. Other days he was Prefontaine, dishing out a long, punishing drive to his competitors over the last several blocks.

His hair grew along with his confidence and his pale, boney frame became sinewy and tan as he shed his shirt on these warm summer runs.

# 18

# The English Channel

One evening after dinner, Del's friends came to pick him up. Del was still up in his room changing so they occupied the lawn furniture in the back yard. When Del came down, they stayed for awhile in the growing shade behind the house. Len could hear them talking through the open windows. They were speculating on whether Bobby Fischer would stay in Reykjavik or leave, and if he stayed, could he still win the match.

After losing the first game, Fischer had complained about the noise from the video cameras in the auditorium, demanding that they be removed. A noise expert was brought in and determined that there was no noise that could be detected by the human ear. Fischer's demand was rejected. At the scheduled start of game two, Spassky again sat alone at the table in front of a sold-out auditorium. He sat there an entire hour, the time a player is allowed to be late before a game is forfeited, waiting for Fischer. Fischer refused to play, choosing instead to stay in his hotel room and brood. At the end of the hour, the game was awarded to Spassky. Spassky went up two games to none.

As these confounding events were reported, most knowledgeable observers concluded that the match was now lost to Fischer, his deficit too great to overcome. There was also speculation that Fischer, now faced with an almost insurmountable task, would leave Iceland. The next day, in fact, it was reported that he had booked a flight back to New York. Cablegrams from across the U.S. poured into his hotel urging him to stay.

The next day Lawrence said, "On again, off again," as he read the paper.

"What is?" asked Len.

"The chess match," said Lawrence, "It's on again."

When Len got home, he read that Fischer had stayed in Reykjavik. But he had demanded that game three be played not on the stage, but in a small room at the back of the auditorium without cameras. Spassky agreed. It was the turning point of the match.

Over the next couple of weeks, Len eagerly devoured the astonishing game reports. Fischer had attacked relentlessly and won the third game. His confidence bolstered, he agreed to move the games back onto the main stage. Staying on the attack, he won five of the next six games, with Spassky winning just one. The advantage had turned to Fischer. Included in Fischer's winning streak, were two particularly brilliant games. At the end of game six, Fischer was applauded not only by the audience, but also by Spassky, who later called it the best game of the match.

But in the midst of Fischer's blitz, another prodigy had made her way onto the front page of the newspaper. The round, smiling face of fifteen-year-old Lynne Cox of California appeared. She had become the first person to swim the English Channel in under ten hours. Her record was nine hours, fifty-seven minutes. In an era when female sports opportunities were severely limited, she had bested all of the men who had swum the channel before her. As intrigued as Len had been by Fischer's focus in the midst of anarchy, he was now amazed by Cox's focus and determination to not only attempt such a daunting feat, but to conquer it better than anyone before her. How did a girl near his own age decide to take on such a challenge? And then, how was she able to put in what must have been extraordinary training to accomplish it?

All of a sudden, Len's world felt small. His thoughts and experience had been limited to the mundane events of his cloistered family and St. Paul neighborhood. He tried to imagine Lynne Cox training in faraway, mystical California, then flying to storybook England, swimming the legendary English Channel, and finally feted on the shores of old, romantic France. It was as much a teen fantasy to him as Bobby Fischer living alone in New York City at the age of sixteen, or Jim Ryun making the Olympic team and running a sub-four minute mile as a high schooler in Wichita, or Prefontaine running along the docks of Coos Bay and setting the national high school two mile record. Except that those were real-life stories, not teen fiction or fables. Len's imagination had been stirred. He thought, for the first time, that there were possibilities open to him beyond his current existence. He didn't know the nature of those possibilities, only that they existed, and that his awareness of their existence had ignited something inside him that he instinctively knew to be important.

# 19

# A Struggle of Heroic Proportions

One day a photo of Boris Spassky sitting at the chess table alone, staring at the chess pieces, appeared in the paper. The photo was taken at the completion of game thirteen of the World Chess Championship, which was called by one international grandmaster, "a struggle of heroic proportions." The nine-hour, seventy-four move game looked to be a draw when it was adjourned for the evening after the forty-second move. Spassky's team analyzed the respective positions throughout the night, concluding that Spassky had no way to win, he could only salvage a draw. Fischer stayed up all night as well and came to the same conclusion about his own prospects. But when play resumed the next afternoon, Fischer applied a slow, grinding pressure that eventually wore down Spassky. Fischer came out with a win that stunned the chess world, including Spassky. Spassky sat staring at the board in disbelief long after the match was over. A former world champion watching the game said it was "the highest creative achievement of Fischer."

The next three games of the championship were drawn, but the audience had become more animated, stimulated by the scintillating play. Fischer recoiled, demanding that the first seven rows of seats be removed from the front of the auditorium. The Soviets were finally fed up with Fischer's petulance. They issued a statement accusing Fischer of using "non-chess means of influence" to unnerve Spassky. The seats remained. The Soviets requested that the stage and Spassky's chair be checked for "electronic devices and chemical substances" which they claimed were being used to weaken him. Nothing was found.

# 20

# This is Going to Hurt

In late July, the appearance of TV commercials for the Olympic Games invigorated Len's running. He felt good, but also felt that it was only a preface, like he was on the verge of something. He was stronger physically than at the beginning of the summer, and felt like there were other, less definable, pieces of a puzzle being subtly put in place.

He began to run farther along the River Road path. One day, he noticed a small trail angling off down the river bank and decided to explore it for a short distance. It was rocky with roots jutting across it like the upper path, but still runnable as it meandered gently down the bluff. It gradually became still and quiet under a thick canopy of oak and cottonwood leaves that spread out from dozens of massive branches reaching out over the bluff from huge, old trees.

Len had gone about a quarter of a mile and decided to turn back when he came to a small, bright clearing where the sun was unimpeded. There was grass in the clearing and a crab apple tree heavy with fruit. He looked out over the river. He had come about a third of the way down the bluff. Even from here, the brown expanse of water seemed alive with light and movement, eddies and swirls, and the air smelled like life itself. Small, unseen creatures rustled through the clutter of leaves, brush and dead wood on the surrounding forest floor. Len stood transfixed. There was no sign from here of the two cities he stood between, just the arboreal bluffs that rose above him on either side and the abiding flow of the Mississippi River. He felt like the first and last man on the world, like the Borstal boy in *The Loneliness of the Long Distance Runner* that he would read in high school, as if this is where running began and where it eventually would end, and all the while in between, it remained immutable and sacrosanct as human frenzy, achievement and degradation occurred all around. A quiescent comfort, that Len would feel always in this place, settled over him. He stayed for several minutes, looking, breathing and feeling.

He jogged back up the path, his muscles loosening up again easily, the flow of sweat resuming where it had begun to dry on his temples. His pace picked up along the River Road path as it always did on his way back. But he eased off the pace as he turned off the path toward home, keeping the profound presence and mystery of the river and the clearing with him as he finished his run.

Len started to run regularly to the clearing, going at whatever pace he felt on the way out and many times pushing up the hill and racing for home on the way back. He estimated the distance to the clearing and back to be somewhere between four and five miles. Sometimes, stepping out into a cool morning after a stretch of hot days, running was easy and fast. On one of these days, he ran swiftly to the river, turned along the River Road path, then down into the woods, his feet moving quickly among the path's obstacles. Suddenly, his foot caught on a root, catapulting him forward. He soared out over the path as it dropped away from him. He was in the air long enough to think, "This is going to hurt when I land." And it did.

Len landed, prone, several feet lower than the ground he had left. His body flattened forcefully onto rocks and roots, then he lay still, cringing in searing silence. Pain spread through his body from several points of impact. Both hands were scraped and one was bleeding a little. One knee and down his shin was also scraped and bleeding. He slowly rolled himself up into a sitting position. As he surveyed his injuries, he was startled to see a man standing on the trail in front of him, looking down at him. He had never seen another person on this trail, and the person he saw now looked disheveled and grungy. He looked up at the man's face. It was the gaunt, ruddy face of an Indian.

"Who are you?" the Indian asked.

"Leonard."

The Indian studied Len.

"Are you hurt Leonard?"

"Not bad," Len lied.

"What are you doing here?"

"I was running."

"Why?"

"I'm on the cross country team."

The Indian's facial features softened. "I was a runner, when I was in prison. It helped me do my time," he said thoughtfully.

This caught Len off guard. "Do you still run?" he asked nervously.

"Sometimes, if I have to go a long ways, but mostly I walk."

Len gently probed around the injured areas on his legs.

"Anything broken?" the Indian asked.

Len stretched one leg, then the other slowly out in front of him, then back in.

"No," he said, now feeling the need to move. He pushed himself slowly up onto his feet.

"Can you still run?"

"I don't know," said Len as he began to limp up the trail. His legs had tightened up, and felt more sore as he moved. The bleeding had stopped but sharp pain continued to radiate from several spots. He got to the path along the River Road and tried to jog. It was jarring. He walked. When he got to the street, he alternated walking and jogging and eventually made it back home.

# 21

# Prison

Tom lays on his back on the bed in his cell with his hands clasped behind his head and his eyes closed. In three months his sentence will be up, eighteen years after he entered the prison. The anxiety of getting out has become almost unbearable, almost too much to think about. He feels dread and apprehension more than anticipation. He wonders if he can even survive on the outside.

Tom doesn't remember all of the details of the murder he committed because he had been drinking heavily. But he knows that he committed it because others saw him do it. On the reservation, he had quit school and gotten kicked out of where he was living. He thought his life would improve when he moved from the reservation to Minneapolis. But the drinking, stealing and fighting continued. He thought he could get a job and an apartment and turn things around. Maybe he could shake off the depression, anger and stigma of the reservation. But he didn't get a job, even when he was sober, which was less and less. He was living on the street with bad people doing bad things. The depression he felt sometimes turned to rage so quickly that it surprised him. The culmination came when his rage burst out in a torrent and he mercilessly beat a man he barely knew, with whom he had been drinking. Once his rage started coming out, it kept coming, and didn't stop until he was physically too tired to go on. He was passed out when the police found him. He had only been off of the reservation for six months.

His first years in prison were what he called his hard time physically. He hadn't lived without alcohol since grade school and he couldn't control his anger. He craved alcohol and was beaten. His depression deepened and he became withdrawn. The only thing he really wanted was to die. He started to talk to the prison psychologist. It helped, but depression and anger still hung over him. Gradually, over the years, it became more subdued. He had become tired and resigned. He felt like his spirit was broken. He had five years left of his sentence. If his first years in prison had been his hard time physically, he now entered his hardest time emotionally. He was given anti-depressants, but he didn't think they did anything except make him feel lethargic.

One day, Mary, the nurse who gave him his medication, told him that when she was angry or sad, it helped to go for a jog. Tom had heard about jogging but thought it was only done by a few health nuts. He had never heard of a woman doing it. Mary said that not many did, but she liked to jog along the St. Croix River near where she lived. It was peaceful and everything seemed in harmony. Peace and harmony were two things Tom had never experienced. She told him he should try jogging when he was in the yard, but he never thought seriously of doing it. He liked talking to her though. It was nice to hear a woman's voice. She began to bring him articles about running and runners and he accepted them politely. Even if he did not read them when he went back to his cell, he kept them because he thought he might read them someday, and he usually eventually did. Then one day she told him that it had been arranged for Billy Mills to come and talk to the prisoners. The only things Tom knew about Mills were that he was an Indian and that he had won a gold medal in the Olympics.

As Mills talked, Tom was taken back to the reservation. Mills grew up on a reservation and had seen all the same things that Tom had experienced: alcoholism, poverty, violence, hopelessness. Mills had been orphaned at the age of twelve. Tom could relate to that because his father had never been around and his mother was an alcoholic who came and went. One day she never came back. Tom was in his teens by then and living mostly with an aunt. But as he became an alcoholic and increasingly violent, his aunt kicked him out. He hadn't had what he would call a home since then. But then

Mills told how he had risen out of poverty, got an education, trained for and won the Olympic gold medal in the 10,000 meters. He looked right at Tom when he said that no matter what someone's circumstances, there was always a chance to do better if you didn't lose hope.

Afterward, Tom went up and talked to Mills. He told him that he had grown up on a reservation too and that the prison nurse told him he should start running. Mills said that running had helped him in many ways. It had given him self-esteem, confidence and hope. His prison had been poverty, and running helped him escape. People still discriminated against him, but he was determined to make the Olympic team. Once he made the team, no one thought he could win a medal. He hadn't even won the U.S. Olympic Trials, and the world record holder would be in the Olympic race. But the important thing, Mills said, was that *he* thought he could win the gold medal. He had never broken 29:00 for the 10,000 before, but he won the Olympic race in 28:24 with a furious sprint down the final straight. Before he began his talk at the prison, Mills played a recording of the radio announcers yelling and whooping it up when he won. They didn't think he would win the gold medal, and when he did, they went nuts. Back in his cell, Tom thought that the bars and walls around him wasn't the only prison he was in.

One day, not long after, when Tom was out in the yard, on a day when his mind was in the darkest of places, he started to run. He could not have said why he made the decision to run, only that at that moment the thought of doing anything else seemed impossibly sad. He ran slowly on the gravel path along the inside of the wall. He began to sweat and feel like he was doing something that came natural to him but that he had neglected. As he ran, a tranquil feeling arose inside of him, like a reprieve from what he had been feeling for a very long time. It was the beginning of his healing.

Tom ran most days during his last five years in prison. He did not know or care how far or how fast he ran. He just ran and let his thoughts drift. It calmed him and took his mind outside of his body and the prison. Sometimes when the whistle blew, ending his time in the yard, it was like he was woke from a dream. He had been far off somewhere.

## 22

# A Boy Lying on the Path

Tom steps down onto the narrow path, carefully placing his feet between the rocks and tree roots protruding up through the dirt. Damp leaves brush against his legs as he descends into the river valley. The cool, spring air is the freshest air he has breathed in eighteen years, since before he went in prison. He breathes it in deeply and feels like he is part of life itself, something he has not felt for a very long time, if ever. The path descends so that the city disappears from view below the bluffs. He comes to a clearing that looks out onto the expanse of the river and feels like this is what it must have been like for his ancestors. He feels the land, forest and river accepting him as if in reconciliation after a long sojourn. He continues down the path as it runs along the top of a limestone cliff, then descends through a break along the bottom of the cliff before turning toward the river. He walks off of the trail toward a shaded area along the cliff bottom. It is a cave that is large enough for him to walk into without bending and is wider than it is tall. The cave goes back into the cliff only about ten yards and is dry. "This will work," he thinks. "This is where I will live." He stands in the cave opening looking out toward the river. He can't see all of it because of the trees, but he smells it and feels its presence. He walks back to the path and continues following it as it becomes sandy, then ends at a small beach next to the dark water. He sits down on the beach and looks out over the river. He can imagine a canoe landing at the beach and his ancestors getting out and pulling it onto the sand. Maybe they walked up into the woods then to hunt or gather food or medicine.

Maybe they started a fire and cooked the fish they had speared. He feels at home.

During the next couple of weeks, Tom gathers some things from Goodwill that he will need to live here. He doesn't have much money, so he walks to the Union Gospel Mission for some of his meals. It is a long walk so once he gets up to the River Road he sometimes breaks into a slow run. He arrives at the mission hungry and in good spirits. One morning he is walking up the path and has just passed the clearing when he hears an anguished voice cry, "Ow!" He walks a little further and comes upon a boy lying on the path. The boy is dressed in shorts and a t-shirt with a school name printed on the front. The boy groans as he pushes himself up into a sitting position, and is startled to see Tom.

"Who are you?" Tom asks.

"Leonard," the boy says.

"Are you hurt Leonard?"

"Not bad."

"What are you doing here?"

"I was running."

"Why?"

"I'm on the cross country team."

"I was a runner, when I was in prison. It helped me do my time."

After making sure the boy is not hurt bad and watching him jog up the path back to the River Road, Tom continues on his way to the mission. As he jogs, he thinks of Mary and what she and running have meant to him, and discerns a pleasant feeling of gratitude.

# 23

# Olympians on the River Road

The reports from the World Chess Championship continued to amaze Len. The games had become a series of long, desperate struggles in which both players sweated, grimaced and ran their fingers through disheveled hair. There were moves and counter moves, then counters to counters. There were attacks and probes, traps and escapes. Yet the result was an unprecedented series of draws, with neither competitor able to gain an advantage.

Fischer arrived late to all of these games, sometimes by up to half-an-hour, and continued to complain about nearly everything surrounding the match. Spassky had begun to show signs of stress. His team was worried about his mental state. He took a three day medical adjournment. He thought his food was being tampered with. His wife arrived from Russia to help him relax and cook his meals. Len overheard one of Del's friends say that what Spassky needed to help him relax was some weed, followed by laughter. Del responded that, "It might help him relax but it won't help his game. It hasn't helped mine," after which there was more laughter.

Over the next few days, Len's soreness slowly went away. The skin under his scabs began to heal and he thought about running again. But he didn't want to run on his path, not only because he didn't think he could take another fall so soon, but because he was a little frightened of the grubby Indian he had met. He was a criminal and Len thought there might be other criminals there too. He felt a loss. The path had been his discovery and his place to run, but now it felt a little less like his.

He ran the other way from his house, toward the junior high school. When he got to the school, he kept going to the park. He started around the outside and ran the same loop he had run in cross country and track. It seemed shorter now and not as challenging. After one loop, Len headed home. Except for the loop around the park, the entire run was on city sidewalks with stop lights at most intersections. Len got home and flopped down. It was not a good run. The stretching skin under his scabs itched as he ran. There was nothing personal or private to look forward to on the route.

A couple of days later, Len ran to the river again and slowly made his way down the path to his clearing. He didn't fall and he didn't see the Indian. He stopped in the clearing and stretched before turning back toward home. A week went by and each time he ran, he went to his clearing and never saw the Indian. Then one day, as he reached the clearing, the Indian was coming up from a trail below.

"Still running?" he asked.

"Yeah, the season starts pretty soon," said Len.

"Maybe you'll be the next great Minnesota runner."

Len didn't say anything.

"Did you know there were Olympic runners from here?" asked the Indian.

"No," said Len. "I watched the Olympic Trials. There was one Minnesota guy in the steeplechase, but he didn't make the team."

"There were two Minnesotans on the last Olympic team and one on the team before that."

"Wow," said Len.

"They started running here just like you."

"Here, on the River Road?"

"Yeah, on the River Road and around the lakes. I read articles about them in prison. They grew up in Minneapolis."

"What were their names?"

"Buddy Edelen, Van Nelson and Ron Daws."

"What's your name?"

"Tom."

That wasn't what Len expected.

"I read a lot about running in prison," said Tom. "There was a nurse who got me into running and brought me all these motivational things to read."

"I read *The Jim Ryun Story.*"

"I saw Ryun run in the last Olympics."

"I saw him run in the Olympic Trials. He won the 1500 meters."

"Maybe he can win a gold medal this time," said Tom. "He was second last time and was real disappointed."

"I hope he can win."

"How far are you running today?"

"It's four or five miles."

"That's great."

"I like to run. It's fun, except if I fall," said Len with a half-smile, "but that's only happened once."

"There's a lot of roots and rocks on the path."

"Yeah."

"Alright, stay on your feet and have a good run."

"Okay," said Len as he started up the path.

Tom walked up to the River Road and then broke into a jog. He thought of the articles Mary had given him about the three Minnesota Olympians. When they were young, just starting to run, they had probably looked a lot like Leonard. Tom had not kept most of the articles Mary had given him, but he liked the stories about the great runners. He had kept them in a folder he called his papers, which contained anything on paper of importance to him. Sometimes he went back and reread parts of the articles. He always felt motivated and hopeful after reading them. He thought he had learned as much, or more, about facing and overcoming challenges from them as from the psychologist. He did not have many possessions when he left prison so had just swept everything into his canvas army surplus bag without sorting through it. When he returned to his cave later that day, he went into the bag and pulled out his folder of papers. The articles were still there. He took them out and put them in his backpack.

Len didn't run the next day, but the following day ran down onto his path. When he got to the clearing, Tom was sitting on the ground looking out over the river.

"I thought this was about the time you usually run," he said.

"It's cooler in the morning and I have my paper route in the afternoon."

"Here," said Tom, reaching for his backpack. He opened one of the compartments and pulled out a sheaf of folded paper and handed it to Len. "It's the articles about the Minnesota Olympians who ran here."

"Thanks," said Len, looking down at the folded papers in his hands.

"They might motivate you. They motivated me."

Len didn't now what to think. "Thanks," he said again. He put the articles down on the ground in front of him and stretched. As he bent over, he looked at the top article. There was a photo of a runner crossing a finish line with his arms raised and his fingers forming a V on each hand. After a few minutes he picked up the articles and said, "I'll see you later. I'm going to finish my run and read about this guy," he said, holding up the photo.

Tom smiled. "I'll see you."

# 24

# Butterball Bud

Len unfolded the articles up in his room when he got home. He sat down on his bed and read the caption underneath the photo he had looked at in the clearing. "Yonkers, NY, May 24 - TAKES TICKET TO TOKYO AND LAURELS - Leonard (Buddy) Edelen makes a double "V" sign as he strides across the finish line to win the 26-mile, 385-yard Yonkers Marathon today." Who was this other Leonard, he thought. He began to read the article beneath the photo.

Buddy Edelen's childhood was not easy. His mother had been institutionalized when he was six and he didn't see her again until he was an adult. His dad traveled a lot so Buddy went to live with an aunt. After Buddy's dad remarried, he went back and lived with him. But his dad drank a lot sometimes and yelled at him.

Buddy started to get into trouble and was overweight. His nickname was "Butterball Bud." His step mother pushed him to go out for a sport. He chose football but got a hernia, so the next year went out for cross country. He liked it right away. He said he could run forever without getting tired. Pretty soon he was the best runner on his team and was winning all of his races. But he didn't just want to win races, he wanted to finish races feeling like he could not have run even one second faster. It was like he was trying to run something out. Once he began to experience success, his life began to change. He lost weight, his confidence grew, his self-esteem improved.

Buddy's running began in the Minneapolis suburb of St. Louis Park. He had improved enough by the end of his junior year of high school to be considered a favorite to win the Minnesota State Cross

Country Championship the next fall. But that summer his father took a job in Sioux Falls and Buddy moved with him. Buddy was undefeated that year in South Dakota. In the fall, he won the state cross country meet, and in the spring, won the mile at the state track meet in 4:28. The next year, he returned to Minneapolis to run for the University of Minnesota. He was good right away at the college level. He was already doing more than anyone else on the team.

After graduating with several Big Ten championships and top five national finishes in track and cross country, Buddy did something very rare for a U.S. collegiate runner in the 1950s - he continued running. He had been talked into it by a man who came out of the stands after the 1958 Big Ten meet in West Lafayette, Indiana and told him he could be a great marathon runner. Buddy already loved to run, so it was not a hard sell. The man was Fred Wilt, who had run the 5,000 meters for the U.S. in the 1948 and 1952 Olympics.

Since his retirement from competitive running, Wilt had been studying the training programs of the world's best distance runners. He had competed against the great Czech runner, Emil Zatopek and witnessed his victory over marathon world record holder Jim Peters in the 1952 Olympics. Although Wilt knew that Zatopek was a talented runner, he also knew that his innovative training set him apart. Wilt felt that Zatopek had not won the Olympic marathon with his endurance as much as his speed. Peters had come into the race as the favorite. He was the first man to run the marathon under 2:20, at a time when 2:30 was considered world-class. Peters was the first runner to inject race pace runs into his marathon training. He ran 80-120 miles each week in 11-13 runs, nearly all of it at marathon race pace or slightly faster. Zatopek was known for his voluminous interval workouts. Before becoming the only man to win the 5,000 meters, 10,000 meters and marathon in one Olympics in 1952, Zatopek ran a workout of 20 x 200 meters followed by 40 x 400 meters followed by 20 x 200 meters. He had also reportedly run 60 x 400 meters ten days in a row. Wilt thought if he combined the strength of Peters' marathon pace runs and the speed of Zatopek's interval workouts, and added one additional thing that neither of them did - long distance runs approaching the marathon distance - he could achieve even better results. Buddy was the perfect candidate to test his theory.

Buddy began working with Wilt in 1959 with an eye toward the 1960 Olympic 10,000 meters. U.S. distance running on an international level was virtually nonexistent. There had been only a handful of isolated successes over the previous three decades. By the spring of 1960, Buddy was running eighteen miles a day, broken into two sessions. Workouts included 25 x 440 yards in sixty-eight seconds with a one minute jog recovery, and 4 x 2 miles with four minutes recovery. His 5,000 meter time improved that spring from 14:48 to 14:29, and he ran a 10,000 meter race in 30:35.

In May, he announced he would attempt to break Lew Stieglitz's American 10,000 meter record of 30:19 at an all-comers meet in Sunnyvale, California. Leading the entire way and running alone for more than half of the race, Buddy clipped off split times of 4:48 at one mile, 9:41 at two, 14:33 at three, 19:21 at four, 24:13 at five, and 29:01 at six miles before finishing with a 66.2 second last lap to run 29:58.9, becoming the first American to break thirty minutes for 10,000 meters. Only a handful of people stayed to watch the race, which ended near midnight. The fact that the Olympic qualifying standard was 29:40, and the world record 28:30, indicated the state of U.S. distance running. The thirty minute barrier had first been broken in 1939 by Taisto Maki, one of the last of the Flying Finns. But Buddy felt that if there had been another high caliber runner in the field that night, he might have gone under the Olympic standard.

Leading up to the Olympic Trials, Buddy's workouts began to suffer. A blood test revealed that he was anemic. In the trials race, he held onto the leaders for four miles before fading to tenth place in 31:26. Once he recovered from the anemia, Buddy turned his focus to the marathon. It was too late to make the 1960 Olympic team, but his training for 1964 would begin now. Wilt felt that the attitude toward distance running and the lack of competition and training partners in the U.S. would be a hinderance to Buddy. It was decided that Buddy should go to train where the best distance runners in the world were training. With his teaching degree in hand, he boarded a boat for England, got a job teaching in a primary school, settled into a small apartment above a pub, and began to train for his first marathon.

In shorter races leading up to the marathon, the English press was incredulous that an American was beating English runners. But Buddy's training had progressed to workouts of 30 x 400 meters, 5 x 2 miles and distance runs in excess of twenty miles. He won a half-marathon in 1:04:37 and a twenty-mile road race in 1:45:30. In early 1962, he broke the American record for ten miles by over two minutes, running 48:31.8. *Track and Field News* called it "one of the finest long distance races of all time by an American." Two weeks later, he set an American record of 12 miles, 151 yards for the one hour run. He was ready for the marathon.

On June 16, 1962, Buddy lined up with a handful of other runners for the Polytechnic Marathon, England's pre-eminent marathon. Queen Elizabeth greeted the runners at the start. When she greeted Buddy, he caused raised eyebrows with his friendly return greeting of "Hi, Queen!" Despite his rigorous preparation for the race, it was his inexperience that turned the race into a nightmare. Against Wilt's advice, Buddy had not reduced his training enough leading up to the race. But even worse, he ate the wrong food that morning, and too much of it. By six miles, the can of sardines he had eaten caused nausea and cramping. Then his legs went and he struggled to the finish in ninth place in 2:31. He wrote in his journal, "Never came so close to quitting a race before."

A month later, Buddy broke the American record for the six mile run in 28:26, but was disgusted to have been beaten by seven Brits. The next week he rested and ran the Welsh Marathon in 2:22:33, winning by over nine minutes. In December, he was invited to run the Asahi Marathon in Fukuoka, Japan. Buddy stuck with three Japanese runners until the last few miles before dropping off, but ran 2:18:56.8. Nine years after Jim Peters had broken the 2:20 barrier, Buddy became the first American to do it.

Over the winter of 1963, Buddy's training increased again. In addition to the high volume intervals and weekly long run, he added another mid-week long run. He was now running up to 135 miles a week. Without resting, he broke the American record for ten miles again, running 48:28. He inquired about running the Boston Marathon, but was offered no travel money or lodging so opted for the Athens Marathon. Boston brought in Abebe Bikila and Mamo Wolde from Ethiopia that year. The Athens course was the same hilly route as the original marathon from Marathon to Athens. Bikila had set the course record of 2:23:44.6 in 1961. On a day that began hot and sunny, then turned to a downpour in the middle and finished sunny but not as hot, Buddy ran alone the final twenty miles. He finished in 2:23:06, breaking Bikila's record by thirty-eight seconds.

One month after Athens, Buddy lined up again for the Polytechnic Marathon. With the temperature at seventy-three degrees for the 1:30 p.m. start, the early pace was conservative. Buddy felt strong and soon grew impatient. He gradually increased the pace to 5:03 per mile and by eighteen miles was alone. Still feeling strong coming into the finish in Chiswick stadium, smiling and waving to the crowd, Buddy crossed the line in 2:14:28, a new world record and the first man to run under 2:15. To the assembled sportswriters, Buddy declared, "The days of plodding the marathon are over. It takes speed work, like the 110 yard sprints I practice, and the hard training on the roads to give you both the pace and the stamina you need." In his journal Buddy wrote, "Happiest day of my life. I never dreamed I'd win or run so fast … I felt good all the way … I simply cannot believe that I have broke the world record."

Buddy continued to race frequently throughout 1963 on the road and track, lowering his American six mile record to 28:00.8. In the fall, he broke the course record at the Kosice Peace Marathon in Czechoslovakia by over two minutes, running 2:15:09.6, a record that would stand for sixteen years. He felt the performance was superior to his world record run because of the rough cobblestones on the course. He now held two of the three fastest marathons ever run.

With 1963 coming to a close, Buddy turned his attention to the U.S. Olympic Trials Marathon, which would be run in May in Yonkers, New York. He wrote an open letter to *Track and Field News*, asking the U.S. Olympic Committee to change the time and venue of the trials to correspond more closely with the conditions runners would encounter in Tokyo. The Yonkers course was hilly, Tokyo was flat. An afternoon race in Yonkers in May could also be hot. The letter was to no avail.

That winter, Buddy's preparation began with increased mileage and increased clothing. He pushed his long run up beyond the marathon distance and began to wear up to four sweatshirts during workouts to prepare for the possibility of a hot day at the trials. At noon on May 24, with the temperature at ninety-one degrees and high humidity, Buddy stepped to the starting line with 127 other men for the 1964 Olympic Trials Marathon. The heat index on the street was well over 100 degrees. In the weeks leading up to the race, runners had urged the AAU to change the starting time, but their request was denied. The out and back course followed the Hudson River from Yonkers to Mount Pleasant and back. There was traffic control in Yonkers but the rest of the route had traffic going both ways along the course, with runners having to fend for themselves. There were few spectators.

Staying in the lead pack for the first ten miles, passed in fifty-five minutes, Buddy became impatient. The pack included two-time Olympian Johnny Kelley, Pan-American Marathon runner-up Gordon McKenzie, Norm Higgins, who was working with the great Hungarian coach, Mihaly Igloi, and Hal Higdon. Buddy increased his tempo and by twelve miles was a hundred yards clear of the field. Taking water whenever Wilt could get it to him, Buddy ran alone the rest of the way. Passing twenty miles in one hour, forty-eight minutes, Buddy's thoughts bordered on the delirious. With the heat getting worse as the race progressed, Buddy composed his obituary in his mind. "Member of the 1964 Olympic Team" was the headline.

Buddy crossed the finish line in 2:24:25, then waited. Twenty minutes later Adolph Gruber, an Austrian marathoner with Olympic aspirations in his own country, crossed the line in 2:44:11. Johnny Kelley was the next U.S. runner, coming in third in 2:44:46. Just thirty-seven men finished under the four hour time limit established by race officials. Anticipation grew for the Edelen-Bikila duel that would come in Tokyo.

After running thirty minutes a day for four days following the marathon, Buddy resumed training with interval workouts of 20 x 440 yards on May 29 and 5 x 1 mile on May 30. After the second workout he commented that he "felt tight in the hips for some reason." It was the beginning of an injury that would end his running career. The tightness turned to sharp pain. With the Olympics looming, Buddy tried to continue training but was finally forced to stop. He took time off of running. The pain continued but at a lesser level. Starting to train again, a sharp pain arose in his left shin. Still, Buddy pushed on.

On the first day of the Tokyo Olympics, Buddy watched as Billy Mills became the first American to ever win the Olympic 10,000 meter run. In the Olympic Village before the race, Billy had told Buddy, "I will win." Buddy had smiled politely. Then Buddy watched as Bob Schul of the United States won the 5,000 meter run and Bill Dellinger took the bronze medal. One of Buddy's motivations when he began training with Wilt five years earlier, had been to show the world that Americans could be competitive long distance runners. He had gotten a portion of world's attention with his world record marathon run, but the Olympics was the ultimate stage. Coming into the games injured and lacking training, he now watched as it was left to others to demonstrate American distance running prowess.

On the last day of Olympic competition, Buddy rejected suggestions to take pain killers and get a cortisone shot, and stepped to the line of the Olympic Marathon, hoping just to finish. The pace went out quick, with Buddy falling behind in anguish. Still he pushed. In the second half of the race, with his legs beginning to feel numb, he started to pass runners who had gone out with the fast early pace as they filtered back through the field. As the stadium came into

Buddy's view, Bikila was crossing the finish line first in 2:12:11, a new Olympic and world record. Buddy drove hard, continuing to pass runners. The last man he passed was 1963 Boston Marathon champion Aurele Vandendriessche. Exhausted and in agony, Buddy crossed the line in 2:18:12, good for sixth place. In his journal he wrote that he had run the last six miles "on guts alone ... I could not have run one bit faster today ... I gave every ounce of strength I had right to the end."

After the Olympics, Buddy moved to Alamosa, Colorado, site of the 1968 Olympic Trials Marathon. Running in the 7,640 foot altitude of Alamosa would require adaptation and Buddy wanted to be more adapted than anyone else, as he had been for the heat in Yonkers. At the same time, he tried to heal the cause of his back pain, sciatica. Over the next two years Buddy trained sporadically as he sought relief. But with training came pain, sometimes so bad he could barely get out of bed. Finally, Buddy Edelen was forced to stop training altogether. He was able to run short, easy runs, but he would not compete again.

# 25

# The Plodder

Len had become engrossed in the article about Buddy Edelen and had read it through in one sitting. Now he felt the dried salt from his run on his forehead and dampness on his bed where he had been sitting in his sweaty shorts. He took a bath and went down to have breakfast. It was nearly noon. Del was home later that day for a few minutes and Len asked if he had ever heard of Buddy Edelen. Del said he hadn't. Len told him Buddy's story.

"Where did you hear that?" asked Del.

"It's an article I read," said Len.

"You're pretty excited about it aren't you?"

"I didn't know there were good runners from here."

"You've been running a lot too."

"Yeah, it's fun."

"You better watch out Squirt, you might get good."

Len smiled.

The next day he ran to the river and down to his clearing hoping to see Tom. He wanted to tell him that he liked the article. He waited in the clearing for a few minutes, but Tom never came. He ran back home as the temperature and humidity rose higher with the morning sun. He thought about Buddy running the marathon in Yonkers all alone with the sun beating down and cars going both ways on the street, and the drivers thinking he was crazy. And near the end, even Buddy starting to think he was crazy, composing his own obituary. "Maybe some day I'll run a marathon," thought Len.

The next day Len looked at the other articles. There was a photo with one that showed Buddy Edelen as a spectator at the 1968

Olympic Trials Marathon. Len began to read. Despite retiring from competitive running, Buddy stayed on in Alamosa to help with the organization of the trials race. Also in the photo was Ron Daws, who had been a teammate of Buddy's at the University of Minnesota. In college, Ron was considered somewhat of a clumsy plodder. He had once been told by the coach to get out of Buddy's way during a workout so as not to trip him up. Ron had not responded to the training at the university nor improved on his times from high school. Gradually, he became frustrated and quit the team and running altogether.

Ron had been out of college and out of running for several months when a couple of friends approached him about forming a running club and putting on road races. He began to run again. Over the next two years, Ron enjoyed running long distance runs and races with his friends. By 1964, he was running enough to enter the Olympic Trials Marathon in Yonkers. Unprepared for the heat, he staggered in to the finish dehydrated, exhausted and sick in 3:25, good for fifteenth place. He was hospitalized and released, but was readmitted after being found unconscious in the shower. He was released six hours later, whereupon he promptly vomited.

Ron's experience in Yonkers was perhaps the most valuable running lesson he would ever learn. Afterward, he talked with Buddy about his heat training technique of wearing four sweatshirts during workouts. Ron would not go into a big race unprepared for the conditions again.

In the early 1960s, there was not a lot of published information on training to run long distances. Ron had been training himself, just running how he felt and what fit into his full-time work schedule. That summer, Ron borrowed a copy of *Run To The Top*, by Arthur Lydiard. Lydiard was a New Zealander who had run marathons and coached several Olympic medalists in the 1960 games. In 1962, Lydiard published his book outlining his training philosophy. Ron became so excited about running as he read, that he finished the book in one sitting. Lydiard's philosophy of high weekly mileage and long runs fit with what Ron was experiencing in his own running. He began following the training schedules Lydiard had written out.

Over the next three years, Ron's mileage increased steadily as he delved more deeply into Lydiard's training. Nonetheless, he was apprehensive as he stepped to the line of the 1967 U.S. Marathon Championship in Holyoke, Massachusetts. He had trained more than ever and had heat trained, but the temperature at the start was already climbing into the mid-90s. He let the lead pack go, but gradually picked off runners as they faltered in the heat. By eighteen miles he had moved from the back of the pack into third place. Two miles later, he moved into the lead and went on to win by three minutes in just over 2:40. He felt that he had won not because he was a better runner than the others, but because he was better prepared.

The win had qualified Ron to represent the U.S. in the Pan American Games, held that year a short jaunt from Minneapolis in Winnipeg, Manitoba. Leaving for Winnipeg, Ron felt more fit than he had ever been. He kept to his heavy training schedule, but two weeks out from the race, during an eighteen mile run, he developed hip pain. After resting for two days, he pushed through a twenty mile run. The pain worsened. The diagnosis was sciatica. He knew this is what had derailed Buddy's running career, and now it threatened to derail his. Despite being unable to run in the last week before the marathon, Ron went to the starting line. He lasted just five kilometers before limping off the course in pain.

A month later, Ron attempted his first run since the race. The pain returned within a minute of running. At thirty-one-years-old, less than a year out from the Olympic Trials, Ron thought his running career was over. In a last ditch effort to return to running, Ron went to see an orthopedic surgeon, who recommended that he start running again but stop and walk whenever the pain returned. Ron's first run lasted two blocks. But gradually he worked up to two miles and by the end of the fall was running nine miles without pain. During this time he had also taken a one week dose of cortisone orally.

With no remaining symptoms of the sciatica, Ron set his sights on the 1968 Olympic Trials Marathon. Even though his best marathon time was slower than many others who would contend for a spot on the team, Ron felt if he prepared perfectly and could capitalize on the mistakes of others, he would have a chance, albeit slim, to make the team. His winter training in Minnesota was good. In April, he placed fifth in the Boston Marathon in 2:29:17, but was seven minutes behind the winner, Amby Burfoot. In May, he ran, and served as the race director, of one of six regional selection marathon races to determine the twenty runners who would receive funding to travel to Alamosa for an expense-paid month of high altitude training before the trials race. Recent University of Minnesota graduate Tom Heinonen won the Minnesota regional in a state record time of 2:18:29. Ron finished a disappointing fourth in 2:24:12, dropping him to eighteenth on the funding list with one regional race still to be run. Unsure whether he would receive funding, Ron headed for Alamosa for a six week training stint before the trials race, prepared to fund himself if necessary.

What Ron learned about the marathon, altitude, pacing, nutrition and himself during those six weeks proved invaluable. He had started out ambitiously on training runs, only to finish at a walk and climb into bed for the rest of the day. He had started out slowly on training runs, only to find that he still could not finish fast at that altitude. He ate raisins because of their high iron content, only to get stomach cramps and diarrhea. He plodded along in his full sweat suit to train for the heat, while other runners flew by him bare-chested and in shorts.

In five of his last six weeks of training before the marathon, Ron covered over one hundred miles, including one week of 129. He had run four runs of 26-30 miles. He ran workouts such as a 14.2 mile run from 7,100 feet altitude up to 12,850 feet; 12 miles "up and down mountains;" a one hour run in sand dunes; 10 x 1 mile at marathon pace with short rest; and 10 x 110 yards + 10 x 220 yards + 10 x 440 yards + 10 x 220 yards. Ten days out from the race, Ron's training had not only brought him fitness, but also a flare-up of sciatica. This time he got a shot of cortisone immediately and took two days off.

The symptoms disappeared and he resumed his final race preparations.

The trials day dawned hot and dry. In the first few miles, Ron watched as several of the favorites pulled away from him. Other favorites went out even more conservative, and lagged behind him. Meanwhile, Ron executed his strategy of trying to run an exactly even pace, to distribute his energy evenly throughout. By seventeen miles he had moved into fourth, looking ahead at the third place runner, Steve Matthews, who had beaten him by four minutes in the regional qualifier. Burfoot and Heinonen had started slowly hoping to finish fast enough to make the team in the late stages of the race, but what they could now muster was too little, too late. Billy Mills had run near the lead early on, but had dropped out of the race. Ron's chance to make the Olympic team rested on his ability to get past Matthews and hold off any late challengers.

Going out for the last 5.2 mile loop, Ron moved past Matthews into third. Despite slowing and fighting off cramps in the last couple of miles, Ron held onto third in 2:33:09. George Young had won in 2:30:48 and Kenny Moore had finished second in 2:31:47. Ron had proved that there was still room for a plodder in the marathon, at least in extreme conditions where superior preparation could overcome superior talent.

In Mexico City, on a sunny day in the mid-seventies, Ron used a similar even-pace strategy to finish twenty-second in the Olympic marathon. The following spring he finished fourth in the Boston Marathon in a personal best of 2:20:21.

# 26

# Moving Van

"The marathon is crazy," thought Len, "Thirty mile runs and cortisone shots." He knew Ron had trained on the River Road and around the lakes, and that Buddy had trained on the River Road when he was at the university. The road had seemed lonely to him sometimes but now it seemed less so. He began to think of what was around the next bend. What had Buddy and Ron seen on the River Road on their long runs that he had not yet seen?

Len ran into Tom on the River Road the next day.

"Those are great articles," he said.

Tom smiled. "I thought you might think so."

"I haven't read them all, just two of them."

"Which ones?"

"I read about Buddy Edelen and Ron Daws."

"The marathoners."

"Yeah, I can't believe how much they ran!"

"Yeah, it's amazing," said Tom, "Van Nelson, the other one, wasn't a marathoner but he still ran as much as Buddy and Ron. I guess that's what it takes. He could really move."

When he got home, Len unfolded the article about Van Nelson. At the top was a photo of Van running underneath a bank sign that had the time and temperature on it. The temperature read twelve below zero. Van was a Minneapolis kid who went to St. Cloud State. He started running as a seventeen-year-old junior in high school and by the time he was twenty-one in 1967, he was ranked first in the U.S. in the 10,000 meters and second in the 5,000 meters. He was ranked eighth in the world in the 10,000 that year and had notched wins over

Kip Keino, Gerry Lindgren and George Young. He had lost a race to world 5,000 and 10,000 meter record holder Ron Clarke by one second.

In high school at Minneapolis Washburn, Van was a good runner right away. Even though the distance races weren't very long, Van enjoyed running long. Cross country races were only 1.8 miles and the longest track race was the mile. He loved to run around the lakes near his south Minneapolis home. Running around two lakes was seven miles, while three lakes was ten miles. On some of these runs during the cross country and track seasons, his coach accompanied him, driving his car alongside. Many of these runs were also at a quick pace. His teammates would go around Lake Harriet and Lake Calhoun for seven miles, while Van added on Lake of the Isles for ten miles and tried to beat them back. Speed work consisted mostly of 20 x 220 yards with a 220 yard jog recovery.

He nearly didn't go out for track because he didn't think he would like running in circles the same as running along the lakes. But he took right to track racing, placing second in the mile at the state meet as a senior in 4:19, just one second out of first.

At St. Cloud State, Van upped his mileage to near 140 miles a week, though rarely running over ten miles at one time. Most days he ran ten miles in the morning and ten miles in the afternoon on the same five mile loop. His morning ten was usually run in sixty to sixty-three minutes, with the afternoon ten run in around fifty-five minutes. He carried a stopwatch in his hand on every run, sticking to a self-imposed rule that the morning run could be over sixty minutes but the afternoon run had to always be under. He kept up his workout of 220s from high school once or twice a week, but increased the volume up to 36 x 220. He ran them in thirty seconds, with a fifty second 220 jog in-between for recovery. The last four 220s of each workout were usually run in well under thirty seconds. He did an interval workout of 440s once but did not think it worked for him, so thereafter all of his interval workouts were kept to 220s.

As a freshman, Van finished eighth in the 1964 NAIA Cross Country Championship. In track he finished second in the NAIA national outdoor three mile in a U.S. freshman record of 13:45, a record that was lowered by Gerry Lindgren later that year in a summer meet.

After finishing third in the NAIA cross country meet as a sophomore, Van's confidence grew with each track race he ran during the winter and into the summer of 1966. He won the NAIA indoor two mile title, and outdoors won the NAIA mile and three mile titles. He won the Drake Relays three mile and six mile, a feat he would achieve three straight years, becoming Drake's first three-time double winner, while setting new records in all six races. In July of 1966, he ran his first 10,000 meter race, a new U.S. collegiate record of 28:55.5, passing through six miles in a collegiate record of 28:02.8. It was a time that ranked him fourth on the all-time U.S. performance list. At the end of the summer, he ran a 13:27 three mile race in Helsinki, Finland, which was the seventh best time in the world that year.

During the winter of 1967, Van was sought by indoor meet directors from Madison Square Garden in New York City to the Cow Palace in San Francisco. He traveled around the U.S., racing against the world's best distance runners on banked, wooden tracks set up in city arenas in front of huge crowds. Runners from around the world flocked to this indoor traveling carnival, racing two miles in one city and three miles in the next. Van lowered his two mile personal best to 8:38 and won the NAIA national two mile title. He finished his indoor season with a third place finish at the AAU national meet in the three mile in a personal best of 13:23.9, number four on the all-time world list. Tracy Smith won the race in a new world record time of 13:16.2, breaking Ron Clarke's record of 13:18.4.

But even his weekend travel schedule didn't interrupt his training. Returning from a race in Winnipeg, a heavy snow began to fall. By the time he got back to St. Cloud, there were sixteen inches on the ground. The snowplows had not had a chance to get out yet when Van went out for his ten miler, which he completed in knee deep snow. Cold was not a factor either. There were days when both of his runs were done in below zero temperatures.

In the spring, Van won the NAIA three mile and six mile titles again. In June, he battled Smith and Clarke down to the wire in a 5,000 meter race in Los Angeles. Clarke came out on top in 13:39.8, Smith second in 13:40.8, with Van third in 13:41.8. He doubled in the three mile and six mile races at the AAU Championships in Bakersfield, placing third in the three mile in 13:16.8, with Lindgren winning in 13:10.6. He came back to win the 6 mile in 28:18.8. In August, Van won the 5,000 and 10,000 meter races at the Pan American Games, both in record times. Then it was on to the U.S./ Great Britain dual meet in the White City Stadium, where he won the 10,000 meter run in 28:48.2 on what a London newspaper called "a dusty, slow track." By the end of August 1967, Van had recorded a 13:09.2 three mile time, good for fourth on the world list, ahead of Lindgren and Keino, and a 13:39.4 5,000 meter time, good for sixth on the world list. Both times were at the top of the U.S. list.

By the Olympic year of 1968, Van had become one of the top distance runners in the world. He started the year by winning the NAIA two mile over Australian Olympian Kerry O'Brien, who was allowed to run the race as an open runner. After running an Olympic standard three-mile time of 13:17.4 at the Drake Relays, Van won the six mile in 28:21.1, missing the Olympic standard of 28:05. So the next week he ran a solo 10,000 meter effort at the Macalester Invitational in St. Paul in 28:54.3, under the Olympic standard of 29:00.

Going into the Olympic Trials, Van ranked first in the U.S. six mile with a time of 27:46.8, twenty-six seconds ahead of the second ranked runner, and third in the three mile, with a time of 13:17.4, ten seconds behind Lindgren. One month out from the Olympic 10,000 meter run, the trials race was conducted on a track outside of South Lake Tahoe at 7,347 feet elevation. In a tactical race that came down to a final sprint, Van finished second in 30:04 to Tracy Smith's 30:00. Billy Mills was fourth in 30:32, with Lindgren, coming off of an achilles tendon injury, fifth in 30:44.

Even though Mexico City was at the same altitude as the track at South Lake Tahoe, the conditions were very different. While South

Lake Tahoe had been cool and dry, the day of the Olympic 10,000 meter run was hot and humid. The pace went out slow, going through 5,000 meters in 15:00, before the runners from the countries at altitude took over and forced the pace. Naftali Temu of Kenya ran the second 5,000 meters in 14:27 to win the gold medal. Van stayed with the leaders as long as he could, but faded back through the pack to have the most disappointing finish of his career, twenty-ninth in a field of thirty-eight. The altitude, heat and humidity had taken their toll on all of the runners from sea level countries. Going into the Olympics, Clarke, the world record holder, had run fifteen seconds faster than the next fastest runner, but in Mexico City he staggered in sixth before collapsing, in need of medical attention. Van was not consoled. He had previously beaten many of the runners who finished ahead of him that day. But at twenty-two-years-old, he knew his best running was still ahead of him.

Back in St. Cloud, Van worked on finishing his teaching degree. He had cut back on his class schedule during his junior and senior years in order to compete internationally. Now he cut back on his training, went to school and picked up hours working for a landscaping company to pay his bills. He planned on picking up his training and competition schedule once his degree was finished and he could secure a teaching job. But just a year into his plan, an accident at a construction site crushed a disc in his back and destroyed a nerve running down his right leg. He tried to run, but the pain was too great. He had surgery, but to no avail. At twenty-three-years-old, the career of one of America's most promising distance runners was over.

"Man," said Len aloud, shaking his head. All of the thoughts and feelings he had about Van and the tragic, abrupt end of his running career were jumbled. His imagination had stirred reading about all of the great races Van had run and all of the great runners he had raced. But he felt almost a physical pain in his chest reading about how it had ended. He had seen one of the Minneapolis lakes but had never been around any of them. He wanted to go there now and run and see where Van had run. He imagined Van chasing his team around the lakes and racing against runners from other countries on banked indoor tracks in front of huge, roaring crowds. He wondered if those kind of races still existed. Then his thoughts turned to Ron hungrily turning the pages of Lydiard's book and training for the Olympic team, and of Buddy setting a world record in the marathon and calling it the happiest day of his life. Olympians were from here! They had gone to school here, run on the cross country courses and tracks here, and run on this River Road. All of a sudden, it didn't seem to Len so much that he was just starting out, but that he was continuing what others had started. He felt their legacy and presence as he ran. It was as if a door in his mind that he never even knew existed, had been opened, revealing possibilities of which he had never thought.

# 27

# Living in Harmony

The next few days were hot and Len pretended to be Buddy in Yonkers, running alone far out in front, driven not by the other competitors, but by an inner drive to be the best marathoner in the world. The more he imagined it, the more it seemed possible. He didn't see Tom during this time, even though he stopped in his clearing to stretch and cool off.

One morning the following week, Tom was sitting in the clearing looking out over the river when Len got there. It looked like he had been there for awhile.

"I read about Van," said Len.

"What do you think?"

"You were right, he could really move. He was one of the best in the world."

"It's too bad he got hurt so young."

"That was rotten luck. I wonder what he's doing now?"

"He's probably around here somewhere."

"The Olympics start pretty soon," said Len.

"Yeah, I went to the library and read the paper. I saw something about Prefontaine. He's a young hot shot. He's got some fire in him."

"I think he'll win."

"He says if it's a pure guts race, he's the only one who can win."

Len smiled, then furrowed his brow and cocked his head to the side.

"He might win," said Tom, "but I learned in prison that sometimes guts aren't enough, and they don't replace brains."

Len had sat down on the grass to stretch as Tom talked. He could tell Tom wasn't going anywhere soon, and even though he was in the middle of his run, Len wanted to talk about running. The stories he had read were as compelling to him as Lydiard's book had been to Ron. He had become immersed in this running lore, and wanted to hear more and be a part of it.

Tom spoke in a soft, smooth voice as he looked out over the river. "People who have a rough early life go one of two ways. Some are hard workers. It takes a lot for them to put their trust in anything because people they counted on left them, or things they valued were taken away from them. So they just rely on themselves. Even when they have success, they don't let up. They don't ever want to go back. For others, it's too much. They can't see a way up or out so they give up. I related to Billy Mills because we came from the same background. And I related to some of the things Buddy went through as a kid. But I didn't have success like they did. I couldn't see a path for myself. I was in prison for eighteen years for murder, but maybe it was a blessing. Maybe if I had been out I would have got killed myself, either here or in Vietnam."

Tom looked at Len. He could tell that Len had tensed when he said murder.

"Don't worry, I'm not like that anymore," said Tom, "My life before I went in prison seems more like a dream or something I read, not what I lived. I was an alcoholic and don't even remember much about it or understand it. But I haven't drank since before I went in. Being by the river is good too. I feel my ancestors here. When I got out I didn't want to go back to my family or any of the places I had been before. I didn't want to end up doing the same things or have bad things happen. So I came to St. Paul, to the river. I sat down and looked out at the river for a long time. It was peaceful here, so I decided to stay. I want to live here like my ancestors, along the river in harmony."

"How long have you been out?"

"Just a few weeks, since spring."

They sat quietly in the peaceful tranquility and beauty of the river. Tom seemed to have become lost in thought. He sat motionless, a contemplative look on his face. After a few minutes, Len got up and said, "I'll see you later."

"Okay," said Tom, without moving.

As Len ran home, he thought about what Tom had told him about his life. Tom seemed intelligent and thoughtful and, Len thought, might have been a good teacher. But his life had gone in a different direction. Len tried to think about what he might be doing if he hadn't started running. He knew what some of the alternatives were and was glad he didn't have to think about them. He felt motivated to run even more, and was grateful that he had discovered running, the River Road, his path and the clearing.

Over the next two weeks, Len's running picked up just thinking about Van, Buddy, Ron, and the upcoming Olympics. He went out more days and, despite the added mileage, felt good on his runs. Sometimes when Tom was in the clearing, he sat on the grass and stretched while they talked. On the days he wasn't there, Len stayed on his feet, stretched for a few minutes, then charged back up the path for home.

# 28

## Meat Grinders and Hills

One night in mid-August, Len received a phone call from Mr. Renner. Varsity cross country practice was starting the following Monday. Len said he had been running and that he would be there. He thought fondly of his junior high team, the free-spirited running in the park and the touch football games, but knew that he was beyond that and would not be satisfied going back.

That Saturday, Len rode his bike to the junior high for his physical. As small as he still was, there were now some smaller boys standing, shivering in their white underwear and t-shirts in the line. Soon they would don their football pads and run through tires with the other scrubs while their boorish coach yelled imprecations at them. Len told a couple of them to go out for cross country instead, but he didn't think they would, at least not this year. He had grown a couple of inches and filled out a bit since his first physical two years earlier. A wispy layer of soft, blonde hair had sprouted over his more defined body. A turbulent bay of sun bleached hair flopped along on his head. He took off his clothes and went to the back of the line, but this year did not shiver in the dank air.

On Monday, Len got up and rode his bike through a warm, muggy morning to the high school for cross country practice. Cars were pulling into the parking lot. There was football practice too. He followed a bunch of guys into the school and continued following a few skinnier guys who split off toward a classroom near the locker room. A couple of dozen guys quickly filled the desk seats in the room, creating a jovial cacophony. Len received a couple of addled looks but otherwise went unnoticed or ignored. Mr. Renner walked in, started an attendance sheet around the room and told everyone to pass their forms up to the front. He went over the practice and meet schedule, then told the team to go to the locker room to get lockers and equipment.

Len ambled slowly toward the door as the others poured out into the hallway. He followed the herd down the hall, taking a place at the end of the line outside the equipment room. Thick cotton sweats, a uniform and a lock with a locker number and combination written on athletic tape on the back were issued. Len found his locker and began hanging up his gear.

"Are you sure you're in the right place?" Len heard next to him. He turned to see a lanky, fair-skinned, red haired boy.

"Yeah," said Len, looking up at the much taller boy.

"You broke my junior high mile record."

"You're Kent?"

"Yeah."

Kent looked at the junior high gym clothes Len had worn to practice and smiled.

"Nice outfit."

Len returned a sheepish grin.

"You going to run with us?" asked Kent.

"Yeah, Mr. Renner called me."

Just then Kent heard his name boisterously abused by someone down the row of lockers and turned to face the offender.

"Someone help Bodine with his lock, he's not good with numbers," he called as he moved away from Len.

"Meet out behind the school," yelled a tall, muscular curly-haired boy.

Len waited for some others to begin walking out, then fell in behind them. The team gathered in the grassy shade next to the school. The practice fields were further out and Len could see the football team beginning to gather there.

"Kent, go over to Summit and down to the river," said Mr. Renner, "That'll be five miles."

"That'll be my longest run of the summer," said Bodine.

"And it's going to show," someone added.

Len knew that several of the top runners had run during the summer, but there was a larger group that had done little or no running. Some of the team was already shirtless and now others took off their shirts and threw them onto the ground next to the building. The team took off at an easy pace. Len thought it would pick up but it never did and he ran comfortably at the back of the lead pack the entire way. A good number of guys stayed up with the pace. The rest of the team straggled out behind.

Back at the school, the team lined up to drink from the coldest drinking fountain inside the gym, each greedily pulling the cold water in on his turn. Then one by one as they finished, they returned to the shaded grass behind the school to stretch.

"You must have run some over the summer," Kent said to Len.

"A few times a week. Not every day."

Bodine strayed in, flopped down and sprawled out full length on the ground. "I forgot what five miles felt like," he gasped.

"Are you going to run with us during the year?" Kent asked.

"Yeah, Mr. Renner said there's a football coach that teaches at the junior high that comes over every day. I can ride with him," said Len.

Mr. Renner came out of the building. "How many stayed up with you Kent?" he asked.

"About a dozen."

Mr. Renner scanned the group but said only, "Stretch out good."

"What are we doing tomorrow?" Kent asked.

"Twelve 440s in two man teams."

Kent smiled and said, "Meat grinders."

"Oh boy, my favorite workout," said Bodine, the only guy on the team with a beard.

Mr. Renner looked at him. "You have to shave that off before school starts," he said.

"I know," Bodine said glumly.

"We're gonna be a clean cut team," said Rich.

"We may not be fast, but we'll be clean cut," said Bodine sarcastically.

"Clean and mean," said Rich.

"I'd rather be slow and scruffy," said Bodine.

"I can't be scruffy," said Rich, feeling his own smooth chin.

People slowly started pealing away. Len was the only one that headed toward the bike rack.

Tuesday morning as the team warmed up around the school practice fields, Len felt like he did before a race. He didn't want to run bad and have Mr. Renner or the top guys on the team think it had been a mistake to ask him to run with them. But he also had never done twelve 440s before and didn't know if he could do it very fast or even at all.

On each end of the field, Mr. Renner had put stakes into the ground to resemble the shape of a track, only it included a slight uphill on one side and slight downhill on the other side. He paired the team up in what he thought would be competitive teams of two. Len was with Rich, who had bounced between being the fourth and fifth man on the team the previous year.

"You want to run first or second?" Rich asked Len.

"Whatever you want to do."

"I want to get it done as fast as possible, so I'll go first," said Rich.

The team stretched out and did wind sprints. Everyone's shirts were off in the warm, humid air as they walked to the start. The first group took off like a shot. Rich settled into sixth place on the backstretch. The leadoff group stayed tight all the way around the first quarter-mile so there was congestion as they came into the tag off area.

"Seventy-three, seventy-four," called Mr. Renner as the leaders tagged off.

Rich passed a runner in the final straight and tagged off to Len in fifth place in seventy-five seconds. Len accelerated out onto the course, a dry taste in his mouth. He got passed right away by the partner of the guy that Rich had just passed. He latched onto him and stuck with him down the back stretch. Len decided that it was a long workout and if he used a lot of energy trying to pass him back now, he might regret it later in the workout. He stayed behind and tagged off in sixth place, as Mr. Renner called out two-thirty-two, two-thirty-three.

Rich moved back into fifth. This time, Len held off the other guy longer but still was passed near the end. Once again, Rich passed into fifth, this time putting a little distance on his man. As he tagged Len's hand, he yelled, "Come on!" not angrily but encouragingly. Len dashed out onto the course determined not to get passed again. He held fifth and lost nothing on the teams in front. He heard the guy behind him, but didn't let him past.

The speed guys had dominated the first part of the workout. Now the guys with endurance began to take over. The team Len and Rich had been battling dropped further behind with each leg. The first two teams had opened a gap on the others, with Len and Rich racing two other teams for third.

Into the second half of the workout, Len had to dig deeper each time out. He barely saw Rich take off after tagging his hand. He was exhausted, bent over with his hands on his knees, sweat streaming down his face, lungs straining oxygen from the thick air. When he did look up, Rich was already across the field on the backstretch, halfway done with his lap. The rest of the team appeared to be in a similar state of distress.

On the last 440, the first runners gave what they had left and came in grimacing and gasping. The first two teams were thirty yards ahead of the next three teams coming down the final stretch. Rich came barreling into the tag off zone fourth, slapped Len's hand and yelled, "Go!" Len sprinted out onto the course. He went out as fast as he could, feeling now within the first few steps like he had at the end of each 440 just a few intervals earlier. He stayed in the same position around the first turn and down the backstretch. Just before the final turn, he pumped his arms as if desperately pulling at a lifeline that would keep him in the pack. He felt his head begin to tilt back. His lungs, craving oxygen, sucked in and blew out great volumes of air that seemed to do no good. He held his place around the final turn and into the finish, then stood bent over, hands on his knees, legs trembling. Rich put his hand on Len's back and said,

"Way to run tough." Len thought he had never run so hard in a race or workout.

The team went into the school and drank lustily from the cold fountain, then came out to begin an easy cool down jog around the practice fields. As they jogged, Kent said, "We could be good this year." He listed several guys who had run well in the workout then said, "and we have Lenny."

Len could tell that he had surprised them during the workout that day, but he was still an unknown to them and not everyone appeared ready to fully embrace him. He was younger than some of their siblings and there was a possibility that he would displace one of them for a spot in the top seven. But neither was anyone unfriendly toward him.

He biked home slowly, took a bath and wolfed down a bowl of cereal. He hung lazily around the house all day until it was time for his paper route. He left the house early so he could go into the market and talk to Lawrence for a few minutes before his papers came. Len's legs were more tired and stiff than they had ever been as he walked to the market. Lawrence was behind the cash register awaiting the late afternoon rush, when people came to get last minute items they would need that evening.

"Hi Lenny," said Lawrence brightly as Len walked into the market.

"Hi Lawrence."

Len paused and looked down the aisle at a woman who was searching for something on the spice rack, then looked back at Lawrence.

"Is that extra food you give to dogs and cats sometimes?" asked Len.

"It's what I trim off when I'm cutting meat to package, or if I cut a box of cereal and I can't sell it," said Lawrence. "Sometimes I put a little gravy or milk on it," he said with a smile.

"Do you ever put vegetables and fruit out there?"

"Not usually. But if it's bruised a lot I don't sell it."

"What do you do with it?"

"I take it home to compost for my garden."

"But it's still good to eat?"

"Oh yeah, it's not rotten, just bruised," said Lawrence, then added, "Lots of questions today."

"I have a friend who lives near here that doesn't have a job and I thought if it was just extra anyway … "

"Have him come by, I'll see what I can do."

"Thanks," said Len with a smile.

"Any time," said Lawrence warmly. "What's his name?"

"Tom, he's an Indian."

"That's okay," said Lawrence, smiling.

Len's legs gradually loosened up but remained tired as he walked his route. The day had grown hot and humid. Len walked slowly through the tranquil neighborhood in the copper August light.

Mr. Jenson, an old, retired guy who had worked at the post office for a long time, was in his yard staring up at the gutters on his house. He turned toward Len when the paper hit the step.

"I saw you running," he said, fixing his gaze on him.

"I'm on the cross country team."

"I was a boxer. We ran when we were in training."

"How far did you run?"

"We ran from the gym downtown up to the capitol and back. It was a mile."

"Oh!" said Len, trying to sound impressed.

"We had already sparred and jumped rope so our legs were tired, but it made a difference in the late rounds. We were able to keep going."

Len was momentarily speechless. He couldn't picture Mr. Jenson as a young boxer, bobbing and weaving in the ring, or even just young. He could only envision this crusty, old guy in boxing trunks in a ring with his arms up in the ready position, waiting to get clobbered.

"We used to weigh in for our fights then go out and have a big dinner of steak and eggs. It gave us energy. Sometimes, if we didn't have a fight coming up we got ice cream after our run. We read that's what long distance runners did to cool down after a run."

"Really?"

"Yeah," said Mr. Jenson, looking slightly wounded that Len would question him.

"I've never heard that."

"Well, times have changed," said Mr. Jenson, then added, "You look like you could use some energy."

"We had a hard workout today. I'm still tired."

"You better get going and have some supper," said Mr. Jenson, then added with a nod of his head, "Steak and eggs."

Wednesday the team ran slowly over to Summit Avenue and down to the river again. No one was interested in pushing the pace. Len liked running on Summit's wide, center boulevard. The ground was soft and there were huge elm trees along it so that almost the entire run to the river was shaded. The team ran in a large group that gradually strung out as they threaded their way through the shrubs and flower beds that had been planted on the boulevard. It was the opposite direction from Len's house than the river, but caught the river at a big horseshoe bend a few miles away from his usual running route. There was a small park at the intersection of Summit and the River Road that had a drinking fountain, so the team invariably stopped to drink before turning back for school.

Thursday the team jogged their warm-up a couple of miles over to a long hill next to the Town and Country golf course, stopping at the bottom of it to stretch under a huge oak tree. The workout was to sprint eight times up the hill and jog down for recovery in-between. Most everyone's legs were still sore and heavy from the meat grinders.

"I don't know if I can get up this even once," said Bodine.

"Yeah, this is going to be a tough one," said Kent.

"If I die at the top, just bury me there," said Rich.

"If I die, I'm going to do it at the bottom," said Bodine. "That's one less hill."

The team finished warming up and walked over to where Mr. Renner was standing.

"The hill's about 500 yards," he said. "I'm not going to time them, but run them hard. Jog on the way down, don't walk. Look up at the top of the hill as you run, not down at the hill. That will keep your head up and your body tall so you can put a strong, efficient force into the ground. Drive your knees and your arms."

The team started up the hill but not with the same enthusiasm with which they had attacked the meat grinders. They ran together, with no one wanting to expend too much energy on the first one. Halfway up, a loud fart punctuated the sound of footsteps and breathing.

"I think that says it all," said Rich, and everyone burst out laughing. This slowed down the run even more.

"Did you guys hear that car backfire?" asked Phil, who had been identified as the offender.

"I thought you were just trying to propel yourself up the hill," said Bodine.

"Ha! I could use some jet propulsion," said Rich.

"Next time wait until I'm not behind you," said Wayne, "my eyebrows are singed."

Mark and Kent pushed the second hill harder and the team began to string out. After getting the stiffness out of their legs on the first hill, and despite the heaviness, the next few hills were gradually faster before maintaining on the last couple.

"Well, that hurt a lot," said Bodine sardonically as the team began jogging back to the school.

"No kidding," said Rich.

"Hills are good for you though," said Mark.

"It went better than I thought it would," said Kent.

"After the first one," said Rich.

"Yeah, I felt better after that one," said Phil.

"I should think so!" exclaimed Bodine. "You should have felt a whole lot better after getting that out of your system!"

Len felt better on the jog back to the school than he had on the jog out to the hill. His legs were tired but, in some perverse way, the hills had worked the soreness out of them. He had never carried over such fatigue from a previous workout, but it had gone better than he thought it would. As he jogged back with the team, he sensed that he had gained something valuable from the workout, something he could not quite identify, but that he knew was going to make him a better runner. His sense was not only for his body, but for his mind as well.

# 29

# Mile Repeats

That afternoon, Lawrence muttered, "What in the world?" as he looked at the front page of the paper while Len folded.

"What is it?" asked Len.

"World Chess Championship organizers rope off the first seven rows of auditorium seats," read Lawrence.

"Why?"

"Fischer said the spectators were bothering him. He demanded that the first seven rows of auditorium seats be removed. He wanted it done earlier but they wouldn't do it. This time he said he would leave if they didn't do it. So they took them out. But they didn't tell the Soviets. When the Soviets found out, they protested and made them put them back in. So they compromised and put them back in but roped them off so no one could sit in them."

Len didn't know what to say. Despite having a commanding lead over Boris Spassky, Bobby Fischer kept up the pressure on the organizers. When he got home, Len read more of the article. Each player had received half-a-point for each game during the long series of draws. Fischer held a three point lead, but more importantly was just two points away from winning the championship. Spassky and his team worked desperately to turn the tide, but Fischer was a master of the kill and moved inexorably toward victory.

Len thought about Boris Spassky. He had been confident at the start, but Fischer's aggressive play rattled him and he had lost an early string of games. He had recovered, but only enough to salvage a series of draws. The article said Spassky was digging deep into his ability to try to win a game, but could not do it. There was something about Fischer that he could not decipher. He went into the games not knowing what would come next from Fischer, and grimly wondered how he would respond to it. Len thought it was like him going into these hard workouts he had never done before. He was not sure if he could do them or do them well enough to stay up where he wanted to be. The difference was that Spassky had to overcome Fischer, while Len had to overcome his own doubts and fears. Fischer seemed to have gained strength and confidence from watching Spassky's frustration. Len marked his own progress by his ability to stay up with the top runners on the team, gaining strength and confidence the more he did it. While Len had struggled on the hills, he hadn't struggled more than anyone else, and knew that he had only struggled because of accumulated fatigue and not because of something he lacked. To his surprise, he had recovered more quickly than most of the others and felt that it was due to having charged up his path in the weeks before practice. He was confident that when his legs were fresher he would be a tough hill racer. But just as important, he was beginning to feel the confidence to push himself without fear.

Friday the team ran five miles out around an A&W that was popular with the team. Mark was dating one of the waitresses and several of the guys yelled, "Hi Janet!" as they ran by. It didn't matter that Janet was nowhere in sight and, in fact, the A&W was not open for the day yet. Len could tell that the A&W played an integral role in the social life of the team.

Saturday morning the workout was three times one mile with three minutes rest over the conference cross country course at Como Park. The team jogged to the park in a good mood. Their legs were tired from the week but, like Len, most of the team's muscle soreness had subsided. He had never done mile intervals and knew, with the training load already in his legs, it was going to be a tough workout in which he would, once again, be pushed to his limit. But he also knew that the rest of the team was feeling the same and if he could stay up, it would mean that he had a good chance to make the varsity. He was prepared to dig deep.

The three mile course was laid out in two conjoined one-mile loops. The course covered the first loop, then the second, then finished by running the first loop in reverse. The ground was rolling with thick grass and a few tight turns. The team finished their warm-up then shuffled, shirtless and solemn, to the start.

"Let's go guys," said Mark. "Run together. We need a pack."

"Ready?" asked Mr. Renner looking the group over.

No one said anything so he said "Go!"

Mark and Kent pushed out to the front right away. Phil and Rich fell in behind them, with Len following closely. Gradually, a gap began to grow behind Len, with the top five separating themselves from the rest of the team. The five stayed together all the way, finishing in 5:20. It felt hard to Len, his acceleration out of each turn requiring progressively more effort throughout the mile.

"Way to go guys," said Mark.

"Keep it going." said Kent.

Len wasn't sure he could continue at this pace, but knew he would try. He looked at Rich. His usual blithe face was fixed in a frown of concentration. Phil looked determined.

"Come on Lenny," said Rich in a soft voice without looking at him as they went to the start of the second mile. But Len could tell Rich was wrestling with his own doubts.

Kent and Mark led out the second one. This time Len ran alongside Phil, with Rich right behind. The grass seemed longer on this loop, and Len felt like he had to lift his feet higher to get through it. By halfway, Rich was struggling and was losing a couple of steps on Phil and Len around each turn. Kent and Mark ran side by side, opening a fifteen yard gap on Phil and Len by the end. They ran another 5:20. Phil and Len came through in 5:23, and Rich in 5:27.

Len's fatigue was becoming systematic, the acrid flashpoint below his sternum radiating out to his extremities. No one talked as they jogged and walked in circles around the starting area seeking recovery. They waited for Mr. Renner to call them to the line, each questioning his own ability to summon the required effort for the last mile.

"Come on guys," said Kent. "Keep it together. It's the last one. This is where we win the race."

"We can do it," affirmed Mark.

Mr. Renner said, "Here we go, last one."

The team took off. It was hard for Len from the first step. There was nothing he could do as Mark and Kent began to pull away after the first quarter mile. Phil ran beside Len, his head oscillating from side to side with the effort. Rich clung desperately to their back. At the halfway point, Phil got a couple of steps ahead of Len through a turn. Len pushed harder onto the next straight and got back up with him. Rich was receding behind.

Mr. Renner, holding a stopwatch, came into view. Kent and Mark, still running side by side thirty yards in front, finished under 5:20. Phil and Len finished together in 5:25. Rich came in just over 5:30. They moved off in different directions, each managing his own torment privately. As the paroxysms subsided Kent said, "Good job guys. We have five guys better than any of us were last year at this time."

The last of the team was trickling in. At the end of the first week of practice, everyone knew where they stood. As they milled about recovering, several guys said, "Good job Lenny."

"You too," Len replied.

He didn't remember all of their names yet, but he could tell that they were no longer skeptical of his ability to be there, nor was he.

# 30

# The Happy Games

Len biked home, ate a bowl of cereal, and waited for the Olympic opening ceremony to come on TV. The stadium appeared, magnificent and futuristic, with an uneven glass spiderweb-like canopy over the seats on one side. Along the top of the other side, the flags of the world fluttered colorfully in a gentle breeze. Jim McKay said the glass canopy was designed to suggest the nearby Alps and a new democratic, transparent Germany, contrasting the last Olympics held in Germany during the Nazi era. "The Happy Games" was the motto.

The athletes began parading into the stadium and Len looked for the American distance runners. He didn't see any of them and began to doze off. He perked up when he heard McKay say, "There they go, 5,000 Bavarian doves symbolizing peace, brotherhood and sportsmanship, which is certainly much in evidence here today," as the birds were released and flew up into, and then out of the stadium. The Olympic flag was hoisted up into the breeze and the Olympic flame roared to life. The games were underway.

McKay and his announcing partner Chris Shenkel, talked about the great east-west rivalry that would play out over the next three weeks. They had seen many instances of the Soviet Union, East Germany and the United States using sports competitions as propaganda opportunities. Hearing this, and following the Fischer/ Spassky match, Len began to understand that no venue was exempt from the Cold War. But he wondered what the athletes from these countries thought, if they felt the same as their governments, or for them, if the Olympic ideal transcended the official animosity and suspicion. Len thought that it would for him, but he could not be sure. Maybe he just didn't know enough about all of it. But it seemed like the Cold War was like a deeply woven fiber that threaded its way through almost everything that went on in the world, and maybe there was just no getting around it.

Len's view of the world derived largely from the afternoon newspaper. As he glanced at the front page each day while unbundling the papers, he learned about the Cold War, Vietnam War, Middle East war, Northern Ireland war, space war, racial war, all of the wars going on in the world. Many of the things on the front page that were not wars, were the causes or effects of wars - demonstrations, assassinations, bombings, kidnappings, hijackings, defections. The Olympics would be a welcome respite, he thought. Even McKay and Shenkel seemed optimistic that, despite the political atmosphere outside of Munich, the Olympics would provide great and fair athletic competition.

Right away, when he saw the athletes coming into the stadium, Len wanted to be an Olympian. To walk out into this stadium as one of the top athletes in the world, along with the other top athletes, seemed the athletic pinnacle. He was excited anticipating the Olympic races. He wondered what Prefontaine was doing right now, and what it was like in the Olympic village and in Munich.

# 31

## All the Victory and All the Loss

Len had planned to take Sunday off from running, but the day was resplendent and he hadn't been to his clearing all week. Late in the morning, he put on his running clothes and went out the door. His legs were tired, so he went slow. The clearing was beautiful and serene. He stretched on the grass in the warm sun. After a few minutes, he heard footsteps and looked up to see Tom coming down the path from the River Road.

"I haven't seen you for awhile," said Tom.

"Cross country practice started so I'm running there during the week."

"How's it going?"

"Hard. I'm tired and sore."

"You running a lot?"

"Yeah, and we had three hard workouts this week. We did meat grinders Tuesday, hills Thursday and mile intervals yesterday."

"Meat grinders huh? That sounds hard."

"Yeah, it was. The other days we ran five miles."

"Is today your long run?"

"No, I'm just doing an easy run."

"Maybe you can work into it once you get used to the training."

"Maybe next week."

"It was the long runs that made Daws good. That and he learned from his mistakes. Everybody makes mistakes but not everybody learns from them. That was one of the most important things I learned in prison. It's not bad luck if you keep doing the same things over and over and bad things happen to you. It's stubbornness, stupidity or fear. People don't like to change though. It's hard. But that's the only way to make things different or better. Sometimes people are afraid of what might happen if they try something new. But once they do, and things are better, they wonder why they were so afraid."

Len didn't know what to say, but he understood what Tom had said and he let it sink in for a minute before he said, "The Olympics started yesterday, but track doesn't start until Thursday."

"I watched some of the last Olympics," said Tom. "They had a TV in the rec. room. I remember watching Jim Ryun and being confused. He was the favorite in the 1500 meters, but he let Keino get so far ahead of him. They kept saying he had a great kick at the end, but I couldn't see how he could make up that much ground. And he didn't. He was either over confident in his kick or he underestimated Keino. Or maybe he was psyched out. He might have been beat before the race even started. Maybe he didn't really believe he could beat Keino at altitude. Maybe he can win a gold medal this time though. All of the great runners come back stronger after they lose. It motivates them. They train harder and don't make the same mistakes again. Ryun was so good so young. A lot of people expected him to win every race. But no one can be great all of the time. He's probably been pushing himself pretty hard since Mexico City."

"I bet Van would have done good in this Olympics," said Len.

"Yeah, he would have been motivated, and in his prime. They might have been talking about him as much as Prefontaine."

"I think they would have. It would have been great to see him run."

"Yeah, it would."

"Do you know Lawrence's Market on Cleveland Avenue?" asked Len.

"Yeah, I've been by it."

"Lawrence is a friend of mine. That's where I pick up my papers. He said he has extra food all the time. He doesn't like to throw it away, so I told him about you and he said you should come by and get some of it so he doesn't have to throw it away."

There was a pause. Tom looked at Len.

"He's a real nice guy," said Len.

Tom's face softened. "Ok, if he's a real nice guy."

That afternoon Len began an infatuation. He had run easily back to his house, had lunch, then turned on the Olympics. The first event covered was the women's gymnastics all-around prelims. He had never seen gymnastics. The Soviet Union was the top team. They had a seventeen-year-old girl who had bouncy, blonde hair and an easy, beautiful smile. She played to the crowd and they responded fervently, which made her play to them all the more. When she finished, they cheered wildly and she flashed her sweet smile and waved. The crowd, the announcers, everyone loved Olga Korbut, with the possible exception of her older teammate, Ludmila Tourischeva.

Tourischeva was like an attractive, but plain older sister trying to compete with a cute, precocious younger sister just discovering the effect she could have on those around her. They were teammates, but also competitors. They were two of the best gymnasts in the world on the best team in the world. Tourischeva was seasoned and serious in her quest for the title of world's best gymnast that the all-around competition would bestow. Korbut seemed not to care, to be doing it just for the pure joy of it, to please the crowd seemed to delight her. Her routines were stunning and daring but she made them look easy and fun, as if she were in the backyard playing on a swing-set or in the grass. She did a back flip on the balance beam in between graceful walkovers and leggy poses. She stood on the top bar of the uneven bars, leapt into space and executed a back flip which brought her hands back to the top bar. But it was her dancing, smiling floor routine set to music that invited the crowd to share her exuberance fully as they clapped in time and cheered her every move. They appreciated Tourischeva, but they adored Korbut.

The coverage then turned to Dan Gable of the United States, wrestling his first match. McKay said he was America's greatest wrestler. He had not lost a single match throughout high school and just one, his last, collegiate match. That loss had haunted and motivated him. It took months for him to acknowledge that maybe it had even made him a better wrestler. He now worked harder than ever because he never wanted to lose again.

McKay narrated a feature on Gable. It began with Gable running in a cold rain in his hometown of Waterloo, Iowa. He finished his run in front of the camera and began to talk as water droplets collected on his face. McKay told about his undefeated high school career and his 181 straight college victories. Then the camera zoomed slowly in on Gable's face. The intensity in his eyes penetrated the lens as he said, "Every time I win a match it fires me up. It feels so good, especially in an individual sport like wrestling because it's all you and it's all your opponent. You're the winner or the loser. You take everything there is to be taken. You take all the victory, you take all the loss."

Gable had verbalized what Len was already beginning to feel about running and himself. Every time Len put on his running clothes and went out the door, running became a little more personal to him, a little more who he was, his own self-definition and image emanating from within him for the first time. The strengths and weaknesses revealed in each race and hard workout began to form the essence of who he was and would become. Everything running had to offer felt like his alone.

During the match, Gable's Yugoslavian opponent lunged at Gable headfirst, butting his forehead into Gable's and drawing blood. The flow was stemmed and Gable dominated the match, holding his foe scoreless before pinning him in the second period. After the match, three stitches were sewn into Gable's forehead.

# 32

# Motivated by Defeat

Monday morning the team ran five miles together out around the Town and Country golf course and back. There was still some heaviness in Len's legs but no soreness. Everyone on the team was still feeling the accumulated fatigue of the first week of practice, but the team spirit was good.

"Did you see that Russian girl, Olga, do that back flip on the uneven bars?" asked Rich as they ran.

"My body doesn't bend like that," said Bodine.

"Even the other gymnasts don't bend like that," said Rich.

"She's a freak!" said Bodine.

"A really good looking freak," said Rich.

"Ha!" Bodine laughed.

"She can use me as an apparatus anytime," said Rich.

"You can be the horse," piped in Kent.

"Women don't have the horse," said Rich.

"You can be the horse anyway," said Bodine.

"Ha!" laughed Rich.

"I don't know how they stay on that balance beam," said Mark. "It's only four inches wide."

"Did you see what Olga did with her legs on the beam?" asked Rich

"Here we go," said Bodine.

"I can't help it. I'm in love," said Rich.

"You're in love every week," said Bodine, "with somebody different."

"It's not my fault, they're all in love with me," said Rich.

"Olga's in love with you?" asked Kent.

"She would be if she knew me," said Rich.

"She's probably in love with some Russian soldier who would crush your face if you looked at her," said Bodine.

"I'd risk it for those legs," said Rich.

That night, Len turned on the Olympic coverage. Del came in, plopped down on the couch and asked, "What are we watching, Squirt?"

"The Olympics," said Len.

It was a rare evening that Del was home, but he was still recovering from the weekend. He had finished his summer job Friday and gone with friends to a Rolling Stones concert at the Met Center on Saturday. He did not get home until Sunday morning just as Len was finishing his run, then spent most of the day in bed. At dinner that evening, Len's dad said, "I read there were some problems at the concert."

"Yeah, there was no air conditioning. It was really hot," said Del.

"I meant the tear gas."

"That's what that was? All the sudden our eyes were watering and stinging."

"You didn't see anything?"

"No, I was inside and didn't see anything but then our eyes started going nuts, but only for a few minutes."

"There were a lot of fans outside the Met Center that didn't get tickets. They wouldn't leave and started getting rowdy. The police used tear gas to disperse them. Some of it must have got into the building through the vents."

"It only got rowdy inside when Stevie Wonder played a long drum solo and people started chanting, 'We want the Stones.'"

"Stevie Wonder was the opening act?"

"Yeah, he was okay except for the drum solo. The acoustics are pretty bad in there though so nothing sounded that good."

His dad paused, then asked, "Do you have everything ready to go back to school?"

"Yeah, I'm ready," said Del with a chuckle.

The Olympic coverage started at the swimming pool, where American Mark Spitz began an epic quest to win seven gold medals in one Olympics. The excitement had built not only in anticipation of his success, but also conversely in anticipation of his potential failure. Before the 1968 Olympics, he had predicted he would win six gold medals. He won just two, both on relays. He underperformed in his individual events, including finishing dead last in the 200 meter butterfly final. His disappointment had fueled his motivation and work for four years. This time he had not predicted winning seven gold medals, but had made his quest known. In order to accomplish this, he would have to race fourteen times in eight days.

Len had never seen a swimming race. The natatorium quieted for the gun, then exploded in a reverberation of sound echoing off the walls as the swimmers dove into the pool for the 200 meter butterfly. Spitz's tall, muscular body extended fully out over, then into, the water, surfacing far out into the pool, ahead of his competitors. His giant wing span went to work churning the water around him and driving his shoulders up into the air with each stroke. With each turn he extended his lead, opening up three body lengths on the field by the finish, winning in a new world record.

"You should've been a swimmer," said Len to Del. "You have long arms like Spitz."

"Not that long, and I don't like to get wet," said Del.

Len smiled and turned back to the TV. The coverage went to women's gymnastics, where the prelims continued in the all-around competition. Len, along with the announcers and crowd, were ready to crown Olga Korbut. The efficient Tourischeva had been performing impeccably, but could not match Korbut's flair, personality or crowd rapport. The crowd and announcers appreciated all of the top performers, but the star was Korbut. Everyone awaited her routines and responded ebulliently to them.

Jim McKay had alerted the viewers that they were in for a special treat when Korbut's turn came on the uneven bars. Now she walked delicately up to the apparatus, leapt forward, catching the bottom bar in her hands. Then, swinging her straight legs underneath the bar, she stretched her body full length out into the air in front of the apparatus and propelled herself through a series of graceful maneuvers that elevated her to the top bar. As she placed both feet on top of the bar, MacKay's announcing partner, Gordon Maddox exclaimed, "Now watch this, watch this! Back summy right to the other bar!"

"Oh!" McKay exclaimed, "Has that been done by anyone before?"

"No, never! Not by any human that I know of," said Maddox.

Korbut now made a daring move down to the lower bar. "Look at that!" exclaimed Maddox, "And she's second best! I don't believe it!" he exclaimed, referring to the Soviet press guide that had touted Tourischeva as the top Soviet.

"This then is a historic performance you're watching right now in gymnastics," said McKay, as Korbut moved fluidly to the top bar, placed both feet on it a second time, and shot herself into a back flip dismount that carried her over the bottom bar and into a perfect landing.

"Oh my god!" exclaimed Maddox, his voice raising a full octave. She raised her arms in triumph and flashed a smile of pure joy before trotting off the platform to rejoin her team.

"I have to say, that was amazing," said Del.

"Yeah," was all Len could manage to say.

The coverage went back to the pool. Len was looking forward to the U.S. four by 100 meter relay, with Mark Spitz on the anchor leg. But the first event shown was the women's 200 meter individual medley relay. The U.S. women's team had several strong swimmers who would contend for medals, but the focus of this race was on a fifteen-year-old Australian named Shane Gould. Len was amazed that here was another great fifteen-year-old girl swimmer! He was watching his first Olympics while she was competing in hers, and while Lynne Cox was celebrating her historic swim across the English Channel.

McKay gave some background on the prodigious Gould. The previous year, at age fourteen, she had broken every women's freestyle world record from 100 meters through 1500 meters, a stunning feat no one else had ever accomplished. Like Spitz, she would be logging several thousand meters of racing in Munich. She was entered in five individual events and one relay, and would race twelve times in eight days.

The camera zoomed in on her as she stepped up onto the starting platform. She was tall, with broad shoulders. But she looked soft also and had a round teenage face like Lynne Cox, not like the gaunt distance runners and the tiny gymnasts Len had seen. The gun sounded and she stretched her long body out over the water, slicing into the surface like a knife. She emerged with an enormous wingspan into the butterfly stroke. She touched the far wall of the pool a split second ahead of the second place swimmer. She was passed by two swimmers on the backstroke leg, but moved back into second on the breast stroke. Going into the last fifty meters of the race, she was half a body length behind. But the final freestyle leg was her specialty, and she attacked it. She took the lead in the midst of the leg and pulled away to win by half a body length in a new world record. After looking to the scoreboard to verify her win, she placed both hands over her face and held them there. On the medal stand, she held a toy stuffed kangaroo and wiped away tears.

"Good for the Aussies," said Del. "I want to go there some day."

Watching the phenomenal, passionate Gould, Len had almost forgotten about Mark Spitz and the four by 100 meter relay, but now those teams came out onto the pool deck. The U.S. team looked confident and serious. They took the lead on the first leg, and continued to extend it throughout the race. Spitz swam the anchor leg all alone and celebrated the victory, and another world record, with the rest of the team at the end. Two down and five to go. He had made the first two look easy.

Then Dan Gable came out for his second match of the competition with a bandage wrapped all the way around his head to cover the stitches in his forehead. Again, he dominated his opponent, a West German, holding him scoreless. The final score was twenty to nothing, a major decision.

"That was brutal," said Del.

"He's only lost one match in his whole life," volunteered Len.

"The guy that beat him deserves a gold medal," said Del. "Even if it wasn't in the Olympics, they should just send him one in the mail."

Watching both Spitz and Gable compete was compelling to Len. The athletes they were competing against had also reached the top of their sport, but Spitz and Gable seemed so much better. And yet, it was failure, not victory, that had motivated them on to this greater height. It wasn't their incredible string of victories and titles that fed their dreams, it was their singular, and to them, devastating defeats. Spitz's letdown in Mexico City and Gable's lone defeat had intensified their Olympic preparations. Losing was loathsome to them. So loathsome that it caused them to reach deeper within themselves emotionally, psychologically and physically to avoid experiencing it again. At this stage of their careers, victory seemed to elicit affirmation and relief within them rather than joy. It proved that what they had been pouring their lives into for so many years had been worth it. A defeat would have caused them to question that conclusion.

Len had already experienced the motivational aspects of losing. The Johnson runners who had beaten him in cross country had been on his mind during the track season, and were perhaps the strongest factor in his running a school record in the mile. He had not beaten them, but he had gotten closer, and as he thought about Spitz and Gable, he knew that chasing the Johnson runners had pulled more out of him than any race he had won. He had trained harder, his attention was more focused, knowing that he would face them in the championship.

# 33

# One Tough Hombre

Tuesday the team jogged slowly around the school practice fields for their warm-up. The workout was five times a half-mile with two minutes rest in between. The course was the same quarter-mile loop on which they ran the meat grinders, only twice around. But they ran these all together, not as a two-man relay. Once again Mark and Kent set the pace, with Phil, Rich and Len clinging together a few yards back. Behind them, Rob and Wayne were beginning to rise above the others in pursuit of the final two varsity positions.

Rob was a good friend of Mark's who had been a receiver on the football team before this year. He was a good athlete who had received plenty of playing time but had been persuaded by Mark to come out for cross country. His main sport was basketball and he thought that running cross country had the double benefit of getting him in better shape with less risk of injury than football. He had always done some running in the summer anyway, but this summer he had run more consistently with Mark. He didn't have Mark's talent for running, but he was a hard worker and had progressed steadily. Mark had told him the team had a chance to make it to state and he was determined to make the top seven. He started most workouts keying on Rich, Phil and Len before falling off. But with almost each workout he was hanging on longer and separating himself from the other contenders.

Wayne had a natural talent for running, but usually did just enough to get by. He ran the minimal amount during the summer that he thought would get him onto the varsity. In workouts, he hung back until the last couple of intervals before pushing hard enough to secure the sixth or seventh spot. There were other harder workers on the team with varsity dreams, who had run more over the summer, who fought to gain the sixth or seventh position in workouts, who it would have meant more to, but who were denied in the final stages of nearly every hard workout when Wayne's talent surfaced.

That night, Len and Del watched as Mark Spitz stood on the pool deck behind his starting platform smoothing his mustache with both hands. This had now become a familiar sight. While his competitors sought to squeeze hundredths of seconds from their times by shaving their bodies of hydrodynamic-impeding hair, Spitz sported a mustache that was quickly becoming iconic.

"Maybe I should grow a mustache," said Del. Len looked over at him, trying to picture it, but didn't say anything. He thought Del might look a little like Frank Shorter with a mustache, only with longer hair.

Spitz stepped onto the platform for the 200 meter freestyle and crouched into his starting position. The gun fired and he sliced into the water, again surfacing ahead of his competitors. In this race, his toughest competition came from his U.S. teammate, Steve Genter. Spitz held the lead through the first fifty meters before Genter pulled even in the second fifty. They turned together at the halfway point. Genter pushed into the lead in the third fifty, but Spitz came on strong in the last fifty to retake the lead. Spitz had won his third gold medal and set his third world record.

"Genter gave him a run," said Del.

"Yeah, he was tough," said Len.

Next came Shane Gould's attempt to win a second gold medal. The 100 meter freestyle was a good event for the U.S. women, but Gould was the world record holder. It was a furious race, just once to the other end of the pool and back. Gould's reaction time off the starting platform was slow. She surfaced from the start near the back of the field. Sandy Neilson of the U.S. was out in front, setting a frenetic pace. Gould moved up through the field one swimmer at a time, but could only move up to third, four 100ths of a second behind Shirley Babashoff of the U.S. A raucous cheer went up from the American section as the results appeared on the scoreboard showing

Neilson and Babashoff of the U.S. going one, two. Gould took the bronze.

"Man, the start is everything in that race," said Del.

Len thought about his seventh grade sprint races. Ten yards in he had already been five yards behind. "Starts are hard," he said.

Len wondered if Gould was beginning to get tired from all of her races or if she would turn out to be like Mark Spitz in Mexico City. Maybe she needed four more years to be able to handle the pressure. Being near the same age, Len wondered how he would handle it. His heart rate had increased before the 100 meter freestyle just watching Gould pacing the pool deck deep in concentration. It was exhilarating for Len to watch this level of individual competition! All of the visages of confidence, poise, doubt and apprehension could be seen on the faces of the swimmers, gymnasts and wrestlers as they prepared for their moment of truth. At the completion of their event, their aspects became those of elation, satisfaction, disappointment or resignation, depending on the degree to which they had fulfilled their expectations. The disappointed Gould swam under the lane markers to congratulate the celebrating Americans, and they embraced her back. Their looks acknowledged their understanding that on another day their roles might easily have been reversed, and they were gracious.

The coverage then went to the wrestling venue for Dan Gable's third match. Again, Gable dominated his opponent from the opening whistle. He scored a second period pin over a Greek wrestler. While his teammates and coaches celebrated each victory, Gable never celebrated, or even looked happy, after his matches. Len wondered what, if anything, he felt as he walked impassively off the mat, and would it be different if he won the gold medal.

"That is one tough hombre," said Del. "Not to be messed with."

# 34

## The Flame Inside

Wednesday the team ran easily along Summit Avenue.

"Can you imagine wrestling Dan Gable?" asked Bodine as they ran. "The guy just looks at you and you want to crap your pants."

"Ha! That's why I'm a runner," said Rich.

"He's tough," said Mark.

"He probably laughed when they put those stitches in his head," said Kent.

"Ha! He wanted more. 'What? I only get three?'" said Bodine.

"How would you feel if, out of hundreds of matches, you were the one guy that beat him?" asked Rich.

"I'd retire," said Bodine.

"You'd kind of feel bad you wrecked his perfect record, but happy you did it too," said Kent.

"I'd be happy," said Mark. "You'd know you were the best."

"I'd settle for second best and not have to wrestle him," said Bodine.

That night was the women's all-around gymnastics final. The world had all but crowned Olga Korbut and this would be her coronation. Despite her fantastic and unprecedented back flips on the uneven bars and balance beam, she was in third after the prelims. But it was very close, even back to tenth place where the first American, the tiny, beautiful Cathy Rigby was placed. Rigby was the top American and was a medal contender in the balance beam by virtue of winning a silver medal in that event at the world championships two years before. It was the first medal ever won in international competition by a female U.S. gymnast.

Del was hooked on the Olympics. He had slowly regained his physical equilibrium from the weekend but stayed in and joined Len for another night of Olympic viewing. The vault was the first event of the all-around final. When the camera zoomed in for a close-up of Rigby, Del said, "Whoa! I have *got* to start watching more gymnastics."

The vault was the only apparatus or event in which Korbut didn't excel. But she was good enough to not have it damage her chances for an all-around gold medal. The places remained the same after the competitors rotated through an uneventful series of vaults. Next up was the uneven bars, where Korbut's breathtaking release from the top bar had become one of the most anticipated events of the Olympics.

Korbut approached the bars, Len thought, with a less uniform, more feminine walk than her teammates. She leapt forward, catching the bottom bar in her hands. But where she usually swung her straight legs underneath the bar and stretched them out in front of the apparatus, she caught her heel on the floor, breaking the elegant, straight line of her legs at the knee and stopping her forward momentum.

"Look at that!," exclaimed Gordon Maddox, "Right off the bat. Oh, that's a shame! And she's in such a tight fight for the championship."

Korbut pushed off the floor with her legs and began the routine again. It was a huge mistake, but she regained her rhythm and beautifully executed her signature back flip off the top bar.

"Here we go," Maddox said hopefully, "There's a back summy to the catch. Wow! Even with her mistake, she's revolutionizing gymnastics!"

But seconds later, she swung low on the apparatus and again caught her feet on the ground.

"Another mistake!" exclaimed Maddox. "Poor kid. This is what we talk about when we say seasoning."

With her momentum broken, she struggled ungainly to get to the top bar.

"She's just lost it all. Lost her composure at age seventeen," lamented Maddox.

"Ha! Done at seventeen, just kill yourself," said Del.

The crowd gasped. It was a disaster. In the course of less than one minute, she had not only dropped out of contention for the all-around gold medal, but also out of contention for any medal. At the end of her routine, she was not smiling. There was no wave. She walked back to her team bench, sat down, lowered her head and began to cry. The usual grim stoicism the Soviet women displayed after a bad routine didn't apply to Korbut, although none had bungled a routine so badly. Korbut's tears seemed to melt the hearts of all who watched and had been enchanted by her, Len included.

The Soviet team now prepared to move on to the balance beam. Korbut gathered her belongings and fell in at the back of the line. They walked in unison in a straight line. As they walked to the beam, Korbut wiped away the last vestige of tears from her high cheek bones, visibly trying to regain the concentration she would need for this demanding and risky event.

When it was her turn, Korbut mounted the beam with confidence and precision. To Len's eye, there were no flaws in her beautiful, difficult routine. She smiled and waved again at the end and the audience embraced her even more. She received the top score.

Del shook his head. "That was amazing!"

"Yeah, I don't know how they stay on that thing," said Len.

"And do all those things," said Del, then added, "back flips!"

As amazing as Korbut was to Del, he was more mesmerized by Rigby. But she could not break into the medals. Nor could Korbut. In the floor exercise, Korbut received the second best score as the crowd blithely clapped along. But it was not enough to move her into the top three. Len had never seen anything more feminine than Korbut's trot off of the platform at the end of her floor exercise. She floated gently on her toes, her arms delicately bent at her sides, her body swaying gracefully. Len had also never seen anyone exhibit such emotion, experience such heartache, in an athletic event, then turn around minutes later and display such steely strength and

146

concentration. There were no girls sports at school and Len wondered if any of the girls he knew would make good athletes. It had never occurred to him that any of them would want to be an athlete. But watching Olga Korbut and Shane Gould compete, he knew that the flame inside them burned as hot as any male athlete he had ever seen. Korbut had displayed the same tenacity and mettle as Dan Gable and Mark Spitz in emerging from a crushing defeat to perform at the top of her sport.

The coverage went back to the pool as Spitz was standing behind the starting platform smoothing his mustache. He stepped up onto the platform, shook his long arms loosely at his sides and crouched into his starting position to wait for the gun to fire. When it did, he once again, stretched his body out over the water and emerged with the lead in the 100 meter butterfly. The race was a full-on sprint to the other end of the pool and back. With each enormous stroke Spitz extended his lead. By the finish he had opened up a full body length. It was his fourth gold medal and fourth world record.

"That guy is made to swim," said Del.

"Just like Gable is made to wrestle," said Len.

Then Shane Gould stepped up onto the starting platform for the 400 meter freestyle. Again, she wasn't the quickest into the water, but once there, the cadence of her arms was noticeably quicker than her competitors. By the 100 meter turn, she had opened up a full body length lead on the field. Her cadence continued unabated, with four or five strokes between each breath. By 200 meters she was up by two body lengths. As the field continued to fall further behind, their strokes slowing and becoming more ragged, Gould maintained her rhythm and precision. By 300 meters she was all alone. In the final fifty meters, with the Aussie section roaring and waving towels in the air, Gould's arms began to splash a little more with each stroke. But she had dominated the race and finished well ahead of the field. At the end of the pool she saluted the Aussie crowd with a wave and smile as she caught her breath. Her time was a new world record. She had clearly put the 100 meter freestyle behind her and summoned all of her energy in this exquisite victory.

The day's coverage finished at the wrestling venue with Dan Gable's fifth match. Earlier in the day he had won his fourth match with a decision over a Japanese wrestler. Now he dominated his Polish opponent before pinning him in the second period. Still, none of Gable's opponents had scored a single point against him. And still, he walked off the mat stoically, workman-like, as if he had just finished with his shift at the factory and was ready to punch out.

"Still no points against him," said Del shaking his head, "and those guys are good!"

"Wrestling's tough," said Len.

Len enjoyed Del's comments. He usually captured what Len was thinking in just a few words and Len was glad that they thought alike. At the end of the Olympic broadcast, Jim McKay said, "We have a report from the World Chess Championship." He announced that Bobby Fischer was now just one point away from winning. The compelling, fascinating, amazing spectacle that had begun at the height of summer had reached a world-wide crescendo of anticipation and interest. Despite the start of the Olympics, the grinding on of the Vietnam War, the frustrating Paris peace talks, bloody bombings in Northern Ireland, jury selection in the Pentagon Papers case, and the intensifying U.S. presidential campaign, the Fischer/Spassky match had remained on the front page of the newspapers that Len unbundled each day.

"He's going in for the kill," said Del. "He's ruthless."

# 35

# A Miscommunication

Thursday the team jogged to Highland Park for a different kind of hill workout. The hill was about 220 yards long and had an equidistant downhill on the other side. It was steep enough to be challenging but not too steep to jar a runner's legs so much on the way down. As the team finished their warm-up and stretched out at the bottom of the hill, Mr. Renner explained the workout.

"Attack the hill, then keep going over the top and run a steady pace down the other side and around to the front again. Then attack the hill again. It's a continuous run. There's no jogging. The loop is about a half-mile, so we'll do six of them," he said.

The team ran a few wind sprints then lined up at the bottom of the hill.

"Go!" said Mr. Renner, and they tore up the hill. The word "attack" obviously meant the same thing to all of them, but as they crested the hill it was apparent that the word "steady" had different meanings. Mark and Kent pushed aggressively down the other side, while Phil, Rich, Rob and Len eased up to recover from the vigorous attack. By the time they got to the bottom and around to the front of the hill again, Mark and Kent were fifty yards ahead. By the third one, the entire team was strung out in a near continuous strand, snaking their way round and round the hill. Mark and Kent had begun by running the steady part too fast and were now slowing so that there appeared to be little difference in their "attack" and their "steady." After seeing the gap in front of Phil, Rich, Rob and Len after the first loop, Mr. Renner had implored them to run faster on the steady part. So on the next one they did, but then their attack was weakened significantly and they were reduced to jogging on the next downhill. This irritated Mr. Renner even more. As the workout progressed, none of the team could get it right and he was frustrated.

Mr. Renner had probably envisioned a workout of his team charging up the hill in a pack, striding down the other side, then moving smartly but controlled around the hill before attacking it again. But the reality was more like the running equivalent of Len's early years in city recreation league football and basketball, where once the ball was put in play, no matter how hard the players tried to execute the plan, confusion reigned. Mr. Renner didn't say much after the workout, but his body language said he had accepted some of the blame. He had either created a workout that the team was incapable of doing or that he didn't or couldn't explain well enough to them. The other possibility was that the concept of the workout was one which the team was incapable of grasping at this point in their running lives.

On the way back Phil said, "I bet that's the last time we do that workout."

"Yeah, Renner wasn't too happy," said Kent.

"We still got in a good run," said Mark.

"Hey Rich, I saw your girlfriend had a rough time on the uneven bars," said Bodine.

"That's cuz she's in love. She couldn't concentrate," said Rich.

"She must have fell out of love before the balance beam," said Bodine, "She killed that!"

"Ha! We're hot and cold," said Rich.

"Maybe she's falling for Mark Spitz," said Wayne.

"You better grow a mustache," said Bodine.

"No fair!" said Rich as he felt his smooth upper lip.

"That thing's like a beaver pelt," said Bodine.

"Ha, mine's like..." Rich started to say.

"A Mexican hairless pelt!" interrupted Bodine, eliciting a burst of guffaws.

"Hey, some chicks dig the smooth look," protested Rich.

"That's good. I'm with you," said Phil, brushing his upper lip with his thumb and forefinger.

"Me too," said Kent.

"I think we all are, except Bodine," said Mark.

# 36

## Spilled Coffee and Flowers

The next day, as Len unbundled his papers, he lifted the top paper off the pile and began to read. Bobby Fischer had won the World Chess Championship. The twenty-first game of the championship began with Fischer arriving late as usual. The playing clock had already been started. Spassky was drinking cup after cup of coffee. Fischer had taken an intriguing new line in this game, and after his surprising seventh move, Spassky spilled his coffee. With the clock running, Spassky scurried to clean up the spill, with Fischer looking on incredulously. As the game began to turn in Fischer's favor, Spassky played on desperately. But Fischer closed in relentlessly. Play was adjourned on the forty-first move, with Fischer holding the edge.

The Soviet team spent the night trying to figure a way out. Fischer went bowling. The next day, exhausted and feeling like the match was lost, Spassky conceded the game and the world championship to Fischer. Fischer had won his war. He had barely overcome his own idiosyncrasies, his own demons, just to make it to Reykjavik, and then to remain there when the match began badly for him. But down by two games, he had pulled, from deep within himself, the fierce, creative essence of his chess genius to win the championship in a way as brutal as any Dan Gable victory.

For the chess experts quoted in the article, it had lived up to its billing as the Chess Match of the Century. For other commentators, and the American public, it was a U.S. victory in the Cold War against communism and the Soviet Union. Fischer returned to the U.S. not only as the World Chess Champion, but as a Cold War hero. But like Prefontaine and his people in Eugene at the Olympic Trials, no one could have predicted that this was Fischer's finest hour. He would choose not to defend his world title, or ever play another major international chess match again.

Len went into the market to give Alice the paper. This was the week Lawrence was at the state fair with his flowers.

"Hi, Lenny," said Alice, as he handed her the paper.

"Hi, Lenny," said Beryl.

"Hi," said Len. "Have Lawrence's flowers been judged yet?"

"This afternoon," Alice replied. "I haven't heard anything yet."

"Every year he says he doesn't think he will win, but he always does," said Beryl.

Alice smiled. "He will come home and won't say anything because he wants to be modest. But I can tell he's dying for me to ask. So I ask, and he tells me all about it: how so and so's flowers looked so good this year and he thought he would be lucky to get second or third; how so and so said their seeds or fertilizer didn't work this year and they will never get them at the same place again; how so and so went to their niece's confirmation out-of-town and it got too cold overnight when they weren't there and their flowers just weren't the same after that. And he finally gets to the judging and how tense it is, and the waiting. But in the end, he always wins, even though he doesn't know 'how in the world' he did it."

"Bless his heart, he knows," said Beryl.

Len smiled. He could hear Lawrence saying all those things. Even if Lawrence really did not know how he did it, the fact was that whether it was plants, animals or people, they all responded to Lawrence. Plants spread their leaves and petals up to the sky, animals lost their fear, and people, especially children, felt his warmth.

# 37

# Triumph and Failure

That night the Olympic coverage started with the women's gymnastics individual event finals. Del was not at home, but Len was in his usual spot. Despite not getting a medal in the all-around competition, Olga Korbut had qualified for the finals in all of the individual events. The vault was her weakest event. Still, she ran gracefully down the runway, hit the spring board with both feet, shot forward with arms outstretched, touched the apparatus, flipped into the air and landed solidly with no extra steps. Others vaulted more athletically, achieved more height, generated more power, but Korbut, to Len's eye, was more aesthetic. She finished fifth then moved on to the balance beam.

She had drawn the last starting position and knew that she needed a 9.9 to win. Her best through the preliminary rounds had been a 9.75.

"It's done by the luck of the draw," said Jim McKay, "but dramatically, that's the way it would be for Olga Korbut. She's in second place coming into the final round. If she gets a 9.9 here she will win the gold medal."

Korbut walked slowly up to the beam, placed her hands on it and lithely lifted herself into a striking full split position to begin her exercise. Every move seemed natural and effortless as she went. There were no balance corrections or close calls. It was an ethereal performance punctuated by a gorgeous handstand in which her legs suggested the bow and shaft of an arrow about to be shot, and a stunning back flip leading into her dismount. She received her 9.9 and the gold medal.

The coverage then switched to Jim McKay explaining the bizarre beginning of the track and field events earlier in the day. Two U.S. sprinters, who were gold medal contenders in the 100 meter dash, had failed to show up for their quarter-final round. Eddie Hart and Rey Robinson had finished first and second in the U.S. Olympic Trials, tying the world record of 9.9 as they crossed the finish line together. They had both easily won their preliminary races that morning, but arrived at the stadium in the afternoon with the quarter-finals already underway. They had missed their race and were out of the competition. The third American in the 100 meter field, Robert Taylor, was in the last quarter-final. Realizing his race was about to begin, he had rushed to the starting line, stripped off his warm-up suit, and got down into his starting blocks with no time to spare. Despite not warming up, Taylor finished second to Valeriy Borzov of the Soviet Union, and moved on to the semi-final round. Borzov was also a gold medal contender. But without Hart and Robinson in the field, he had become the prohibitive favorite.

McKay then turned to a live interview with the distraught Hart and Robinson, who sat alongside their coach, Stan Wright. The athlete's could hardly speak, their voices barely audible. The anguished Wright explained that he had been following an old schedule that was incorrect. He had brought his athletes to the track at the wrong time. He took full responsibility. It was heartbreaking for Len to watch. They had trained four years for a ten second race and had missed it. Hart would get one more chance in this Olympics as the anchor of the four by 100 meter relay. But Robinson was done. He had missed his only chance.

McKay then reported that, also earlier in the day, Frank Shorter had qualified for the final in the 10,000 meters, running an American record of 27:58 in his prelim. None of Shorter's race was shown and McKay moved on to Dave Wottle's first round 800 meter race. Only the last 200 meters of the race was shown. Wottle, running in the fourth of eight heats, used his magnificent speed to move through the tight pack of runners on the final straight. He finished second in 1:47.64, moving on to the semi-final.

The coverage then went to the swimming venue for the finals of the men's four by 200 meter relay. The U.S. team took the lead in the first leg and continued to build it over the next two legs. By the time Mark Spitz dove into the pool for the anchor leg, the U.S. was all alone. Spitz extended the lead, earning his fifth gold medal and fifth world record.

Next came Dan Gable's gold medal match. He had made it to the final without any opponent scoring a single point against him. "Dedication is the name of Dan Gable," said Frank Gifford's announcing partner, Ken Kraft, as the match began. "He works out seven hours a day, seven days a week. I have never seen such dedication."

Gifford added, "Dan has said, 'Wrestling is my life,' and his life is on the line tonight."

Gable had won the world championship and been named the meet's outstanding wrestler the previous year in the Soviet Union. Afterward, one of the Russian coaches had said they were going to scour the Soviet Union to find a man to beat Gable in the Olympics. They came up with Ruslan Ashraliev, who Gable now faced in the gold medal match. The U.S. had not won a gold medal in Olympic wrestling since the 1960 games, said Kraft. Gable said before the Olympics that he didn't just want to win the gold medal for himself, but for all U.S. wrestling fans. Now, he dominated Ashraliev, holding the Russian, like his previous opponents, scoreless.

Gable's U.S. teammates carried him off the mat victoriously on their shoulders. The team's spirits were high. Gable had set the tone and began what Ken Kraft called the "greatest night in the history of United States wrestling." Wayne Wells and Ben Peterson followed Gable's gold with golds of their own. Richard Sanders and John Peterson, Ben's brother, won silver medals. Chris Taylor, the enormous, kind-hearted super-heavyweight, won a bronze medal. Len watched the guys receive their medals. Standing on the gold medal platform while the U.S. national anthem played looked like the best feeling in the world.

The coverage then went back to the individual gymnastics finals. There were two events left, the uneven bars and the floor exercise. Korbut was a favorite in both. Her uneven bar routine that had been a disaster yesterday, was a triumph today. She performed it flawlessly with confidence and energy. She received a huge ovation. She smiled affectionately and waved. When her score of 9.8 appeared on the screen, the crowd turned on the judges. Whistling, the American equivalent of booing, filled the arena along with jeers that held up the competition for several minutes. Korbut had narrowly lost the gold medal that the audience felt she deserved. The competitors moved on to the floor exercise. Korbut had again drawn the final starting position.

"As I said, there's one more gymnast to go," said Jim McKay. "You might have guessed, it's Olga Korbut. She has a gold now and she has a silver. To win another gold, she needs a performance of nine point nine zero. That's what she got on the balance beam."

Korbut had finished her dainty walk to her starting position and struck her starting pose. The music began and she leapt freely into her routine.

"What an exciting move!" exclaimed Gordon Maddox. "Watch how she beams and plays to the crowd."

The crowd was captivated, clapping to her airy music and cheering her major moves. Korbut was buoyed by them and did play to them with every move, gesture and smile. She punctuated a tumbling sequence across the floor with a high swan-dive back flip, landing gracefully in a horizontal position on the floor.

"Isn't that something!" effused Maddox.

McKay could hardly contain himself, "You can tell, nothing can stop her now!" he said.

"Gee, I hope she gets it," Maddox gushed. "She had a couple of little form breaks, but so did her teammate."

Korbut smiled and made a delicate little gesture to finish her routine.

"Oh yeah!" exclaimed Maddox.

The crowd erupted into enthusiastic applause.

"Ho, ho," McKay laughed. "She feels like she can fly to the moon under her own power right now."

She trotted delicately off of the platform, her beautiful smile responding to the prolonged applause. Her exercise had radiated youth, exuberance and, to Len, romance.

"She got it!" burst Maddox.

"She got the 9.9 and another gold medal!" added McKay. "Can you believe that!"

It had been a fantastic, unpredictable, inspiring night of Olympic events for Len. Korbut, Spitz, Gable and the rest of the U.S. wrestling team had been rewarded for their years of dedication and work. Shorter and Wottle had moved closer toward their ultimate goal. Hart and Robinson had been devastated. It seemed that every day the range of emotions shown by Olympic athletes covered the entire spectrum from elation to desolation. Len had never seen such personal and open displays of emotion at athletic events. The few sports he had previously watched on TV had been team sports. There was celebrating or disappointment in those games but nothing like he was seeing in the faces of these Olympians. This was raw emotion from deep within them that wasn't contingent on a team or teammate's performance, only their own. The passion that drove their bodies to the limit, was also their harshest judge. In triumph their ecstasy burst forth. In failure their despondency seeped out.

# 38

# Fifteen-Year-Old Girls

Friday the team ran easy over to Summit and down to the river and back. Len looked forward to these runs. They were slow and allowed him to recover well for the next hard workout. He had run faster sometimes during the summer, especially returning from the river, but with the accumulated fatigue from the harder workouts, he was glad for the casual pace. Plus, Len was getting to know the team better and, in less than two weeks, had begun to feel like a full, accepted member of the squad. He enjoyed listening to the banter of the team while running.

"Olga's not in love with you anymore, Rich?" asked Bodine, "She concentrated pretty good last night."

"Ha! I think it's over," said Rich.

"She moved on to Dan Gable," said Kent.

"Beauty and the beast," said Bodine.

"He could take care of that Russian soldier," said Kent.

"That was the Russian soldier that he beat for the gold medal," said Rich.

"How about those guys that missed the hundred?" said Mark.

"I would be so pissed!" said Phil.

"I can't believe the coach had the wrong schedule!" said Mark.

"You'd think he would have checked it out just to make sure," said Kent.

"I wonder if they fired him," said Phil.

"They should have, that was bad," said Mark.

"They sicked Chris Taylor on him," said Bodine.

"Ha! That guy is so huge!" exclaimed Rich.

"He could still catch you though. He looked pretty quick," said Phil.

"In the first five yards," said Rich, "after that I hope I could out run him."

"If you can't out run Chris Taylor after five yards, you shouldn't be out for cross country," said Bodine.

That afternoon, Len delivered his papers for the last time. Once school started, the varsity cross country practices would start later in the afternoon and last longer than the junior high practices. The papers would get out too late. He brought his replacement along to learn the route. Lawrence was done at the state fair and had relieved Alice and Beryl for the last couple hours of the day. Len had told him he had to quit the route the previous week.

"This is Diane," said Len. "She's taking over my paper route."

"Nice to meet you Diane," said Lawrence.

"Hi," said Diane.

"She lives next door to me," said Len.

"We've never had a paper girl before," said Lawrence.

Diane just smiled.

"I told her she can fold the papers in here if it's bad out," said Len.

"Oh yeah, right over here beside the counter," said Lawrence. "It's out of the way."

"Thanks," said Diane.

"I'm going to miss Lenny," said Lawrence, looking at Len, "but I'm sure he'll come in to visit sometimes."

"Yeah, I will," said Len.

"I'll make sure he does," said Diane.

"Okay," said Lawrence with a smile.

That night, Len eagerly turned on the Olympics. Track and field was finally on! In the 800 meter semi-final, Dave Wottle once again laid back early in the race, then threaded his way through a crowded field of runners to qualify for the finals. The finish had been tight, with six runners finishing within one second of each other. Only two of them moved on to the final. Wottle had won the tactical race in a slow 1:48.7 with another great finishing drive over the last 100 meters. He was both exciting and maddening to watch. He was always easy to spot, even if the camera panned out, because of the old golf cap he wore in every race. Jim McKay thought it looked goofy, but Len thought it was cool.

There had been two semi-finals of the 100 meter dash earlier in the day. Valeriy Borzov won one in 10.21 and Robert Taylor the other in 10.30. Borzov was clearly the best sprinter in the field and it would take an extraordinary effort for anyone to beat him. The only potential challengers, Hart and Robinson, were now sitting in the stands. The 100 meter final was the last track event of the day. The muscular Borzov lowered himself into his starting block in lane two, Taylor ran in lane four. At the explosion of the starting gun, Borzov drove low and hard down the middle of his lane. He was the last runner to come up to his full height, continuing to accelerate even as the speed of the others began to level off. When he did rise fully, his knees drove high in front of him, each powerful stride propelling him over large sections of the track. He pulled away easily to a convincing win in 10.14, crossing the finish line with his arms raised high, both palms facing forward. Taylor took second, one place higher than he had in the U.S. Olympic trials, in 10.24.

The day's Olympic coverage finished at the pool. Shane Gould stepped up onto her starting platform for the final of the 200 meter freestyle looking relaxed and confident. A couple of lanes over, another fifteen-year-old was readying herself for the race, but looked nervous and fidgety. Keena Rothhammer of the U.S. was a long distance specialist. This was a short distance for her, but long enough that she could swim down her competitors late in the race.

"Another fifteen-year-old girl swimmer!" thought Len.

Lynne Cox, Shane Gould, and now Keena Rothhammer had all excelled to the top of their sport. Len wondered what they were all like, what their lives were like, how they had done it. He wondered if they were like other girls his age when they weren't swimming. Did whatever it was that made them great swimmers, also make them different from their peers?

Gould dominated the race, pulling further away from the field with each length of the pool swum. She won her third gold medal and set her third world record. She was nearly the female equivalent of Mark Spitz, but at the age of fifteen. Rothhammer finished strong to win the bronze medal, with her U.S. teammate Shirley Babashoff winning the silver medal. With Len's fifteenth birthday approaching, he began to feel a rising desire to up his own athletic game.

# 39

# A Good Team

Saturday the workout was three times a mile at Como Park again. Mr. Renner said he wanted the team to get on the conference cross country course a few times before the conference race. He said it would help with tactics. He had worked a lot on his house over the years and said that using the right tactic was like using the right tool on a home project. If you used the right tool, it made the job a lot easier and it was done right. Using the wrong tool made for more and harder work, and you probably would not be happy with the result. He said that the goal was to walk away from the finish line satisfied that on that day you had given your best, not only physically, but mentally. That meant planning and executing a strategy. "It doesn't always turn out the way you want," he said, "but if you give your best you can still have pride in your effort. Don't just let the race happen to you," he said. "Plan it out the way you want it to happen." Len told him that his strategy was to hang on as long as he could. Mr. Renner said that the better shape a runner is in, the more tactics are available to him. "You're just starting out," he told Len, "but as you get better, you won't have to hang on to others, you will be able to set your own pace and make them hang onto you." That made sense to Len. He thought about Jim Ryun and Steve Prefontaine. They had each found the best strategy for them, but they were also superior runners. He imagined himself running in the lead pack in a race and everyone in the pack thinking the pace was tough. Then when they were all starting to strain, he would start his long, hard drive to the finish and leave them struggling in his wake like Prefontaine had done in the Olympic Trials.

There was a good spirit on the team as they jogged to the park. The returners knew that the team was much improved over last year's team. The top seniors: Kent, Phil and Rich had decided in May that they would run more over the summer than they ever had before. In their junior year, they had discovered that they had some talent for distance running. But they also knew they could work a lot harder, that they had not given their best effort yet. They had talked about seeing what they could do as seniors, how good they could be if they put in the work. It had inspired others on the team to run more too. They knew Mark, who was a junior, would also run so they would have a good top four. They had pushed Wayne to run more to make a strong top five, and he had, though not to their level. Still, they felt like they had a team that could compete for a top conference finish, and if everything went right, a shot at making it to state. Len's presence, which had at first been a curiosity, then a cautiously optimistic hope, had become an integral piece of the puzzle. Rob, who Mark had hoped could fill the fifth spot, was a bonus. In addition to the top guys, there were others on the team who had run more and strived to make it into the top seven. There hadn't been a top conference finish or a trip to the state meet in a long time, before the memory of anyone on the team, except Mr. Renner. He saw it and felt it too. He seemed cautiously optimistic, excited to have a dedicated group, but not wanting to invest too much emotion too early.

Physically the team seemed to feel good going into the workout since the Thursday hill workout hadn't taken too much out of them. It was a warm, muggy day so their shirts came off as soon as they got to the park. They stretched and did their wind sprints.

"Pack it up today guys," said Kent. "We need seven guys up there."

"I'll just hang on you guys," said Rob to Phil.

"Start out with us today," said Rich to Wayne.

"That might be suicide," said Wayne.

"Stay as close as you can," said Phil.

"It's a good day to die," said Bodine.

The team moved to the start. Mark and Kent led out the first mile. At the half mile, there were six guys still together. Rob dropped off in the second half mile but there was a pack of five at the end in 5:18. Len was feeling good. Running side by side as usual, Mark and Kent set a faster pace on the second mile. They began to pull away from Phil, Rich and Len in the second half. Len thought about going with them but by the time he decided, the gap was already there, so he stayed with Phil and Rich. Len pushed their pace, trying to keep the gap in front of them from opening more. They finished together in 5:17, three seconds behind Mark and Kent.

"Lookin' good guys," said Mark.

"Alright, finish strong," added Kent.

Len's recovery from these miles was much better than last week's. As they coalesced at the start for the third mile, he made the decision to try to stay with Mark and Kent all the way this time, if he could. The pace set was faster still than the previous mile. Len was working hard, but still feeling like he could stay there. With a half mile left, Rich was off the back and Phil was beginning to fade. Len ran a step behind Mark and Kent, determined to go all the way. As they came to the finish, Mr. Renner called out, "5:12!" They walked off to the side to recover as other runners came in. Len was tired but it wasn't the exhaustion he had felt the previous week.

"Attaboy Lenny," said Mr. Renner.

"Good job man," said Mark.

"All right!" said Kent as he shook his head yes.

Phil, who had been the third runner a few times the previous year, didn't say anything to Len. He had run the miles faster than he ever had, but Len could tell he was disappointed that he had fallen behind. Rich, as always, came up to Len and said, "Good job Lenny," but was subdued as he recovered from his own effort.

The team collected their shirts and stopped at a picnic shelter in the park to get a drink before jogging back to the school. As they jogged Len heard Kent say, "If we run like we did today at conference we might have a shot at South."

"I wonder how they're doing this year?" asked Mark.

"Their top guys are back," said Kent, "but I'm not sure after that."

"We're a good team though," said Mark.

"We were today," said Kent.

# 40

# Dave Wottle's Bid

That afternoon, Len was on the couch as the U.S. team blew out another overmatched opponent in Olympic basketball. Frank Gifford said that most countries hardly played any basketball other than in the Olympics, so it was no wonder the U.S. had won every gold medal. The U.S. team was made up of top college players who had been playing since they were kids. Len dozed off during the game, but kept it on, waiting for the track events to start.

After the interminable basketball game concluded, Dave Wottle's 800 meter final came on. Del had come in and joined Len. McKay said that Evgeni Arshanov of the Soviet Union was the heavy favorite. He hadn't lost a race in three years. He looked serious but confident standing in lane one waiting for the race to start. Wottle nervously shook out his arms and legs in lane three. They were called to the set position and the gun was quickly fired. The race went out fast.

"Two laps around," said McKay as the runners rounded the first turn, "They stay in lanes for the first 100 meters then they'll break. Boit is looking strong already. We have Arshanov on the inside in the lead as they break, but Boit on the outside is going for the lead right now. Ouko, the other Kenyan on his inside, and Wottle is way back, exactly where he was in the semi-final."

At the end of the first 100 hundred meters, Wottle was ten meters behind the pack. By 200 meters, Mike Boit and Robert Ouko, were gracefully, but relentlessly, pushing the pace side by side in the front. Wottle had dropped fifteen meters behind the second to last place runner.

"We don't know right now if he's just trying to stay out of trouble," said McKay's announcing partner, Marty Liquori. "It'll be a few more hundred yards before we know if Dave is seriously injured or just laying back to stay out of trouble."

"What's he doing?" asked Len. "He's got a good kick, but he's not even in the race!"

"Yeah, he looks out of it," said Del.

Len felt edgy, leaned forward on the couch. Del looked at him with raised eyebrows. Len thought Wottle had blown it already. He was too far behind the pack to even be in the same picture. The camera panned back to him, a solitary runner in last place on the screen.

"He's not too bad," said Liquori, "because it was quite a fast pace through that first two hundred meters."

In the second two hundred meters, Wottle began to close the gap.

"Here are the Kenyans in the lead coming up to the bell lap," said Liquori.

"The split is 52.3," said McKay.

Wottle made contact with the back of the pack for the first time in the race just past the 400 meter mark, and stayed there around the curve and onto the backstretch.

"At least he's in there now," said Len. "He's got a chance."

"If Dave can just pull up here and get on the outside of Arshanov, he would have him boxed in perfectly," said Liquori, "Let's hope Dave can make a move down this backstretch."

"The Kenyans running like a mirror reflection of each other in first and second," said McKay.

With 300 meters to go, Arshanov burst out of the pack and into the lead.

"There he goes," said Liquori, "There's Arshanov of the Soviet Union going up to the lead right now," he said as the crowd noise rose.

Wottle began to move up through the field.

"Dave Wottle is making his bid," said McKay, "He's not in too bad position right now," he said as Wottle moved from last place past two runners into sixth.

"I think Dave's in great position at this point," said Liquori, "He's in perfect position on the outside, good striking distance for this last 100 meters."

Into the final turn, Arshanov led the two Kenyans. Wottle moved out of sixth position into fifth, and then fourth.

"Come on Wottle!" said Len.

"Stand by for the kick of Dave Wottle, if he's got it, he could make it!" exclaimed McKay as the runners came off the turn, "But he's gotta catch Arshanov and the Kenyans, and here he comes! This is the bid for a gold medal of Dave Wottle!"

Arshanov hit the final straight with a burst that opened up three meters between him and the Kenyans. Wottle came off the turn wide, still seven or eight meters behind Arshanov and had to get by the Kenyans first. The Kenyans were in full sprint.

"He's got one Kenyan!" said McKay as Wottle went past Ouko fifty meters from the finish. But as he came alongside Boit, the lanky Kenyan fought back, matching his pace. They ran side by side, gaining incrementally on Arshanov.

"Oh man!" said Del.

"Can he make it?" exclaimed McKay.

Wottle began to inch ahead of Boit in the final ten meters, his momentum carrying him closer to the slowing Arshanov. He pulled even with the Russian only in the last two strides as he leaned for the finish line. A desperate Arshanov dove for the line beside him.

"I think he did it!" yelled McKay, "Dave Wottle won the gold medal! The man who came out of nowhere in the U.S. Olympic trials! The man who then got married and some people said he shouldn't have got married, it would ruin him! He came up with two bad knees! He couldn't train for weeks, and he has come in and won the gold medal, the first tremendously exciting moment in track for the United States in these Olympic Games!"

"Whoa!" exclaimed Del.

"An amazing race!" exclaimed Liquori, "In that last 25 meters he pulled it out and took it from Arshanov."

"Well what can you say about this fella," said McKay, as Wottle and the others wandered around the finish area waiting for the official results to be posted. "He started wearing that golf cap because he had real long hair that used to come down into his eyes, and then he kept it as a superstition."

The camera zoomed in on Wottle's face.

"He never changes expression," said McKay.

"I think Dave is stunned," said Liquori, "I don't think he realizes what he's just done."

"That may very well be," said McKay, "From Canton, Ohio. He lives two blocks from the pro football hall of fame, recently married, recent graduate of Bowling Green State."

Arshanov picked himself up off of the track as Wottle walked around the finish area looking dazed. The results came up on the scoreboard with Wottle's name at the top followed by Arshanov's, both with the exact same time of 1:45.8. The scoreboard couldn't show the three 100ths of a second that had separated them.

Len got up off the floor, where he had been on all fours closer to the TV during the last 200 meters of Wottle's race.

"Man!" he exclaimed, shaking his head.

"Are you alright?" asked Del.

Len laughed. "Yeah, that was unbelievable!"

"Yeah, talk about leaving it to the end," said Del.

On the medal stand, Arshanov barely acknowledged Wottle. He seemed to be either in disbelief or embarrassed that he had lost. He had most likely never even heard of Wottle before the Olympics. McKay said Wottle had barely been on the U.S. middle distance running radar, let alone the world radar, the previous year. Until recently, even in the U.S., he had been known more for his golf cap than his Olympic gold medal prospects. The U.S. national anthem began to play. Wottle stood at attention with his hat still on his head. McKay charitably said that in the excitement he was sure that Wottle had probably just forgot to take it off.

"Arshanov does *not* like Wottle," said Del.

Next came the final of the 400 meter hurdles. Ralph Mann of the U.S. was one of the favorites. He had set an American record of 48.4 at the Olympic Trials, just .28 off of the world record, and the fastest time of the year going into the Olympics. The world record holder and defending Olympic champion, Dave Hemery of Great Britain was also in the race. Another medal contender was John Akii-Bua of Uganda, who Hemery had narrowly defeated earlier in the year. Akii-Bua had been running the event just two years. He hadn't won many races, none on the international level, but was improving rapidly as he adapted to the rigorous training and honed the technical aspects of the event.

McKay introduced a pre-recorded story about Akii-Bua. It showed him training in Uganda on grass and jumping over rudimentarily constructed hurdles on a dirt track that was little more than a circular, single lane path. He ran cross country for endurance and did track workouts wearing a twenty pound weight vest for strength.

"That's not even a track!" said Del.

"And those aren't real hurdles," said Len.

Akii-Bua's story may not have been told at all were it not for the tumultuous events going on in his home country while he was away at the Olympic Games. Just as the small Ugandan Olympic team, competing in just three sports, was about to leave for Munich, Uganda's dictator, Idi Amin, made world headlines by issuing an edict expelling 80,000 Asians from the country. The Asians were remnants, and descendants of remnants, of British colonial rule. Amin despised the British and wanted all vestiges of them out of Uganda. He gave the Asians ninety days to leave.

Len had seen Amin's picture on the front page of the newspaper the day after he had issued the edict, but Uganda was a small, far away country and he hadn't paid much attention. The story that now unfolded was crazy and gruesome. Having taken control of the African country just a year earlier in a military coup, Amin had also begun carrying out executions of political opponents along tribal lines. Akii-Bua's tribe, the Langi, was one of the tribes taking the brunt of Amin's killing spree. But Amin dared not touch the country's star athlete, yet anyway. In fact, Akii-Bua's success had been held up by Amin in a cynical gesture of how well he was treating the Langi.

"Amin sounds like a real fun guy," said Del.

Akii-Bua had won his semi-final in Munich, with Mann and Hemery close behind, but they had eased up once they were assured of qualifying for the final. The lane draw for the final was random. Akii-Bua drew lane one. The gun was fired.

"It's a good start," said McKay, "And it's Ralph Mann going particularly hard."

Down the backstretch, Hemery began to move.

"Hemery now beginning to get him back," said McKay.

Entering the final turn McKay said, "And it's Hemery with a clear lead now. Akii-Bua on the inside is getting left behind a little bit."

The race began to tighten coming off the final turn, with Akii-Bua driving furiously onto the straight.

"And it's Hemery still leading, with Akii-Bua coming on the inside. Akii-Bua coming on the inside! Two hurdles to go and Akii-Bua is coming and so too is Ralph Mann. They're at the last barrier and Akii-Bua leads with Hemery! The last hurdle to go and the African's going to win it! Akki-Bua wins with a new world record, taking the distance into a new era!"

Mann caught Hemery at the line to take the silver medal.

Akii-Bua had become the first man to run the 400 meter hurdles in under forty-eight seconds. His time of 47.82 would last for four years. McKay now wondered what would happen to him when he returned to Uganda. Would his gold medal be enough to keep him safe from the murderous Idi Amin?

# 41

## Sisu and Hana

Sunday morning was sunny, beautiful and warm. Len ran through his tranquil neighborhood to the river under a canopy of maple, oak and elm leaves that was penetrated intermittently by shafts of sparkling sunlight. He turned onto the River Road and ran easily along the dirt path before descending down to his clearing. Emerging from the cloistered path, he was surprised to see Tom sitting cross-legged in the clearing looking out over the river. He sat serenely in a sunny spot and had a content look on his face. He turned his head and looked at Len.

"How was your running this week?" he asked.

"Good. I'm not as tired."

"You're getting in better shape. Are you racing soon?"

"We have our first race Thursday."

"Are you doing a long run today?"

"Yeah, I want to go a little longer."

"This trail goes a ways farther, another couple of miles."

"Is it ok to run on?" Len asked anxiously, thinking not just of the condition of the path.

Sensing Len's apprehension, Tom said, "Yeah, it's ok."

Len had never been past the clearing. He started down the verdant path. It continued gradually down the bluff, into a deeper, quieter realm. There were portions where the trail narrowed and wound through breaks along a limestone cliff, finally emerging below it. The path ran along the bottom of the cliff for a ways before angling off toward the water. A flash of bright orange ahead surprised Len as he came around a slight bend. It was gone the instant he saw it. He stopped cold, his stirring heart and lungs the only discernible movement in the still woods. He looked at the rogue sun spot that had dropped through the trees and lit up the path where he had seen the flash. Still, nothing moved. Only then did he recognize that what he had seen was the bushy, sun-splashed tail of a fox he had startled as it darted into the underbrush with a flamboyant wave of its tail.

Len felt far removed from the city in the primitive woods below the cliff. The path became sandy as it neared the water. He breathed in the musty, muddy scent that pervaded the lower path. The trail continued to drop before coming to a small, sandy beach next to the water. He stopped on the beach even though the path extended on along the flat next to the water. Large volumes of dark water swirled around the sandbank. The far shore looked a mile away. An ebony colored log bobbed past on the enduring current. It was easy to imagine it soon being miles away down the river now that it was free of its moorings. Being here for the first time was both exhilarating and calming to Len. He felt at ease as he stretched on the soft sand. He glanced along the bank at the path as it continued next to the water, and resolved to explore it on a future run. After a few minutes he started back up the trail.

The climb back to the clearing was tougher than he anticipated. He estimated that he had run another mile or so down the path, but it had seemed more gradual on the way down than the way back up. Tom was still sitting in the same place when he arrived back at the clearing.

"How was it?" he asked.

"It was great! Tough on the way back though. I saw a fox!"

"Yeah, all kinds of creatures live down there."

"It's like you're not in the city anymore."

"How far did you run?"

"All the way to the river."

"Is that your longest run?"

"Yeah, it will be about seven miles when I get home."

"You'll get strong if you do that every week."

"Yeah, especially with that hill in there."

"The river will be for you what the lakes were for Van."

Len liked that idea. He already had an affinity for the river like no other place. The more he came to it and the closer he had got to it, the more he felt its strength and the sensibility of all those before him who had lived here and been a part of it. He had become a part of it. It was his place to run, but even more than that.

"I went to the library and read the paper," said Tom. "The Olympic 10,000 meters is today. Maybe Frank Shorter can do what no other American except Billy Mills has done."

"He set an American record in the prelims."

"He might still be tired from that."

"That's gotta be tough, running a 10,000 meter prelim, then coming back four days later and running the final."

"In the article about Shorter, they also talked about this Finn, Lasse Viren. He's doubling in the 5,000 and 10,000. He's trying to be the next Flying Finn. They haven't won anything for awhile, so Viren is their big hope. The tradition they lost is called Sisu. It's their toughness. They're trying to get their Sisu back so they brought Lydiard over to Finland to motivate them. Viren says he has Sisu. We'll see."

"Did you read about Dave Wottle in the 800? That was the best race I've ever seen!"

"There was a picture of him with his arms raised right after the finish line and a Russian on the ground."

"The Russian was in the lead and Wottle caught him right at the end. Wottle started out way behind in last place on the first lap. He caught up in the second lap and out-kicked everyone on the final straight. The Russian dove at the line, but Wottle won. The Russian was undefeated for three years. I was going nuts! I thought he was too far back and waited too long. I've never seen a kick like that!"

"He had the confidence to stick to his plan."

"They said he had a knee injury before the Olympics too."

"Maybe that was a good thing. He might have been training too hard and needed the rest. If he wouldn't have got injured, his legs might have been more tired and he wouldn't have won."

"Did you see those American sprinters missed their race?"

"Yeah, their coach blew it. Too bad for them."

"And Mark Spitz has won five gold medals and set five world records. He still has two races."

"Swimming's not as hard on your body so you can do more. Jim Ryun's coach was a swimming coach before he was a running coach. He trained his runners the same way he trained his swimmers. Twice a day and a lot of miles, and a lot of intervals. Only in the pool it's a lot of meters not miles. In high school, Ryun ran fifteen mile runs and did twenty 440s or twenty 220s."

"The most we've done is meat grinders. That's twelve 440s."

"That's okay. Lydiard probably wouldn't have you doing any intervals at all yet. He would build up your mileage for awhile first. All of the Minnesota Olympians ran a lot of miles. As soon as Buddy started running more, he set the American record in the 10,000 meters. He probably could have run a lot faster in the 10,000 after that but he didn't race it on the track anymore. And he probably would have made the Olympic team in 1960 if he hadn't got anemia. He was always worried about his weight since he had been a fat kid. That's probably why he got anemia. He just didn't eat, and he was training a lot. His body broke down. He didn't learn his lesson about eating until after his first marathon, when he crashed. Wilt had been telling him to eat more, but sometimes you have to learn those things on your own. He had been telling him to rest more before races too, but Buddy learned that the hard way too. Runners make a lot of those kinds of mistakes because they lack confidence. Once Buddy learned those lessons, he set the world record. Sometimes you have to relearn them though. He didn't rest after the trials, and that's when he got injured.

"In an article I read before the 1968 Olympics, they told a story about a Japanese runner who had won the bronze medal in the marathon in Tokyo. He was in second place coming into the stadium, but got out-kicked on the track by an English guy in front of the huge Japanese crowd. He was so ashamed that, after that, he started to train harder than ever. But he kept getting injured. Then early in 1968, when he saw that he couldn't win another Olympic medal, he became so despondent that he committed suicide. He left a note that just said, 'Cannot run anymore.'"

"Wow," said Len.

"The marathon was huge in Japan in the Olympics. Hundreds of thousands of people lined the course and cheered loudly for every runner. Buddy said sometimes it was so loud from both sides of the street that it was one big noise in his head. The Japanese call the marathon Hana. That means "the flower." It's more than a race. They see it as a Zen experience, a way of gaining personal enlightenment and understanding. One Japanese runner said, 'The challenge you get from the marathon is like a rose. It is so painful when you get the sting from the thorn, and so beautiful when you look at the flower.'"

"What's Zen?"

"It's what you learn about yourself from the experience, not the knowledge of how to do things. After I read that article, I read more about Zen. It helped me a lot, and I talked to the psychologist about it. It helped me make sense of things that had happened in my life. When I ran in the yard, I felt like all of the bad things that had happened to me were dripping out of my body with the sweat. It cleared my mind and soul for peace and understanding to enter. I felt the same thing when I came here to the river."

Tom stopped talking then and looked lost in his thoughts as he stared out over the river. The two sat in silence for a few minutes. Len felt suddenly that Tom, the river and running were all parts of the same thing. He couldn't have explained it, but inside, he understood it. He felt a part of it too, but in a way that they had let him become a part of it, not that he had done it on his own.

"Did you meet Lawrence?" Len asked.

"Yeah. You were right, he's a real nice guy. He filled up a whole bag with groceries and kept saying he didn't want to throw it out. But some of it hadn't even been opened."

Len smiled. He felt grateful, both for Lawrence and Tom.

"All this talk of food is making me hungry," said Len.

Tom looked at him with a small smile. "You're still growing. You better go get something to eat."

Len got up slowly, stretched a little, then started up the path.

"See you later," said Len.

"See you later," said Tom.

# 42

## Shorter's Mettle

Len jogged a little stiffly up the path but felt good running once he got back up to the River Road. He felt buoyed that the connection between Lawrence and Tom had worked out. His mind was full of Tom and the river, the Tokyo Olympic Marathon, Buddy, Van, and the sad story of the Japanese runner. He wished he could see Buddy and Van race when they were at their best. He wondered what they were like, what they did, in school at his age. He wanted to run where they had run. But most of all, he wanted to run in the Olympics.

That afternoon, he turned on the TV to watch the 10,000 meter final. But the first track event shown was Rod Milburn of the U.S. running the 110 meter high hurdle prelims. The cool Milburn, sporting a full beard and an Afro parted down the middle, was smooth and graceful as he powered away from the other runners. His body rose in one quick, fluid motion as he cleared each hurdle. The idea that Len had tried to be a hurdler was comical to him now.

Then the 10,000 started. David Bedford of England, with high, red socks and long, flopping hair, shot out to the lead like it was a mile race, stringing the field of fifteen out into a single file line. He hit the 400 meter mark in sixty seconds flat, well under world record pace not only for the 10,000, but also for the 5,000. Emiel Puttemans of Belgium followed Bedford, with the little Ethiopian Miruts Yifter next in line. Then came Mariano Haro of Spain. Viren and Shorter ran near the end of the line, coming through 400 in a still fast sixty-three seconds. Just in front of Viren ran Mohammed Gammoudi, the Tunisian with three Olympic medals already to his credit, including the 5,000 meter gold from Mexico City and the 10,000 silver medal behind Billy Mills in Tokyo.

Len was enthralled seeing the best distance runners in the world battle each other: the gutsy Bedford, putting the race on the edge right from the gun with his long, loping stride; the smooth Puttemans getting right up behind Bedford, not ceding an inch, no matter what the pace; the two small runners, Haro and Yifter sprinting around runners to get up to Puttemans; the rest of the field holding their place in line as Bedford took them through 800 meters in 2:04, 1200 in 3:09 and the 1600 in 4:13. Their faces were set in grim determination. There would be no coasting in this race. The medalists would have to earn every step.

Bedford kept the pressure on in the second mile. One by one, runners dropped off the back of the line until, passing two miles in 8:39, just nine remained in the lead pack. Shorter was the ninth. The pace had slowed but still averaged a sub-world record pace of sixty-five seconds per lap.

In the third mile, Bedford's pace became increasingly erratic. As fatigue set in, he slowed, only to increase the tempo again when Yifter came up to his shoulder. Then as Yifter backed off, the pace slowed again. On the backstretch of the eleventh lap, during one of the slowdowns, Shorter moved to the outside and began passing runners. He had come up to Viren, running in fifth, when the line of runners slowed more and Viren cut his stride to avoid Puttemans, but tripped and fell to the track. Shorter wobbled but stayed up. Abdel Zaddem, Gammoudi's teammate, sidestepped Viren. But Gammoudi could not avoid the downed Finn, tripped over him and flew onto the infield.

Len cringed and said, "Whoa!" out loud.

Viren was on the ground only a couple of seconds. That was all it took to fall thirty meters behind. He re-accelerated and regained contact with the pack within 100 meters, receiving an ovation from the crowd. Gammoudi lay motionless, stunned for several seconds, before getting up and tacking onto the final runners. Off of the lead pack and disheartened, he dropped out of the race soon after.

There was now a line of eight behind the tiring Bedford as the 5,000 meter mark was passed in 13:43. Just before four miles, passed in 17:43, Viren moved into the lead for the first time. Two laps later, Bedford was gone from the lead pack. Viren hit five miles in 22:17 with just four runners still in tow. Finnish flags began to wave in the crowd.

With two laps to go, Haro went to the lead. Yifter and Puttemans followed. Shorter struggled to stay in the lead pack, but could not. Viren surged back into the lead with 600 meters to go. Puttemans followed, then Yifter, and the race was down to three. Haro had run the first 200 meters of the penultimate lap in thirty-one seconds, then Viren dropped the second 200 meters to twenty-nine seconds. Onto the backstretch of the final lap, Viren was in full flight with Puttemans five meters back and Yifter fading. The race for the gold medal was down to two. Puttemans made his move with 200 meters to go. He closed up to Viren's shoulder on the final curve, but that's as close as he could get. Viren accelerated into the final straight and pulled away to win by eight meters in 27:38.35, one second under Ron Clarke's world record. Viren's last lap had been run in fifty-five seconds.

Puttemans took the silver in 27:39, Yifter the bronze in 27:40. Shorter came in fifth, setting another American record of 27:51.32. Viren removed his shoes and, holding them high, jogged barefoot around the track to the cheers of the crowd. A couple of Finnish teens jumped out onto the track and jogged behind, waving a large Finnish flag.

"The Flying Finns are back!" thought Len. Viren was impressive to him, but so were the other runners who had been there all the way until the end. They all had guts. Four different guys had pushed the pace, and kept it fast, during the race. Shorter had not led, but time and again, as the pace surged, he had fallen off the back of the lead pack, and each time, to Len's amazement, he fought his way back up to it. He had won easily in Eugene, but was extended to his limit in Munich, and had shown his mettle. Someday Len wanted to be in a great 10,000 with great runners, where he would have to fight every step to run his best. You would really know what you were made of then, he thought.

The final events of the night were in the pool. Mark Spitz faced his biggest obstacle to winning seven gold medals in the 100 meter freestyle final. He had not won either his prelim or semi-final in the event. The defending Olympic champion, Michael Wenden of Australia, had beaten him in both of the earlier rounds. At the gun, Spitz pushed hard out into the lead. He had a quarter body length lead at the turn. He held this, but no more, the final length of the pool to the end. Hard charging Jerry Heidenreich of the U.S. took the silver. Wenden failed to medal. The top three places were separated by only five tenths of a second. Spitz had his sixth gold medal and sixth world record.

What was it that had changed about Spitz since Mexico City, Len wondered? From being the guy with the talent who tanked in the big races to being the guy who rose to every challenge and came out on top. Whatever it was, he thought, it was the same thing that made Viren get up after falling and win the 10,000.

Shane Gould then swam her last race, taking the silver medal in the 800 meter freestyle, beaten out by Keena Rothhammer. In the early stages of the long race, the two fifteen-year-olds paced themselves with the rest of the field. Just after halfway, Rothhammer moved out to the lead and began to open a gap. Gould could not respond. She battled for the silver medal as Rothhammer locked up the gold.

Len had never thought of girls his age as being tough, but they clearly were. To him, watching the teenage girls compete in the Olympics was both the same and different as watching the men. The same because they proved to be just as tough and resilient, different because it was new to him. He wondered why women competed in all of the same races as men in the pool but not on the track.

# 43

# Groovy Superman

Monday was Labor Day, the last day of summer. Len woke up early and looked out on a fresh, pleasant morning, with the sun spreading a brilliant fuchsia out across the sky from the east. The initial stiffness he felt coming down the stairs quickly gave way to a lively, strong feeling in his legs as he biked to the high school for the last morning practice. The team ran five miles out around the Town and Country golf course.

"Did you guys see Dave Wottle's race?" asked Kent.

"Man, I can't believe he won!" said Phil.

"That was a great race," said Rob.

"Amazing," said Mark.

"I wish I had a kick like that," said Kent.

"He came from so far back even in the last one hundred!" said Phil.

"The Russian looked pissed," said Kent.

"I'd be pissed if the only race I lost in three years was the Olympics," said Mark.

"How about Viren," said Kent, "He falls down and still wins the gold medal and sets a world record."

"He had a great kick too," said Rob.

"I wish I could run a fifty-five in the open four-forty," said Phil.

"Yeah, can you imagine running fifty-five after running twenty-four laps first?" asked Kent.

"I can't imagine running twenty-four laps at all," said Bodine.

"Shorter ran tough," said Mark.

"Two American records in one week," said Kent. "He's in great shape! Now he has the marathon."

"Man, if you count the marathon and his two 10,000s, that's over thirty-eight miles of racing!" said Phil.

"So far, it's been good racing too," said Kent.

"He's a machine," said Mark.

That day, the Olympic coverage began at the pool with Mark Spitz's seventh, and final, race. It was the four by 100 meter medley relay. Del sat watching with Len. The first two U.S. legs, swimming the backstroke and the breaststroke, stayed at or near the front. The U.S. was tied for the lead when Spitz stretched his muscular frame out over the pool for the butterfly on the third leg. He opened up more than a full body length lead by the time he had finished, assuring his seventh gold medal and a seventh world record. He looked so satisfied to Len as he received his gold medal with his teammates.

"He did it," said Del, "seven gold medals. I wonder if he'll make a lot of money from that."

"He looks like he could be an actor," said Len.

"It would be hard not to think of him as Mark Spitz though."

"He would kind of look like Super Man without his mustache."

"Ha! Can you imagine Superman with a mustache?"

"No."

"He'd be like a groovy Superman."

Len smiled.

The coverage then went to the track for the men's 200 meter dash finals. Valeriy Borzov was attempting the sprint double. But unlike the 100 meter dash, the top American was in the field. Larry Black of the U.S. had recorded faster times than Borzov in both the quarter-final and semi-final rounds. Black drew lane one, Borzov lane five. The gun fired and the field accelerated around the turn. Black and Borzov came into the straightaway even, clear of the rest of the field.

"Ooh, dead even, come on Black!" said Del.

But on the straightaway, Borzov powered away from Black, and once again raised his arms in victory as he crossed the finish line. He had confirmed that he was the fastest man in the world. Whatever doubt anyone had was dispelled. It was only for Robinson and Hart to wonder how they would have faired.

"Oh man, that guy is pure speed and power," said Del.

As Len lay in bed that night, he wondered what Olga Korbut was doing now that she was finished competing. He imagined her in his school, standing by a locker holding her books and coyly smiling. He drifted off to sleep, looking forward to the first day of school.

# 44

# Death at the Serene Olympics

The next morning, Len came down to the kitchen early, as always on school days, to the low, reassuring sound of the morning news on the radio to which his parents always listened. As soon as he stepped into the room, a report with the magical words "Munich Olympics" caught his ear and he perked up. But he immediately became confused when he heard, "The peace of what have been called the 'Serene Olympics' was shattered just before dawn this morning about five o'clock when Arab terrorists, armed with submachine guns, faces blackened, a couple of them disguised as guards or trash men in the Olympic Village, climbed a fence, went to the headquarters of the Israeli team, and immediately killed one man, Moshe Weinberg, a coach, two shots in the head, one in the stomach. And the latest report is that one more has been killed. Now at this moment, eight or nine terrified, living human beings are being held prisoner." It was the voice of Jim McKay. He said that the terrorists were demanding that 234 Arab prisoners held in Israeli jails be released.

Stunned, Len sat down to the Cream of Wheat his mom had made for breakfast. He knew about Arabs and Israelis from the newspaper, and the fact that they were constantly fighting. But why were they bringing this to the Olympics? He left for school perturbed and bewildered, trying to imagine what was going on in the Olympic village, and what was going to happen to the Olympics. Despite the events in Munich, once he got to school he felt more comfortable than ever beginning a school year. He was in the oldest class in the junior high. But it was more than that. The confidence he had begun to feel with his success on the track the previous spring had continued to grow with his increased running over the summer. He hadn't been a runner long, but he knew it was what he wanted to do and what he wanted to be, and that he could be good at it.

At the end of the day, he grabbed his duffle bag from his locker and went to the parking lot behind the school. Mr. Johnson, the math teacher who was also an assistant football coach at the high school, was just getting there as well. He waved Len over as he continued walking to his car without breaking stride. Len had never been in his class and had only talked to him once. Mr. Renner had made the arrangement. As he pulled out of the parking lot, Mr. Johnson said, "Have you been watching the Olympics? It's too bad what's going on."

"Yeah, is it still going on?" Len asked.

"Yes. They've stopped the competition."

They rode the rest of the way in silence. Len wondered what it was like in the Olympic village and what Olga, Shorter, Prefontaine, Wottle, Gable and Spitz were doing and thinking. Mr. Johnson pulled into the high school parking lot a few minutes later and said, "Here we are." He quickly put the car in park and threw open his door. Len scrambled out his side and hurried after him into the school.

Even though he had been going to practice at the high school for the past two weeks, the ambience felt unfamiliar walking into the hallways full of kids other than football players and cross country runners. Len threaded his way quickly, and largely unnoticed, through a bustling hallway to the locker room, changed and jogged out to the team meeting spot behind the school. The rest of the team had already begun the warm-up. Len started around the practice fields and came in a couple of minutes behind them.

"Did the teacher make you stay after?" Rich teased as he joined the group.

"I have to come over with Mr. Johnson," said Len.

"Old Stone Face!" said Bodine.

"Ha! He didn't smile the whole time I had him," said Rich.

"He only has one way of explaining things - monotone," said Bodine.

"The challenge wasn't learning the stuff, it was staying awake," said Rich, "If you could stay awake, you could learn it. But I couldn't stay awake!"

"Get your sprints in and we'll get going," called Mr. Renner as he walked toward the team from the practice field, where he had put up stakes to mark out a 220. The workout was twelve times 220 in two man relays on the grass. Mr. Renner told the team to pair up. Rob looked at Len and said, "What do you say, Lenny?"

"Sure," said Len.

He knew Rob had more raw speed than he did, but less endurance. They went full bore the entire workout but were a ways off of the lead group. Len thought that was fine for this workout. He could not have run any faster no matter who he had for a partner, and he knew his legs would be sore the next day. They always were sore after a sprint workout. As the team jogged the cool down Kent said, "I can't believe they stopped the Olympics?"

"I can't believe this is going on at the Olympics," said Wayne.

"Nobody notices anymore if they kill people at home," said Bodine. "They have to do it somewhere else where it will get attention."

"Prefontaine is supposed to run tomorrow," said Kent.

"They talked like it might be over by tonight," said Wayne.

Len turned the TV on as soon as he got home. It was dark in Munich, and the cameras showed the complex where the hostages were being held. Nothing was happening, so Jim McKay was reviewing the events of the day. Olympic officials were shown in the morning talking optimistically about restarting events as soon as this "incident" passed. Calling what was going on an "incident" seemed to trivialize it to Len. Murder had occurred. He wondered if it would be characterized the same if a German had been murdered instead of a Jew. He knew what had happened to the Jews in Germany during World War II and thought it was an eery coincidence that, even though this wasn't perpetrated by Germans, it was Jews taking the brunt in Germany once again. Len didn't know any Jews, but he wondered why so many people seemed to hate them so passionately.

As the TV cameras zoomed in on a shrouded terrorist holding a machine gun and occasionally poking his head out a balcony door, Len didn't feel the same optimism as the officials that the "incident" would pass easily or soon.

Throughout the day the terrorists had issued deadlines for meeting their demand, threatening to shoot more hostages if it was not met. Deadlines came and went as the terrorists negotiated with the Munich police. Video was shown from the late afternoon of one of the terrorists, a nylon stocking over his head, coming out onto a balcony and peering over the railing. The camera then panned back to a nearby building, where two sharpshooters were creeping into position.

"There are men with guns beginning to train those guns on the rooms where the two heads were sticking out a moment ago of the Arab guerrilla lookouts," narrated McKay. "This is happening now, if you can possibly believe that, at the games of the twentieth Olympiad. A police spokesman said a squad of thirty-eight volunteers would storm the house if a deal had not been worked out with the Arabs by the deadline. Now we've gotten an official time check. It is five o' clock. This is the deadline. The storming, if it is going to happen, could happen at any moment." But this deadline passed as well without incident.

As McKay's live coverage returned in the dark of Munich, the terrorists had changed their demand. They wanted to be taken to the airport and flown to an Arab country.

Suddenly, there was a flurry of activity. The area around the building occupied by the terrorists and their hostages was cleared of vehicles and the hundreds of spectators, who had been allowed to watch the drama unfold all during the day. As the area was finished being cleared, a bus rolled up to the outside of the building. It was reported that the terrorists would be coming out in five minutes.

The lights of two helicopters appeared in the sky at the edge of the Olympic Village. As the helicopters were landing, the terrorists and hostages boarded the bus, which began making its way toward the helicopters. The transfer from the bus to the helicopters was swift and the helicopters were airborne quickly. The TV cameras, which had been showing the events all day, were not allowed at the airport. The lights of the helicopters flew out of sight and Jim McKay and Chris Shenkel again recounted the events leading up to the present. Time crept on. Len was getting sleepy and beginning to doze, but didn't want to go to bed without knowing the outcome.

Suddenly McKay, who had in an earpiece, said, "The latest word we get from the airport is that quote 'All hell has broken loose out there.' There is still shooting going on. There is a report of a burning helicopter." Len perked up.

Then nothing. Minutes, then tens of minutes, passed with no additional information being brought forth. McKay and Schenkel gravely kept the broadcast going. Then suddenly, McKay said he was hearing a report that all of the hostages had been saved and most of the terrorists killed. Visible relief spread across his face, but he wondered aloud if the report was true. Minutes later, McKay looked into the camera and said, "I've just gotten the final word," then paused. "You know, when I was a kid my father used to say our greatest hopes and our worst fears are seldom realized. Our worst fears are realized tonight. They have now said that there were eleven hostages, two were killed in their rooms yesterday morning, nine were killed at the airport tonight. They're all gone," he said as he shook his head.

Len went to bed more confused than sad or angry, although he was those things too. It seemed that it had been too easy for the terrorists to take the hostages, and then that the whole response had been bungled badly.

The next morning on the radio, Len heard that there would be no Olympics that day, and there was speculation that the rest of the Olympics would be cancelled. A pall had descended over Munich that enveloped all those around the world who watched or listened. "What are Prefontaine, Jim Ryun and Mark Spitz thinking?" thought Len. This was Pre's first Olympics, his first chance at his sport's highest achievement, and that chance may now be denied. This was probably Ryun's last Olympics, his last chance at the one prize that had eluded him, and might now continue to elude him. Mark Spitz, a Jew, had already been taken out of the Olympic village and sent back to the U.S. for his safety. He wouldn't have been able to celebrate his great accomplishment in Munich anyway. He had been robbed of that.

That day in school, Len was disconsolate. In social studies, Mr. Touhy asked if anyone was watching the Olympics. About three-quarters of the class raised their hands. He asked if the terrorist's actions would further the Arab cause. Len usually didn't talk in class but raised his hand along with a few others. A somewhat surprised Mr. Touhy called on him.

"This shouldn't happen at the Olympics," said Len, "The idea of the Olympics is to bring people together from all over the world for friendly sports competition. If they want to fight, they should do it someplace else. It's not fair to the athletes who have been training for four years. Now they might not even get a chance to compete. It doesn't advance their cause."

Mr. Touhy nodded. There was a brief silence in the room. Len felt warm all of a sudden and hoped someone would talk. Finally, Mr. Touhy called on someone else. Len glanced to the side, relieved. He caught Randi looking at him with a more serious, and he thought mature, look than he had ever seen. They looked at each other for just a second, then she looked away.

The team ran five miles slowly along Summit that day. The first meet was the next day and the sprints the previous day had made all of their legs sore.

"They blew up the helicopter," Len heard Wayne say.

"The police stormed it but couldn't shoot 'em before they blew it up," said Bodine.

"It must have been crazy out there," said Kent.

"I wonder if they'll cancel the Olympics," said Mark.

"Prefontaine is probably so pissed," said Phil.

"All those athletes that haven't competed yet are probably pissed," said Rich.

"All that training," said Mark, shaking his head.

That night, Len watched the memorial service in the Olympic stadium, which was filled to capacity. But even the memorial service was politicized. McKay said that all of the flags from all of the countries that flew along the top of the stadium had been put at half-mast, but the Arab countries had objected to their flags being put at half-mast for dead Israelis. The Arab flags were put back up to the top. The Israelis were insulted.

Len thought that any country that didn't want their flag at half-mast didn't belong at the Olympics. It was a small gesture to honor the dead athletes. He wished they would leave and let the games go on and be what they were intended to be. He wanted to see the competition, not their hatred and vindictiveness.

Avery Brundage, the President of the International Olympic Committee, came to the podium. "We cannot allow a handful of terrorists to destroy this nucleus of international cooperation and goodwill," he said. The games would go on. Len thought maybe they would continue because the thousands of athletes who had trained for this for so long were now looking back at Brundage as he surveyed the stands. Maybe they would continue because the Olympic ideal was higher than the ideal of using violence to achieve a political end. But Len knew now that in some parts of the world, and in some people's minds, the ideal of political vengeance was held higher than the Olympic ideal.

# 45

# Dual at the School

That night Len pulled the spikes he had bought the previous spring out of his closet. They were white leather with three black stripes on the sides and had four, half-inch spikes in the bottom. He slipped them on. They felt snugger than last spring, but fit better he thought, more like racing shoes should. When he had asked at practice if the team raced barefoot like in junior high, he received dubious looks, as if they had never heard of, nor would ever consider, such a thing. He guessed that it had been Gary's personal philosophy that he had passed on to the impressionistic junior high team. Gary was at the high school now but was not out for the cross country team. A couple of guys on the team knew him but did not know why he was not out.

Len took off the spikes and put them in his duffle bag. His varsity uniform hung in his locker at the high school. He had tried it on and it was only a little big, but he thought it would be fine. Anyway, it was the smallest one available, so it didn't matter. It was going to be cool, but a little intimidating, putting it on and running out onto the course in front of high school spectators. This was his first three-mile race but he felt more prepared for it than he had for his first two-mile race the year before.

Throughout the next day, he felt the increasingly frequent chest pangs when the race crept into his thoughts. At lunch, he forced down a little of the goulash that had been deposited on his plate along with half of a thin, pre-made peanut butter sandwich he picked off of a pile of sandwiches at the end of the lunch line. He chased it with a small glass of milk and still felt a little hungry as he left the lunch room. He wondered how anyone could eat steak and eggs before a competition. He had felt slightly nauseous coercing down the little he did eat.

Riding with Mr. Johnson to the high school his throat felt dry, his body weak. He went right into the bathroom when he got to the high school. After changing, the team left the locker room together to begin the warm-up. The team from St. Paul South had already started their warm-up so Central followed them around the course. It was a dual meet on a multiple loop course run around and behind the school practice fields. The South team stopped at one point to look at a hand-drawn map that Mr. Renner had given them, wondering if they were on course. Central caught up to them.

"Do you need any help?" asked Kent.

"Do you go around this part twice?" asked the guy holding the map.

The team stopped.

"Yeah, the first time you make this loop, you go out that way," said Kent, pointing on their map. "That's right over there," he said, waving his arm toward the far side of the field. "The second time, you'll be coming from the other loop so you'll go that way," he said, waving his arm in the other direction, "then you go into the finish."

"Thanks," said their spokesman. They jogged off toward the finish. Central jogged over to their usual gathering place in the shade next to the school to stretch.

"Fifteen minutes!" Mr. Renner yelled.

The team put on their spikes.

"Run together," said Kent, as they moved out into the front of the starting area.

"I'll do my best," said Rich, "but my legs feel like the time my friend ran over them with his bike when I was a kid."

"Ha!" laughed Bodine, "Who was your friend, Wile E. Coyote?"

"Woody Woodpecker, heh, heh, heh, ha, ha!" said Rich, with a big smile.

Everyone smiled and suddenly the atmosphere felt more relaxed. More banter broke out as the team finished their strides. The warm-up had helped Len's sore legs only a little. They felt heavy doing the wind sprints. Mr. Renner had said the team was training through this meet, that they had to learn to run hard when they were tired. "Mission accomplished," thought Len. This was his longest race ever and his legs were already tired.

"Five minutes!" yelled Mr. Renner.

Both teams jogged and walked slowly toward the starting line. They gathered behind the line and Mr. Renner gave some final instructions, then stepped off to the side. He pulled a starter's pistol out of his pocket, asked the timers if they were ready, then raised the gun.

"Runners set!" he yelled, then fired a shot into the air.

Len swallowed a big gulp of air and took off behind Kent and Mark. Going up the first rise onto the practice fields, Phil ran on one side of Len, and Rich on the other. Kent and Mark were already moving out with South's top runners. There was some bumping as the two teams merged into one pack approaching the first turn. Suddenly, Phil swore and came to a dead stop. Runners behind jumped to sidestep him as he turned and started running back toward the start. Len looked back to see him stooping to pick up his glasses.

"Come on Lenny," said Rich. Len turned forward. They rounded the turn and headed down along the long back fence. Coming up to the first mile mark, Len could see three South runners together in the lead. Kent and Mark ran with another South runner about ten yards back. Rich and Len ran another twenty yards back. Around the next turn, Len glanced back to see Phil and Rob running together about ten yards behind them with three more South runners.

In the second mile, the pace continued to feel hard to Len. He hadn't heard the mile split because the student Mr. Renner had got to read the times was standing too far away and mumbling. Len could see that the top three South runners had split apart. Mark was running alone in fourth, gaining on their third man. Kent was battling their fourth man a little further back. Rich and Len still ran together with Phil now close behind. Rob had dropped off but was still running with the three South runners. Len felt like he was running as hard as he could but wasn't sure he could maintain the pace. He thought of Frank Shorter battling, battling, battling every step in the Olympic 10,000, and resolved to do the same.

Into the last mile, the race stretched out more. Mark moved into third and Kent ran alone in fifth. Phil and another South runner had come up with Len. Rich had dropped back and was battling the next two South runners, who had dropped Rob. Len fought every step of the last mile to not slow down, but knew it was happening anyway. Coming down the last rise, his legs burned as Phil and the South runner began to pull away from him. He came across the line in eighth, exhausted. He glanced back as he wobbled into the small finish chute to see Rich get out-kicked by the two South guys with whom he had been running. Len was handed a card with an eight on it at the end of the chute, then stepped out to wait for Rich.

"Good job Lenny," he said as they walked slowly back to their warm-up area, "I had nothing that last mile."

"Me neither," said Len.

They came up on Phil.

"Did you break your glasses?" Rich asked.

"No, I got 'em before anyone stepped on 'em," said Phil.

"Way to get back in the race," said Rich.

Len remembered what Frank Shorter had said after the Olympic 10,000 when he was asked about Viren and Gammoudi falling. He said that he thought Gammoudi was the kind of runner who could only win when everything went his way, but Viren was the kind of runner who was going to win no matter what.

"Yeah, you ran great," Len said to Phil.

"I was just pissed off," Phil said.

"Well, it worked," said Rich.

South won the meet twenty-two to thirty-four. Mr. Renner told the team it was a good start. Only a few seconds faster by a few of the Central runners would have made it a very close contest, he said. He was happy because the team had done a lot better against South this year than last year, and they were the defending region champions.

196

As they sat changing out of their spikes Kent said, "By the end of the season Mark and I can run with their top two and Phil, Lenny and Rich can get up with their three and four guys."

The team's sights had been set. They moved slowly out on a cool down jog, knowing rather than just thinking, for the first time, that making it to state this year was within their grasp.

# 46

# A Bizarre Display

That night as Len waited for Prefontaine's prelim to come on, he thought about Viren falling and Phil going back for his glasses. He thought that having someone say that you were the kind of runner who was going to win no matter what, not just when things went your way, was probably the best compliment you could get as a runner. Len had never thought of the possibility of getting tripped or going down in a race. But as he now imagined it, he saw himself popping back up, like Viren, and getting back into the pack. Just having thought about it, he felt confident in his ability to do it.

Only the top two from each of the five 5,000 meter heats were guaranteed a spot in the Olympic final. Prefontaine and Emiel Puttemans traded the lead throughout their prelim. They kept the pace strong the entire way. Only Harold Norpoth of West Germany stayed with them into the final lap. Puttemans forced the pace all the way to the finish, setting a new Olympic record of 13:31. Prefontaine eased up the last few meters to finish second in 13:32.

"Step one has been taken by the confident young man from Oregon," said Jim McKay.

Then the camera focused in on the U.S. trio of Vince Matthews, Wayne Collett and John Smith, three of the top 400 meter runners in the world, now lining up their starting blocks for the Olympic 400 meter final. McKay said there could easily be a medal sweep for the U.S. in this event.

The gun was fired and the Americans all got out well around the first turn. But coming off the turn onto the backstretch, Smith pulled up, and out, of the race, grabbing at his hamstring. Matthews and

Collett continued down the backstretch, moving out ahead of the field. Coming into the homestretch, Matthews pulled clear of Collett, who was holding off the rest of the field in second. They held their form down the final straight to take the gold and silver medals.

Matthews and Collett came to the Olympic podium to receive their medals. But as the ceremony began, the crowd stirred and the announcers wondered aloud what kind of statement they were attempting to make. Matthews stood with his U.S. warm-up jacket unzipped and a sweat-stained t-shirt underneath. Collett appeared barefoot, wearing no warm-up pants and his jacket unzipped. As the U.S. national anthem played, Matthews gestured for Collett to join him on the top of the stand. They stood casually talking, purposefully facing away from the flag during the anthem. If they were trying to make any statement other than blatant disrespect, they failed spectacularly, said McKay. Following the ceremony, the two were kicked out of the Olympic village and sent home.

It had been a bizarre display to Len. He had seen many medal presentations that were the emotional culmination of the years of dedication and training for the athlete's receiving the medals. It was the moment that made everything they had been through to get there worth it. This appeared not to be the case for Matthews and Collett.

The coverage then went to a U.S. basketball game, which was another blowout. Parts of several games had been shown already and all of them were won easily by the U.S. It was America's game. But there was also talk of the imminent showdown between the U.S. and the Soviet Union. The basketball announcer, Frank Gifford, said that this Soviet team was a tough, physical team that had been playing together for seven years. The U.S. team was the youngest basketball team the country had ever sent to the Olympics and had been together just a few weeks. The Soviets had also won all of their games easily.

# 47

# Ryun Denied

Friday the team ran easily through the soft, amber light of the early autumn afternoon out around the A&W. Friday night was looked forward to by most of the guys on the team, and the A&W usually played some role in their plans. As usual, when they ran by, several guys on the team yelled, "Hi Janet!" This time the A&W was open and Janet was delivering a food order out to a car. She was carrying a tray with burgers, fries and frosty mugs of root beer so couldn't wave. But she smiled, and that was enough for the yellers to claim victory with a cheer.

On the way back the team felt tired from the race, but upbeat.

"We're only going to get better," Kent said as they ran.

"Everyone else is going to get better too," said Rich.

"We can run with those guys," said Mark.

"Even if we don't beat South, if we run with them, we'll beat everyone else," said Kent.

"I just have to stick with this little shit," said Rich giving Len a shove. He had a big smile on his face.

"We'll all have to stick with that little shit," said Mark, "he might be beating all of us pretty soon."

"We can't go too far today, Rich has to get ready for his date tonight," said Bodine.

Rich got his big smile. "I have to start the year off right!"

"Wayne, are you going to the football game?" asked Kent.

"I'll get there at some point," said Wayne. He looked at Phil. "I'll pick you up at seven."

"Lenny's probably got a big date," said Bodine.

"Yeah, but his bike's only a one-seater," said Rich.

"She can ride on the handlebars," said Bodine.

"They're going to the drive-in," said Rich, "she'll have to hold the speaker."

Kent looked at Wayne. "Why don't you swing by after you get Phil."

"Oh, oh, this sounds serious," said Bodine.

"Nah, we're just cruisin'," said Wayne.

"I have to work for my old man," said Bodine.

Kent looked at Mark. "What are you going to do?"

"We're going to the game," said Mark.

"Well, go home right afterward. You know what Renner says about hanging out with girls too much - it gives you weak legs," said Bodine.

"Ha!" laughed Rich, "I forgot about that."

"We did have weak legs after homecoming last year," said Kent.

"I don't know if it was the girls, or the dancing," said Rich.

"Or, maybe it was because we hadn't gone to bed yet," said Bodine.

"Ha!" laughed Rich, "A lethal combination!"

Kent went into his Renner impersonation, "I don't know why we even bother going to meets if you're just going to stay out all night and dance the night before."

"That's my point exactly!" exclaimed Bodine, "Don't schedule meets when we're going to stay out all night and dance!"

Rich looked at Len. "See what you got yourself into," he said.

"You'll be corrupted in no time," said Bodine.

That night, Jim Ryun began his quest to get perhaps the only thing he still wanted from running, an Olympic gold medal. To Len, no one was as exciting to watch as Ryun. He loped along looking relaxed and strong early in his races. But everyone knew what was coming, and waited for the great kick. When it came, no matter how often you had seen it, it was still stunning. Winding up his long stride, his head rolling from side to side, few had ever matched it - none when he was at his very best. Kip Keino, his long time rival who had won in

Mexico City, was back to defend his Olympic title. But there were other, younger runners contending as well. Keino was in Ryun's prelim along with a fast, young New Zealander, Rod Dixon. There were seven heats with the top four in each heat plus the next two fastest moving onto the semi-finals, for a total of thirty.

In the first heat, Dave Wottle had come from behind to finish second. Ryun ran with nine other runners in the fourth heat. The pace through the first half of Ryun's heat was slow so all of the runners stayed tightly bunched. Keino had chosen to run from the front, Ryun stayed at the back of the pack.

With 500 meters left, coming into the penultimate homestretch, Ryun ran in the back on the inside next to the rail. Keino ran in front on the outside. Ryun made a move to get to the outside, cutting closely in front of Billy Fordjour of Ghana. Suddenly, their legs became tangled. Ryun tripped and went down, with Fordjour tumbling over him. Ryun rolled to his back and lay still. Fordjour lay on his side, still. The pack pulled away.

"Jim Ryun is down on the track!" exclaimed McKay.

"No!" said Len out loud. He couldn't believe his eyes.

"The United States seems to be jinxed in this race," said Liquori, "we haven't had a winner since 1908."

As the pack began the bell lap, the stunned Ryun and Fordjour pushed themselves up onto their feet. Ryun slowly accelerated, limping noticeably. He gradually got his long stride going again, but it was too late. The pack battled for the qualifying positions 100 meters in front of him. Keino finished first followed by Dixon. Ryun finished ninth, eleven seconds behind.

As Ryun crossed the finish line, an anguished look spread across his face. Keino turned, took Ryun's hand in his and put his other arm around his shoulder in a show of genuine sympathy. Ryun was inconsolable. Len cringed. Ryun filed a protest to be allowed to move onto the semi-final. It was denied. His Olympics were over almost before they began.

# 48

# Three Seconds

The team didn't have practice that Saturday so Len decided to do an easy run down to his clearing. He stepped out the door and imagined Viren training in the early Finnish morning. As Len began running, he emulated Viren's form as he ran to the river, feeling a tinge of guilt because of the many days he had run like Prefontaine. It was easy to feel like Viren as he jogged down into the woods. In an interview, Viren said he lived in a small town and did all of his running on forest trails. He had a secret trail where he ran a specific workout. He said that when he could do that workout well, he knew he was ready to race. But he also said, with a sly smile, that the secret to his success was reindeer milk.

Len stopped and breathed in the sensuous air of the clearing. His was not a religious family, but standing here felt like standing at the center of creation itself to him. He stretched out for a few minutes before running back up his own forest trail. He didn't see Tom that day and wondered where he lived, what he did, where he went. He felt good running like Viren on the way home and gradually increased his pace as he went. Len finished his five miles and walked into a quiet house as he imagined Viren had done countless times in his small town in Finland.

That afternoon on the track, the men's four by 100 meter relay semifinals were run. Eddy Hart anchored the U.S. team into the final. Valeriy Borzov anchored for the Soviets, who also qualified for the final. Hart would now get his chance to test himself against Borzov.

In the 1500 meter semifinal, Dave Wottle stuck with the fast-closing formula that had brought him so much success. But this time he fell just short and missed making the final. The U.S. would have no one contending for the 1500 meter gold medal.

McKay then said the women's 1500 meter final would be run. There were no U.S. runners in it so the broadcast would go to the gold medal basketball game between the U.S. and the Soviet Union. But McKay added that this was the first time that women would run the 1500 in the Olympics. The longest race up until now had been the 800. Len thought this was strange because in the spring he had seen in the paper that the Boston Marathon had officially added a women's division. If they could run a marathon, he thought, why not all of the other Olympic distance races? McKay said a Russian woman had broken the world record in both the prelim and semi-final rounds and was the heavy favorite. Her world record now stood at 4:05, which he said was equivalent to a 4:23 mile. "Whoa!" thought Len. He wanted to watch this woman run. But the basketball game came on.

Frank Gifford said that both teams were undefeated in this Olympics, but the U.S. was 63-0 in Olympic basketball since the sport had been added to the games in 1936. Len was drawn into the game right from the start because the Soviets jumped out to a 5-0 lead, and Jim Brewer of the University of Minnesota was one of the U.S. starters. Both teams played a slow, cautious game in the first half, with the Soviets holding an edge over the U.S. 26-21 at halftime.

Early in the second half, the game became more physical with Dwight Jones of the U.S. and a Soviet player both being ejected from the game after almost coming to blows over a rebound. Jones had been the leading scorer for the U.S. The Soviet player ejected was a substitute playing in his first Olympic game. Had this been a calculated plan by the Soviets to gain an advantage, Gifford wondered? A few seconds later, Jim Brewer fell to the court coming down from a jump ball and hit his head on the floor. Soon after, he came out of the game and did not return. The Soviets immediately opened up a ten point lead.

With two of their big men out, the U.S. battled back with a full court defense. With three minutes left, the U.S. had cut the deficit to two points, the closest it had been since the game began. But thirty seconds later, the Soviets had opened it up to five points again. Once again, the U.S. fought back and cut the lead to one point with 1:30 to go.

"The streak is on the line, sixty-three straight, seven gold medals," said Gifford.

Then another of the U.S. inside big men, Mike Bantom, fouled out.

"What a situation for this young team," lamented Gifford. "They're down by two points. Fifty-five seconds remaining in the game. Now they find themselves with their backs totally to the wall."

The Soviets sunk a free throw to lead by three, and the U.S. inbounded the ball with fifty-three seconds left.

"Alright, the U.S. now down by three, the clock moving with fifty-three seconds," said Gifford.

The U. S. brought the ball down the court.

"Jim Forbes, Texas at El Paso, hits! Inside forty seconds, the U.S. down by one," exclaimed Gifford.

The Soviets took the ball out, brought it down the court and began passing it around.

"Inside twenty seconds. This machine-like Russian team running the clock out," said Gifford.

"Into Belov. Shot blocked by McMillen!" exclaimed Gifford.

Belov got his own rebound and tried to clear the ball by passing it to the outside. Doug Collins stole the pass and went the length of the floor.

"Five seconds, four seconds!" counted Gifford.

Collins shot a lay up with three seconds remaining but was fouled hard by a Soviet player. He missed the lay up and fell to the floor well out of bounds, hitting his head on the base of the basket standard.

"Three seconds shows on the clock as Doug Collins, desperately driving for that lay in, crashed into the support of the basket," said

Gifford. "Doug Collins of the United States, Illinois State University, shaken up."

Collins lay still. A medical team came out and a few seconds later Collins was up and walking around. The camera zoomed in on the scoreboard as Gifford said, "That's the story, 49-48, three seconds on the clock. Doug Collins coming to the bench, and he'll stay in. And here's the story, he will be shooting two fouls. Doug Collins, and what pressure you put on a young man."

Collins put the first foul shot in to tie the game for the first time since the game had begun. The U.S. fans erupted!

"This place goes insane! Doug Collins has tied it up," said Gifford.

Collins stepped to the line for the second shot, and immediately sunk it, putting the U.S. into the lead.

"Doug Collins has perhaps won the game!" Gifford exclaimed, "Two seconds."

The frantic Soviets grabbed the ball. The referee waved them to play on. They threw the ball in and got up to mid-court before calling a time out with one second left. Then suddenly, a conflux of coaches, officials and players began arguing along the sideline and out onto the court.

"Somebody has gone down on the floor," said Gifford, "The Russian coach, or a Russian official and Hank Iba are yelling at each other and bedlam has taken over here at the basketball hall."

"The United States leads now 50-49 with one second showing on the clock," said Gifford. "But what neither team wants is a technical foul. Everybody is trying to calm everybody else down. The officials are trying to get everyone settled down. They come over to talk to Hank Iba. Now you have me totally confused. They're changing the clock. They're going back to three seconds."

Gradually, the officials moved everyone off of the court. An official handed the ball to the Soviet player back at the baseline, who immediately threw it in bounds the length of the court. It tipped off of Belov's outstretched hand, bounced off the backboard and onto the floor. The horn sounded and the hall erupted, the U.S. bench and fans ran out onto the court.

"It's all over. Wow! What a finish!" exclaimed Gifford, "The United States winning their eighth consecutive gold medal. This place has gone crazy! The United States wins it 50-49!"

On the court a large circle celebration was taking place. "Hank Iba in the middle along with assistant coach Johnny Bach," exclaimed Gifford. "Great performances, particularly by Kevin Joyce, who came on to spur the United States attack with six points."

Photographers came onto the court. An American flag waved in the crowd.

Suddenly, shoving erupted between the U.S. players and a guy in a suit. Hank Iba pushed the man away. Officials began clearing the celebrating assemblage off the floor.

"Now we're being told the scoreboard is not correct," said a bewildered Gifford. "They are running the clock down. Hank Iba comes to the bench. The horn had sounded. But apparently, they're going to put the clock back down to three seconds. Confusion reigns as the United States still has that one point lead 50-49 as a result of two pressure packed free throw shots by Doug Collins of Illinois State. Now the clock shows three seconds."

The floor was slowly cleared. For the third time, an official handed the ball to the Soviet player to inbound. The Soviets had set up their team on the floor and now the U.S. players were being told to go out onto the court. They looked confused and unsure which of them should be going out.

"There is time for the Russians to go to their big man, Alexander Belov," said Gifford, "They're going to try. Alexander Beloz between two American defenders back there with him," said Gifford.

McMillen, who was guarding the inbounds pass, was waved back by the referee, leaving an open passing lane down the court. The ball was thrown the full length of the court toward Belov, who was guarded by the six-seven Jim Forbes with six-three Kevin Joyce, running over to help. Forbes and Joyce caromed off Belov as he leapt for the ball. Belov came down with the ball and laid in an easy shot under the basket. Now it was the Soviet bench and fans that rushed onto the court in a victory celebration, as the shocked U.S. players watched.

"The Russian team has mobbed Alexander Belov. And this time it is over," said Gifford. "First, it was indicated the United States had won 49-48. Now again, an official is talking to head coach Iba on the side. And that looks like the final score, although there is a big rhubarb going on in front of the bench. Meanwhile, the Russians are mobbing Alexander Belov. And apparently, the argument is over. The amount of seconds on the clock was wrong. The Russians put the ball in play with one second, they threw it the length of the court, the gun sounded, the United States apparently had won the game. Then the official came over to the score keepers table. He was told that that clock was unofficial, that there were really three seconds remaining in the game. So they ran the clock back to three seconds. Russia inbounded the ball. It went the length of the floor to Alexander Belov. He put it in to put the Russians ahead 51-50. But the debate still goes on."

Len was stunned! He couldn't believe how this could happen in the Olympics! Like the U.S. basketball team, and many people around the world who watched the game, he felt the U.S. had been cheated. But maybe this is how the Cold War worked. It wasn't just about propping up third-world dictators, fomenting rebellions, arming guerrillas and swapping spies. It was about using all available means, including sports, to gain a strategic or propaganda advantage. It had galled the Soviets that Bobby Fischer had beaten them at their national game. Now, somehow, the Soviets had beaten the U.S. at its national game. Both contests had been close and could have gone either way. They were both controversial, with the loser blaming outside forces. It was hard to see it as a coincidence.

# 49

# Where Tom Lives

Sunday morning Len went out for his long run. He wasn't sure how far he would go, but he felt good after two easy days and wanted to explore the farthest reaches of the path down by the water. When he got to the clearing Tom was there sitting and looking out over the river.

"Today is the last day of the Olympics," said Len, "Prefontaine and Frank Shorter are running. Jim Ryun fell in his prelim and is out."

"That's bad luck for Ryun. He's a great runner, like Ron Clarke, but neither one of them could win a gold medal."

"It would have been great to see him beat Keino in the final like Keino beat him in Mexico City."

"Life doesn't provide many chances to get even."

"I wonder if Shorter is tired from the 10,000?"

"That's a good question. He's had a little more than a week to recover, but he ran two hard races in four days."

"The U.S. basketball team got robbed out of the gold medal yesterday."

"How did they get robbed?"

"They won the game but the officials put three seconds back on the clock. They won it again, and the officials put three more seconds back on the clock. Then the Soviets won but they didn't put anymore time back on the clock."

"Sounds like prison. Everything is rigged against you. Even when you play by their rules and think you will win, they change the rules or make new ones and you lose anyway. How did your race go?"

"It was hard."

"What man were you on your team?"

"Fourth."

"Did your team win?"

"No, they're the defending region champions."

"Maybe you can get them back later in the season. Are you doing a long run today?"

"Yeah."

"That's good. Are you doing morning runs?"

"I'm going to start. I like running in the morning."

"All of the great runners run twice a day almost every day."

"I read that Prefontaine runs five miles in the morning."

"There you go."

Len continued his run down the sylvan path, through the silent trees, along the limestone cliff to the water. The river was higher, and looked swifter, than the last time he had been here, but he could still stand on the sand bar. The dark water swirled around it, spinning small eddies off the end. It was easy to imagine Tom's ancestors standing in this same spot seeing, hearing and smelling everything that Len was now. The whole expanse of the great river spread out before him, looking like he thought it always had and how he hoped it always would.

Len continued along the path past the beach. It was narrower and wound through the bottom flora along a gentle curve in the river for another mile or so before dropping down to the water and ending. It was more rocky than sandy here. The water looked deep and foreboding even right next to the shore. The cliff was closer to the water and more sheer. It felt remote and primeval, like he had stumbled onto some ancient and secret landing. There was a rugged crag jutting out from the cliff and covered in wild vines that hid the landing from any river mariner that didn't know where to look for it. From behind the crag, one could easily push a canoe out onto the river, seeming to appear on the water out of nowhere. It was quiet except for the soft lapping of the water onto the rocks. Len crouched down and put his hand into the water, feeling as though he had completed some connection. He stood up and breathed in deeply of the water, rock and mud that smelled like they had been here for a thousand years, then turned back toward the beach and began to run. As he approached the rise through the cliff, his eye caught an unnatural blue color off the trail a ways in a shady area. He slowed and saw that it was a tarp hung up on the side of the cliff. It was attached to the cliff at the top somehow but the bottom was loose. Len eased to a walk and made his way to the tarp. There was a small, matted down area in front of the tarp where there had been a fire. An uncut log, that looked like a good place to sit, rested near where the fire had been. Len pulled the loose part of the tarp out from the cliff and saw that it covered a cave that was apparently being lived in. Inside, there was a canvas army surplus bag full of something and tied shut at the top, a smaller backpack next to it that he recognized as Tom's, a rolled up sleeping bag, and a plastic gallon milk jug half full of water. Len had seen the water container hanging off of Tom's backpack sometimes.

Len dropped the tarp covering the cave and turned to look at the campsite. It was a beautiful, tranquil spot with a nice view of the river through a stand of aspen trees on one side, and gradually rising forest up to the limestone cliff on the other. Len knew now where Tom lived. He felt a little uncomfortable, like he was invading Tom's sanctuary, so he returned to the main path and started the climb back up to the clearing. Tom was gone when he got there, so he continued on up to the River Road and home. He decided not to tell Tom that he had found where he lived.

# 50

# That's Not Frank

That afternoon, Jim McKay began the Olympic coverage with a follow-up to the U.S./Soviet basketball game. The U.S. had filed a protest overnight. A five man panel was appointed to adjudicate the protest. Three of the five were from eastern block Soviet allied countries. The protest was denied three to two, with the eastern block voting as one to uphold the Soviet victory. "That figures," thought Len. The U.S. team had subsequently voted unanimously to refuse to accept the silver medals. They had reserved seats on the first available flight home.

McKay provided new details about the debacle on the court. The person who had come down out of the stands after Doug Collins sunk his free throws to put the U.S. into the lead, was William Jones of England, head of the International Basketball Federation. Though he had no jurisdiction over the game or officials, he ordered that the clock be reset to three seconds and the ball be given back to the Soviets. While admitting that calling a timeout in that situation was not allowed, the officials complied, with no technical foul being assessed to the Soviets. The U.S. coach, Hank Iba, had argued the decision vociferously. McKay said that additionally, one of the game officials, a Brazilian, refused to sign the official scoring sheet in an act of protest, saying the Russian victory was "completely irregular and outside the rules of the game of basketball."

Video was shown of the basketball medal ceremony. The Soviet team stood on the large gold medal platform and the Cuban team stood on the bronze medal platform. In between, the silver medal platform stood empty as the national anthem of the Soviet Union was played.

The broadcast then went to the Olympic stadium as Jim McKay said, "Here comes the race of exhaustion. The race that will grind most of this field of seventy-six scheduled runners into the streets of Munich before it is done. This is the marathon. Twenty-six miles, three-hundred-eighty-five yards. There's your man, Frank Shorter, wearing the mustache, all the way on the outside, wearing the white shirt with USA."

McKay's announcing partner, Erich Segal, said, "Frank Shorter of the United States has a real chance in this race. He finished fifth in the 10,000 meters, that's about the best he could possibly do. But today he is the fastest man in the marathon field. No one has run 10,000 meters as fast as Frank Shorter. He was the top-rated marathon runner in the world last year. He beat the world at Fukuoka, Japan. He is a heavy favorite."

The marathon started with the runners taking two laps around the track in front of the over 80,000 spectators packed into the stadium. Frank Shorter ran near the front along with Kenny Moore and Jack Bacheler. The camera zoomed in on Shorter.

"There's Frank Shorter," said McKay, "One of America's last two hopes for an individual gold medal today, the other being Steve Prefontaine."

"America has not won a gold medal in the marathon for over half a century," said Segal, "and I think Frank Shorter has a chance."

Segal, who was a marathoner and had taught Shorter in an English class at Yale, said the weather would not be a factor. It was cool and partly cloudy. He said Shorter was mainly worried about Derek Clayton of Australia, the world record holder in the marathon, and Ron Hill of England. It seemed to Len that the world record holder should be the race favorite. Shorter had won some big marathons but his best time was a couple of minutes slower than Clayton's. The defending Olympic champion, Mamo Wolde from Ethiopia, was also in the field, but he was now forty-years-old. But

Ethiopians had won the last three Olympic gold medals in the marathon.

The marathoners ran out of the stadium onto the streets of Munich with Shorter running in fifth place. The coverage stayed at the stadium, where the final of the men's 5,000 meters was about to begin. Jim McKay said that Prefontaine planned to run his last mile in four minutes, then asked Erich Segal for his prediction.

"Steve Prefontaine will be the Olympic 5,000 meter champion," said Segal, "I think he will break the world's record at 5,000 meters. But I think he will have to do it in Montreal. Because today, Steve Prefontaine, twenty-one-years-old, is running up against the very big boys."

The runners sprang off of the starting line into the first turn. But on the backstretch the pace slowed to a crawl, and remained slow through the first mile, passed in 4:26.

"Boy, what strategy must be going on out there," said McKay, "This is the thinking time, isn't it?"

"Nobody was thinking during that first mile," countered Segal.

No one had dropped off the pace as the tight pack bumped and tripped its way into the second mile. This wasn't the race Pre said he was going to run, thought Len. No one had expended any guts on the pace so far. But Pre would move soon, Len thought, as he leaned anxiously forward. But the second mile was even slower than the first, 4:28, yet Pre stayed behind. Len wondered what he was doing, why he wasn't pushing the pace. At the Olympic Trials, Pre had made his move with six laps to go. Where he had run a sixty-four second lap with six to go in Eugene, the same lap in Munich was run in sixty-seven.

"Go Pre!" Len thought, "Push the pace!"

With five laps to go, Pre remained in the lumbering pack. Finally, with four laps to go, Pre moved into the lead, but ran just a sixty-four second lap. With three laps to go, Pre's time was well off what it had been at this point in the trials, and this field was full of more potent kickers.

"Prefontaine has got to run that four minute mile, he's got to!" exclaimed Segal. But would this drive be long enough or fast enough? With three laps to go, the pack was still intact. Now, Pre ran a sixty-one. The lead pack was whittled to five.

With two laps to go, Viren and then Puttemans went by Pre. On the turn, Gammoudi went by. England's Ian Stewart stayed in fifth. This was not the hard driving Pre Len had expected to see, with head cocked to one side, confident in his ability to take more pain and break any would-be followers. It was a more tentative, indecisive Pre. On the backstretch, he moved out into lane two and shot back into the lead.

The group of five was now clear of the rest of the field. Coming around the turn with 600 meters to go, finally he looked like the Prefontaine everyone was expecting, head cocked, brow furrowed, arms driving. But as the bell sounded for the final lap, Prefontaine again let Viren go past. Gammoudi stayed on Pre's shoulder. Puttemans was off the back and a gap was opening in front of Stewart. That lap had been run in sixty seconds.

"It's going to be a last lap fight," said McKay, "It seems impossible that Prefontaine can out-kick Viren."

"Or Gammoudi," added Segal.

It looked to Len like it was going to be a three man race. Pre would get a medal, it was just a matter of which color. Into the turn, Gammoudi went by Prefontaine and moved up to Viren's shoulder.

"Lasse Viren is going for his second gold medal of the games," exclaimed McKay. "Mohamed Gammoudi is right with him, and so is Steve Prefontaine! The kid is showing all the guts in the world. He's hanging in there with the kickers."

On the backstretch, Prefontaine burst to the outside of Gammoudi as if to go by, but eased up and stayed at his side. Gammoudi got spooked and accelerated away into the lead. Prefontaine again burst to Gammoudi's outside shoulder, but again stopped short of passing.

"Go! Pass! Take the lead!" Len thought.

And again, Gammoudi accelerated away and began to open a gap on Prefontaine. Prefontaine looked for Viren on his outside, but at that same moment, Viren went by on his inside and chased after Gammoudi into the final turn. Viren came up to Gammoudi's shoulder, then accelerated past him and began to pull away down the homestretch. Gammoudi and Prefontaine shifted into a full sprint in second and third. Stewart came off the turn fourth, ten meters behind Prefontaine.

Coming to the finish line, Viren had opened up ten meters on Gammoudi. Prefontaine was another three meters back. Stewart was closing fast on Prefontaine. Viren won in a new Olympic record of 13:26.42. Gammoudi crossed second in 13:27.33. Stewart went past Prefontaine in the last ten meters to claim the bronze in 13:27.61. With five meters to go Prefontaine staggered, then nearly fell over, but made it to the line fourth in 13:28.25.

Prefontaine had run his last mile in 4:04. This was two seconds faster than his last mile at the trials, but his last six laps had been one second slower than in Eugene. It had been good enough against the best U.S. runners, but not good enough to win an Olympic medal.

It had been a great, frustrating race for Len to watch! He was disappointed that Pre didn't get a medal, and was confused why he had run the way he had. It would be the race that he would think about more than any other as he honed his own racing ability.

The next event was the men's four by 100 meter relay. McKay wondered if, despite going up against a strong U.S. team that had looked good in the prelims, Valeriy Borzov could anchor the Soviet Union to victory, winning his third gold medal of the games.

The U.S. team ran in lane one, keeping the Soviets in their sights out in lane four. Larry Black ran a strong lead-off leg for the U.S. and executed a near-perfect hand-off to Robert Taylor, propelling the U.S. into the lead on the backstretch. Taylor executed a similarly smooth hand-off to Gerald Tinker on the third leg. Tinker came into the final hand-off two steps ahead of the Soviets. Eddy Hart took the baton into the homestretch and held those two steps, but no more, on the hard driving Borzov, all the way to the finish. Hart had earned his chance to stand on the gold medal platform.

The coverage went out to the streets of Munich for the marathon as the leaders passed the ten kilometer mark in 31:09. Derek Clayton was in front setting the pace, with a pack of just under a dozen runners right behind. Shorter was at the back of that pack, with Kenny Moore and Jack Bacheler running nearby. Len wondered if Shorter was having some problem or didn't feel good.

The coverage returned to the track for the last three Olympic events. The men's 1500 meter final began slow. But just before the end of the second lap, Kip Keino made his move to the front and clipped off a fifty-five second lap. "The long, hard drive!" thought Len. The field strung out behind Keino and going into the final straight only Finland's Pekka Vasala remained on Keino's shoulder. On the straight, Vasala pulled out to lane two and made his move, passing Keino with fifty meters to go. "Another Flying Finn," thought Len. Lydiard *had* inspired them.

Then came the four by 400 meter relay. The U.S. had been the heavy favorite coming into the games, borne out by the top-two sweep in the open 400 meters. But the dismissal of Vince Matthews and Wayne Collette for their petulant antics on the medal stand had cost the U.S. its chance. With Matthews and Collette back in the U.S., the U.S. was unable to field a team.

When the marathon came back on, Shorter was out in front, running all alone. He had taken control of the race. His pace was steady and efficient, his face calm, as he ground out the miles. Kenny Moore of the U.S. had pushed into second, with Wolde dogging his heals and Karl Lismont, of Portugal, lurking within striking distance.

"Alright, Shorter!" thought Len, "And Moore, going for silver!"

Passing thirty kilometers in 1:32:49, Shorter had opened up a 1:05 lead on Moore and Wolde, with Lismont another twenty seconds back. Clayton held fifth place thirteen seconds behind Lismont, with Bacheler running sixth, another five seconds back.

Len had never seen a full marathon or any race not run on a track or cross country course, only the short video of the top finishers at the Olympic Trials. Large crowds lined the streets of Munich as the compelling battle for Olympic medals unfolded before them in the final seven miles. Most of the TV coverage for the next forty minutes focused on Shorter's solo journey past the notable sights of Munich along the course. But even watching him wind through the crowded streets with his slightly pigeon-toed, metronomic stride and drooping mustache was compelling to Len. He knew some day he wanted to run a marathon through spectator-lined streets.

Approaching the stadium, Shorter's lead had stretched to almost two minutes. Lismont had closed on Moore and Wolde, and the three now battled fiercely for the last two medals. Moore's sweat-drenched hair flopped on his head as his face began to grimace. Lismont's head rolled from side to side as he pumped his arms harder. The smooth Wolde showed little outside sign of fatigue. Clayton and Bacheler had fallen off.

Shorter disappeared into the tunnel leading into the stadium. The camera switched to an inside view of the stadium and almost immediately a runner came out of the tunnel onto the track. The crowd rose to a standing ovation. But the runner was not Frank Shorter. Erich Segal was incredulous!

"That's not Frank!" he cried, "That is an imposter! That used to happen in the Boston Marathon! That is an imposter! Get him off the track! This happens in bush league marathons. This doesn't happen in an Olympic marathon!"

MacKay said, "This looks like a fake at the Olympic Games! They ought to throw him out! Many in the stadium don't know that a fake has come into the grounds."

"C'mon Frank, you won it!" yelled the inconsolable Segal as Shorter emerged from the tunnel onto the track.

The fresh-looking charlatan, wearing yellow shorts, his long, red hair flopping on his head continued running on the opposite side of the track from Shorter. Len sat watching in disbelief.

"I wonder what Frank is thinking, if he see's that guy up ahead," said Segal, "Look at his face. He looks worried. He's looking at the guy. It's a fake Frank!" he yelled.

Shorter didn't look too worried to Len. He looked tired, but pressed on the last few meters toward the finish line, looking as stoic as he had the entire race.

McKay said, "We came out this morning and said, 'What in the world can happen today that will surprise us.' Well this is it. An imposter entering the Olympic stadium, appearing to win the marathon. Shorter is dazed, he doesn't know what to do."

Some in the crowd of 80,000 had now caught on and began whistling. The imposter veered off the track and ducked into another tunnel.

"Frank Shorter is not getting the tribute he should get for the most grueling, the most wonderful, in its way, races that there is in the world," said McKay.

Shorter ran down the final straight and crossed the line in 2:12:19 looking exhausted, shaking his head.

"Whether Frank thinks he lost or not, I have no idea," said McKay, "He may think that other guy took a complete victory lap and then left the stadium. Has this ever happened? A man, who perhaps does not know, that he's won the marathon in the Olympic Games?"

The whistles from the crowd continued.

"Tremendous confusion here in the Olympic stadium in Munich," said McKay, "The Olympics of total insecurity and unpredictability are continuing here in Munich right down to the last gasp."

Shorter began to jog around the curve and onto the backstretch as Lismont ran into the stadium, arms pumping, head oscillating, sweat flying off his brow, to claim the silver medal in 2:14:31. Then came the still smooth, yet disappointed looking Wolde, taking the bronze in 2:15:08. Thirty-one seconds after Wolde finished, the exhausted, dejected Moore crossed the line in fourth.

As more marathoners trickled into the stadium, preparations were being made for the Olympic closing ceremony. Len turned the TV off. It had been a stunning, fantastic, sad Olympics. Len wondered what they all thought of it, Olga, Pre, Shorter, Viren, Wottle. Were they all as exhilarated and amazed as he was?

# 51

# Running Like Shorter

Monday morning was cool as Len stepped out the door just after sunrise in a long sleeve t-shirt and shorts. He started running quickly to shake off the chill. After the humid summer mornings, running in the cool dawn was invigorating. Some of the leaves were just beginning to turn and a slight reddish hue glowed over the top of the waking neighborhood as the sun touched the peaks of the maple trees that lined the street. Len made good time to the river and turned onto the River Road under a canopy of still mostly green oak leaves that were now tinged with yellow and red. He jogged down onto his path through the dew-soaked woods to his clearing. He stretched for a few minutes, watching the sun begin to burn off the ethereal morning mist from the river. Steam rose off of his damp shirt. He moved quickly back up the hill to the River Road and kept a strong pace all the way home. He felt good and was hungry. He had just enough time to wolf down a bowl of cereal and two pieces of toast before leaving for school.

That afternoon the team's five mile run was a harder run than usual. The team warmed up over to Summit and stretched out on the boulevard. Mr. Renner rode his bike along with them.

"I can't believe that guy got him," Len heard Rich say about Prefontaine.

"I thought he was going to fall over," said Kent.

"I wish he would have got a medal," said Phil.

"He just waited too long," said Mark.

"It was a great race though," said Rich.

"How about that fake guy running onto the track ahead of Shorter!" said Bodine.

"Ha! Someone must have paid him to do that," said Rich.

"His friends were probably going nuts," said Bodine.

"Nobody did anything!" said Rich. "He just kept running."

"Ha! He only stopped because he got tired," said Bodine.

"Erich Segal was going nuts," said Kent. "'You won it Frank! It's a fake Frank!'"

"He looks worried! He looks confused!" said Bodine.

"Segal was ready to run out and tackle the guy," said Kent.

"That's the only thing that would have made the whole thing better," said Bodine.

"Yeah, it was cool that Shorter won," said Kent.

"How would you like to be Kenny Moore," said Phil, "run all that way in second or third then end up getting fourth without a medal?"

"Yeah, he looked pretty shot at the end," said Kent.

The team got to the boulevard on Summit and started to stretch.

"Run quick but relaxed on the way out," said Mr. Renner, "then pick it up on the way back. It shouldn't feel like a race, but it should be a hard, steady run."

"Try to stay together," said Kent.

The team finished stretching and started down Summit toward the river in a tight pack, but began to string out after only a few blocks. The pace seemed quick to Len right away, but he felt better after a few minutes and was able to relax as he ran. He felt the morning run in his legs, but it wasn't inhibiting.

There were seven guys still in the lead pack as the team followed Mr. Renner down the slight hill at the end of Summit and turned onto the River Road. In addition to Kent, Mark, Phil, Rich and Len, were Rob and Wayne. No one had said anything for awhile. There was just the sound of communal breathing and drumming footfalls as they ran. It was energizing to Len, running in this pack, the single ambition just to run together, and fast, as one unit. He felt like he could, and wanted to, run like this for a long time. He felt more a part of the team than ever.

Mr. Renner rode his bike up ahead to the two-and-a-half mile turnaround point and stopped.

"Fifteen-fifty," he called as the pack reached him and made the turn.

The pace picked up as they headed back to Summit. Phil, Rich and Len hung onto Mark and Kent. Rob hung onto the back of them. Wayne began to fall off. They turned onto Summit and pushed up the hill onto the boulevard. By the time they got to the top, Rob was off the back. Mark looked back at the four remaining.

"Way to hang tough guys," he said.

"Keep it going," said Kent.

The pace seemed to gradually pick up every couple of blocks, but Len continued to feel good even at the faster tempo. Halfway back, a gap opened behind him to Phil and Rich. Len stayed with Kent and Mark. Into the last mile, the pace picked up again. Len was surprised that his legs felt no worse than they had at the beginning. Despite the increasing speed, he was keeping up, and even felt like he had more to give if needed. Into the last half mile, he did need it as the pace picked up again, but he stayed with them all the way to the finish. Mr. Renner had rode up ahead and was waiting.

"Twenty-nine-fifty-eight," he called as the pack of three finished.

"Good job," said Mark to Len.

"Yeah, you're getting good" said Kent.

"I'm just better at the long stuff," Len said, thinking of his long Sunday runs.

They jogged back to the school and sat on the grass stretching. Rich looked at Len. "You ran like Shorter today" he said, smiling.

"I felt good," said Len.

"I told you he'd be beating us all pretty soon," said Mark.

"We'll see what we're made of Saturday," said Kent.

Bodine had come in and flopped onto the ground. "I know what I'm made of," he said.

"Jello?" asked Rich, with his big smile.

"Melting Jello," said Bodine, "A pool of Jello."

"It would be nice to get a trophy," said Kent.

"We can if everyone runs good," said Mark

"How many trophies do they give?" asked Rich.

"Top three," said Kent.

"Me and Lenny and Phil gotta be tough," said Rich.

# 52

# Morning Runs

Len felt a palpable void that night with no Olympics to watch. He wanted to watch or talk about running, or go for a run in Munich or Eugene. He felt an agreeable tiredness in his legs from that day's runs, as if he could feel his body getting stronger. As he lay in bed, he thought how great it was running fast up in front with Kent and Mark, like he could go on forever. He was looking forward to the Midland Invitational Saturday.

It was cool again Tuesday morning as Len ran through a radial pink sunrise. He ran easy to the river and onto his path. He was going to turn around at the clearing without stopping, but the peace and beauty he saw as a white mist hovered over the brown water held him there for a moment. Tom appeared from the lower path.

"You're out early," he said

"I'm psyched from watching the Olympics."

"You're running twice a day now?"

"I want to a few times a week."

"I read that Shorter won the marathon."

"Yeah, by a long ways. When he took off, no one went with him."

"He had a good Olympics."

"And Prefontaine got fourth, Viren won."

"I read about the race. Viren showed that he has Sisu. It sounded like Prefontaine ran a good race though."

"Yeah, but he didn't run like he did at the trials. At the trials, when he took the lead, he stayed there and just kept pushing the pace. He didn't let anybody pass. But in the Olympics, he let Viren and a couple other guys pass him twice, then he had to sprint to get past them again. He just kept speeding up and slowing down, and the pace was slower."

"Maybe he wasn't as confident against those guys. It was probably a lot different for him running in Munich than in Eugene."

"I don't think he would have beaten Viren anyway, but he might have got second or third if he had pushed the pace earlier. Those other guys might not have been there to out-kick him."

"Confidence is a hard thing to have all the time. He was probably trying not to make a mistake by going too hard too soon, and waited too long."

"If he wouldn't have waited so long, I think he would have got a medal."

"It's a tough thing. You only get one chance every four years and if you make a mistake, it's a long wait."

"I have to get to school."

"See ya."

Len pushed the pace home because he had lingered at the clearing.

"You shouldn't run in the morning if you're going to be late for school," his mom said as he breezed through the kitchen toward the stairs.

"I won't be late," he said, taking two stairs at a time in his damp socks.

That afternoon the team ran easy around Town and Country. Len's legs were heavy from running more miles in the days since the race. But it was a good heavy. He liked that he was running more, and was more tired than others on the team but was still staying with them, or ahead of them, in workouts. He knew this would make a difference by the end of the season. Some of the others ran in the morning occasionally but there was no coordinated effort to get together. But he was already beginning to like running on his own in the early morning.

Len didn't run Wednesday morning because meat grinders were scheduled for the afternoon. After the warm-up, Rich smiled at Len and said, "Ready for battle, Lenny?"

"Sure," said Len.

"Ha! That didn't sound real confident," said Rich.

"I'm good."

"Okay, you want to go first this time?"

"Alright," said Len, as a pang hit his chest.

"Everyone ready?" asked Mr. Renner.

No one said anything, but they all moved to the start.

"Set!" called Mr. Renner.

They tensed into a slight crouch.

"Go!"

The teams took off in a conflux of sideways elbows, driving legs, bobbing heads, flopping hair, and flying sweat. Len went around the first turn behind several runners he knew he would beat who had got the jump on him off the line. He relaxed and stayed behind them around the curve then pulled to the outside on the long backstretch. As he moved past runners, he knew that it might cost him more than he should be spending so early in the workout. He had moved up to fifth by the time he tagged off to Rich.

Rich moved up into fourth on his leg and Len ran hard to maintain that place over the next few legs. Half-way through the workout, things began to spread out, with Len and Rich holding fifth and running close to the third and fourth place teams. The first two teams were running together a little ways ahead, but less than the first time they had done this workout.

Into the last third of the workout, Len and Rich moved into the third spot and held it. They looked up at the top two teams, but couldn't close the gap. But they didn't lose anything either.

"Good job," said Len to Rich as he bent over after finishing.

"We got better this time," said Rich.

# 53

# A Trophy and a Night Out

The next two days, the team ran easy. Len didn't run in the morning on those days. Saturday was the biggest cross country race he had ever run. There were sixteen teams with almost two hundred runners. Mark, and the seniors who had been to this race, were focused on winning a trophy. Len didn't know what to expect but was ready to do his best.

Len got dropped off at the school early that morning. The yellow school bus was already idling along the curb in front of the school in the orange dawn, but no one was in it yet. Len got on and took a seat in the middle. One by one over the next several minutes the rest of the team climbed into the bus. The bus ride to the meet was quiet. Everyone looked out the window at the expanding florid sunrise or tried to get into a position that would allow for a few more minutes of sleep. The ride took a little over an hour, out past the distant suburbs on the far side of Minneapolis, into the country. There were large fields of corn and soy beans, and small farms with well-kept yards and buildings nestled in groves of trees. Len's mind drifted looking at the rural scenery but every now and then, the race surfaced in his thoughts and the pang in his chest brought him back to the purpose of the trip.

The bus pulled into the large parking lot of a rural golf course where other buses were already lining up to park. A few teams were already walking out onto the course. The team got off of the bus and hauled a tarp out of the back to the edge of the course, spread it out on the cool, damp grass and put their spikes on top.

"Everyone ready?" asked Kent.

"Ready for what?" asked Bodine.

"Ready to hurt," said Rich with a smile.

"I'm ready to hurl," said Bodine.

"Save it for the end," said Rich as they took off for the warm-up.

They jogged slowly onto the course, which was quickly becoming crowded with teams.

"It'll go out fast," said Mark as they jogged.

"Don't get sucked out," said Kent.

"It's hard to pass too," said Phil.

Len wasn't sure what to do. He didn't want to go out too fast and die later, but he didn't want to go out too slow and not be able to pass. He decided he would follow Mark and Kent out the first quarter or half mile and just see how he felt from there. They jogged the first half of the course then came back to stretch. Some of the guys continued on to the clubhouse to use the bathroom, which had a line coming out the door. Spectators had started to arrive and wander out onto the course. The parking lot was full and cars were being routed to a newly-mown alfalfa field next to it, where they parked in scraggly lines. Some parked out along the side of the road and a line began to form there.

An announcement was made for the teams to report to the starting line. As the teams coalesced in the starting area, the first hundred yards of the course became crowded with runners doing their final warm-up sprints. The Central boys put on their spikes and walked along the starting line until they found their starting box. It was lined with white chalk on the short green grass and had room for no more than four runners in the front on the starting line. They stood in the box for a few seconds looking out onto the course, then sprinted out among the other runners. A man with a megaphone called out that it was five minutes to race time and that all runners should return to their starting boxes.

Gradually, all of the runners massed behind the starting line. Len lined up behind Kent, ready to execute his strategy. The rest of the team piled into the box alongside and behind him. A man in a reflective vest walked out to the middle of the course about thirty yards from the starting line and turned to face the fidgeting runners. The teams fell silent and turned their attention to the starter. Mark looked back at the team and said, "Let's go guys." Len tried to swallow but couldn't.

The starter slowly raised a red flag in one hand and a starter's pistol in the other hand above his head. He had a whistle in his mouth that now sent a shriek through the cool morning air. The team leaned forward and tensed, waiting for the pistol to fire. For several long seconds nothing moved, and there was no sound across the vast country. They stood like burglars in the dark bedroom of a sleeping victim who had suddenly stirred. Finally, the pistol fired. The runners tore off the line. Within the first few strides the field began to close in on Len from both sides. He felt arms and elbows bumping him right and left. Mark and Kent disappeared into the crowd in front of him. He felt as if he were running in a stampeding herd of buffalo, not knowing where he was going, and unable to stop or control his pace. He was pulled along at a pace that felt too fast, but he didn't think he should, or even could, slow down.

He came through the mile, still in the midst of a thick stream of runners, passing a loud man calling out, "5:23, 5:24" as he passed. Len realized he had been following a couple of guys from two different teams closely for a couple of minutes. Even though they weren't teammates they seemed to be working together, side by side, or at least were very close in ability and were employing the same strategy. The pace they set was challenging, but manageable for the time being, so Len clung to them into the middle of the stream. The three of them made their way up through the field, passing those who had started too optimistically. The middle mile was hillier and, with each hill, Len could feel the growing fatigue in his legs. They bumped elbows and brushed legs going around some of the tighter turns. Len didn't know if he could stay with the duo, but he knew if he dropped off of them, the race would be much harder for him. The indistinct din yelled from the sidelines by coaches, and spectators during the first mile, had subsided on the farther out second mile. It was just the breathing of the dozen runners around Len, the footfalls thudding into the ground, and the sounds of exertion emanating from those around him on a hill or turn, that filled the air. Around a clump of trees, they came to a larger crowd and the din began again. Just above it Len heard the two mile split of 10:54. He hung onto his cohort desperately, but was unsure for how much longer.

Len felt like he was running as hard as he could, not knowing how far he had left. He had still not seen any sign of the finish when they charged up a small rise where, despite his best effort, a small gap opened between him and his partners. But as he crested the rise, he saw the finish line a couple of hundred yards ahead, and pushed down the other side back up to them. His legs wobbled coming down onto the flat, but he stayed upright as they pressed harder for the finish. He felt his face contort into a grimace as he strained to stay with them. Where he had been incrementally crossing over his red line during the race, he now crossed it fully. His breaths came in wheezes as he gave everything he had left. He wasn't able to pass his companions, but he stayed near them and they pulled him into the finish. He knew he would not have run as fast or placed as high without them. Even though he had never met them and didn't know them, they had brought out his best that day.

Len crossed the finish line hearing 16:36 and within a few steps ran into the backs of his partners as they entered the chute. It was backed up and runners were now coming in three and four per second.

"Keep moving! Keep moving!" was yelled over and over by the meet workers as the spent runners bumped and stumbled their way toward the back of the chute. Len took the card that was thrust in front of him at the end and walked toward the tarp. He looked at the card. Thirty. He was surprised it was so low. Even though he had been steadily passing people, he had thought he was farther back during the race. He didn't know where any of his teammates had finished either, but he knew that he could not have run any faster.

Mark and Kent were already at the tarp.

"How did you do?" asked Kent. Len held up his card.

"16:36," said Len, "eighteen seconds faster than last week.

"Good job," said Mark.

"How did you guys do?" Len asked.

"Sixteenth," said Kent.

"Eleventh," said Mark.

"Way to go!" said Len.

Just then Phil walked up. "Thirty-nine," he said.

Len saw Rich and Rob making their way through the growing crowd of runners. Rob was talking animatedly. He looked happy. Rich smiled now and then but wasn't talking much.

"How'd you do?" asked Mark looking at Rob as they got to the tarp.

"Forty-fifth!" exclaimed Rob.

"I thought he was going to out-kick me," said Rich.

"I was just trying to stay as close to Rich as I could," said Rob excitedly. "I was elbowing guys and cutting guys off trying to stay with him. I had more contact in this race than I had all last year in football! That was a blast!"

"He came up on me with a half mile to go and said 'Let's go!' and I was like 'Oh shit, I can't let Rob beat me,'" said Rich. "I was holding on, trying not to lose any places, but when he said that, I took off and caught three guys."

"Way to go," said Mark.

"We should have put Rob out in front as a blocker the first half mile," said Kent.

"Ha! Full contact cross country," said Rob.

"I wonder what place we got," said Mark.

"Top five for sure," said Kent, "maybe higher."

Wayne came back, slumped to the tarp and began changing his shoes. He dropped his card next to him. It was sixty-seven.

Phil looked at Len. "I saw you up there the last mile but I couldn't catch you."

"There were two guys in front of me the whole way, and I just hung on to them," said Len.

"I saw you and Harris up there," Kent said to Mark.

"Yeah, after I beat him last week, he was killing himself to beat me," said Mark. "He ran tough. He was South's third runner. I'm pretty sure they won the meet unless their fourth and fifth guys tanked."

The team headed out onto the course to cool down.

"We had six guys in the top forty-five," said Kent.

"I did better than last year," said Rich. "I was fourth man last year. This year I was fifth in a better place."

"I did better than last year," said Mark.

"Me too," said Kent, "I think everyone did."

"Yeah, me too," said Phil.

"We're right there to go to state," said Kent.

Mr. Renner was back at the tarp by the time the team finished jogging.

"We got third," he said. "Let's get over to the awards ceremony."

"Good job guys!" said Mark.

"All right!  A trophy!" exclaimed Kent.

A lusty cheer went up from the boys as the team was announced as third. Mark and Kent went up for the trophy, and the boys cheered again as they brought it back. The team went back to the tarp, rolled it up and walked toward the bus. Mr. Renner came up alongside Len.

"That was a nice run today Lenny," he said.

"Yeah, it was hard though," said Len.

"You're doing fine," said Mr. Renner.

The bus ride back to school was boisterous.

"Jeff can get us in," Len heard Bodine say among the cacophony.

"Let's go!" said Rich.

"Wayne, Phil?" asked Bodine, then looked at Len, "Lenny?"

"Sure," said Wayne with a smile.

"Yeah," said Phil.

"All right!" said Bodine. "Now it's just Lenny."

"What are you talking about?" asked Len.

"*Slaughterhouse-Five*," said Rich, "It's rated R but Jeff Nelson works at the theater and can sneak us into the balcony."

"I don't know if I could get a ride," said Len.

"We'll pick you up," said Bodine, "You're already partially corrupted, we might as well finish the job."

"Ha!" laughed Rich, "His parents are going to love us."

"Okay," said Len.

He knew right away that this meant he was going to have to come up with a story that would allow him to get picked up in a car by high school guys, even if they were from the team. He had heard some of the guys talk about *Slaughterhouse-Five* and Kurt Vonnegut before. He had not talked about it with Del anymore after he had seen him reading it a couple of years earlier. The movie had just come out and some of it had been filmed in Minnesota. Bodine, Rich and Wayne had also talked about *Welcome to the Monkey House,* a collection of Vonnegut's short stories. Len had seen Wayne carrying it once after a summer practice. It was Bodine's copy but he had lent it to Wayne. On one of the easy runs, Bodine had told about reading it during the summer on his job at his dad's gas station.

"My old man and Al don't want to be bothered with pumping gas," he said. "They stay in the garage and work on cars. So I have to sit in the front. It's so boring! It's a long time between cars sometimes. My old man hates it when I read though. He says it looks like I'm not paying attention. I asked him if it looks any better if I'm sleeping, which is what I'd be doing if I didn't have a book and had to just stare out at the pumps. So he doesn't say anything anymore but I can tell he doesn't like it.

"Al says, 'Ooh, you going to be a college boy, reading all the time?' I was out pumping gas once and he came in front and picked up *Welcome to the Monkey House.* When I came back in he said, 'You're reading about monkeys? That figures. That's what they teach in school these days. You might have come from a monkey but I didn't.' I told him he was still a monkey, a grease monkey. 'So's your old man,' he said. Screw him. They're great stories."

"*Slaughterhouse-Five* could be a crazy movie," said Bodine, "It's a crazy book. I don't know how they're going to do some of those things. There's a part where Billy Pilgrim, the main character, and Montana Wildhack, a gorgeous movie star, are captured and put in a zoo on the planet Tralfamadore. They make it like a regular apartment on earth but with no ceiling or roof, just a clear dome, so the Tralfamadorians can watch them moving around the whole apartment. They're naked like zoo animals would be. Whenever they take a leak, the Tralfamadorians go wild."

"Ha!" laughed Rich, "I thought it was about World War Two."

"It is," said Bodine, "But he time travels and goes between all these events in his life. Being abducted by the Tralfamadorians is one of them."

"If they're naked on Tralfama-whatever, that's probably why it's rated R," said Rich.

"That's what I'm hoping," said Bodine.

Len had only seen nude pictures of women a couple of times. He had never seen a live one or in a movie. He felt depraved preparing a lie to go to a dirty movie, but he knew that this would not stop him from doing it. Being invited on a team activity of this sort meant his position in the brotherhood was secure.

When he got home, he drank a big glass of milk with a peanut butter and jelly sandwich, took a bath and fell asleep. When he woke, he went to the back yard, where his dad was and told him he was going to celebrate the race with the team that night. He said nothing was planned, they were just going to hang out. His dad studied him for a few seconds, then said it was fine, but he needed to be home by 10:30.

Len had never been picked up in a car from the house except by a friend's parent. He waited, trying to act casual, as if he really wasn't waiting. He was looking at the TV, but not watching it. Rich's red Mustang pulled up in front of the house.

"Bye," said Len.

"10:30," said his dad.

Len went out to the car quickly. The back door opened as he reached it. Bodine and Phil were already in the back. Wayne was in front with Rich. Len got in the back and closed the door. The car pulled slowly, quietly away and turned at the next intersection.

"We don't want to frighten your parents," said Rich.

Immediately after the turn, Rich hit the gas and pushed in an eight track Alice Cooper tape. The opening guitar strains of *School's Out* blasted from a pair of speakers behind Len. If the team had an official band, it was Alice Cooper. Someone had read that the band members had all been on their high school cross country team. The team easily saw how this could happen.

They parked near the theater and walked past the front as if not the least bit interested in whatever was playing. That was Nelson's cue. The team walked around to the side of the theater, where a door opened slowly and Nelson's head popped out. They hustled in and up a back stairway to the balcony. There were only a few people sitting up there. They sat down a couple of rows up from the rail in the center. The theater was already dark and previews were done. The movie was just beginning.

It was a strange, haunting movie to Len, not like anything he had seen before. It was split into three different parts of Billy Pilgrim's life that he traveled between. There were the World War Two parts, where he was a young prisoner of war in Dresden, Germany and survived a horrendous fire bombing of the city. There was his middle-aged life as an optometrist in Illium, New York, with an overweight wife and two kids. The third part was Billy's life on Tralfamadore, where he lived in a clear, geodesic dome with the beautiful Montana Wildhack for eternity. They had Billy and Montana wearing clothes except for a couple of brief scenes where Montana was topless, during which Len sat transfixed without blinking so as not to miss any of it.

He didn't think it could be classified as a dirty movie, so at least if he got found out, he would have that to lean on. But Bodine said the book had been banned in a lot of schools. He said a judge in Michigan called it, "depraved, immoral, psychotic, vulgar and anti-Christian." Len didn't see all that, but he also knew he wouldn't be reading it in school.

The music in the movie was classical and Len saw in the credits that it was by J.S. Bach. He liked the opening, called Largo. It was a simple, beautiful piece played by a solitary piano that had a melancholy feel. It was repeated occasionally throughout the movie with good effect. For the rest of Len's life, whenever he heard it, it brought him back to that darkened theater, his cross country friends, and the beautiful Montana Wildhack.

After the movie, they went to the A&W. They went inside and piled into a booth. There were a few other tables occupied as Len glanced around the room. But he froze and felt the pang in his chest when his eyes got to a table across the room in the corner. Randi and three other girls from his class were there. He could tell that they had noticed him. They stole glances and whispered. He hoped no one at his table would talk too loudly about what they had just seen, especially the topless woman. He would be labeled a pervert before he even had a chance to date.

"How'd you like to spend eternity with Montana Wildhack?" asked Bodine.

"I'd settle for a half-hour," said Rich.

"Fifteen minutes," said Wayne.

"Five minutes," said Phil.

"What about you Lenny?" asked Bodine.

"Yeah, I guess," said Len, smiling.

"You guess what?" asked Bodine.

"I could spend some time with her," said Len.

"Ha! She would eat him alive!" guffawed Rich.

"I'd pay to see that in a geodesic dome!" said Wayne.

"Nah, I think Lenny could hold his own," said Bodine,

"Yeah, underneath that calm exterior lurks a tiger!" said Rich.

"Wouldn't she be surprised?" said Wayne.

"Ha!  She'd be like 'Hey little boy' and he'd be all over her!" said Bodine.

Len just shook his head and smiled.

"It's always the quiet ones," said Wayne.

"Oh, now we've embarrassed him," said Rich, smiling.

Len glanced furtively over at the corner table. The girls didn't appear to have overheard, and in fact, didn't seem to be paying any attention. It looked like they had been done with their drinks for some time, but had been talking and playing with the condiments and straw sleeves for awhile. Len wished they would leave. They had seen him hanging out with high school guys but it was better to keep the details surreptitious. He felt that mystery was his ally in any new relationships that might develop with girls.

A pretty, high school waitress named Twyla, who all of the guys knew, came and took their order. Rich ordered, then said, "Lenny will have a burger and fries and a date with you."

There was good-natured laughing all around. She smiled and gave Len a dreamy look.

"Oh Lenny," she said softly, "really?"

Suddenly, Len couldn't breathe. When she had turned her gaze toward him it was like a spotlight had been turned just on him. He began to open his mouth but had nothing to say.

"What do you really want Lenny?" she asked kindly.

He thought he said fries and a root beer float, but even seconds later, as she walked away, he wasn't sure what he had said.

"You're a smooth operator," said Bodine.

"Ha!" laughed Rich, "I think she likes you."

As they waited for their food, the girls stood up from their table and walked across the room. Len glanced their way and saw a couple of glances back, but Randi was looking straight ahead. Then, just as he looked away, out of the corner of his eye, he saw Randi's delicate hand gracefully sweep her honey colored hair back from her face, and raise her eyes toward him. But did she look? He wasn't sure. They went out the door, and the self-confidence that had drained from Len under Twyla's gaze came rushing back as he realized they had seen a high school girl flirt with him. This had been a great night.

Len was back home by 10:30, as his dad was turning off the nightly news.

"Did you have a good time?" he asked.

"Yeah, we went to the A&W," said Len, and went upstairs.

# 54

# Running in the Rain

Sunday morning Len was as stiff as he had been after the first meet. He also had two small puncture wounds on the front of one shin that looked like a vampire bite where he had been spiked during the race. He had felt a sting when it happened and afterward saw the dried blood on his leg. He felt like he had been bumped, pushed and stepped on almost the whole race.

A cool, light rain was coming down as he stepped out for his long run. He had a windbreaker on and warmed up quickly. Rain had always had a calming effect on him. He slept better when put to sleep by the soft, steady beat of rain outside his window. Today was a good temperature for running he thought, and he felt good doing it in the rain. His hair flopped more heavily on his head by the time he got to the River Road, with droplets running down his face.

He ran carefully down his path through the dripping trees. He passed through the clearing and onto the path on the other side, continuing down to the river. It was drier under the limestone cliffs except for a few trickles. As he got nearer the water, sand began to cling to his shoes. At the water's edge, he looked out into the misty river valley and saw no sign that humans were, or ever had been, here. The river disappeared into the gray drizzle in both directions and the tops of the bluffs were obscured. He thought this is how it had always looked on rainy days, and probably always would. He turned back toward the bluff and ran up through the ashen mist to the top. Tom was coming down the path from the River Road in a rain coat with the hood up.

"Out for a long run?" he asked.

"Yeah, it's nice down here in the rain."

"A little slippery in places."

"That's okay, I'm going slow today because we had a race yesterday."

"How did you do?"

"I got thirtieth. There were almost two-hundred runners."

"That's pretty good."

"I got spiked," said Len, pointing to the two dots on his leg.

"What man on the team were you?"

"Third."

"You're moving up. How did your team do?"

"We were third. We got a trophy," said Len proudly.

"That's good too."

"I think we can make it to state."

"Maybe you *will* be the next great Minnesota runner."

"I hope so. I want to go to the Olympics."

"You know how the Minnesota runners made it. Just do what they did."

It started raining harder then so they parted, with Tom continuing down the path and Len running up to the River Road. Len's shoes started to squish as he neared home and his windbreaker was plastered to his skin. But he had enjoyed the run and stayed out on the front step to stretch for a few minutes.

# 55

# Three Abreast

There were no big meets now until the St. Paul City Conference, just a series of dual meets that Mr. Renner said the team would train through. The boys could tell that Mr. Renner was as excited as they were about the team's success and prospects, but he was also more guarded with his emotions. He had coached successful teams in the past but not for several years. Some years there wasn't anything he could do to motivate the team to do any more or better. Those were the worst years of coaching for him, when he wanted it more than the team. He came home from meets, and ended those seasons, frustrated, especially when he could see there was talent that had been wasted. Other years, the team had been motivated but did not have the talent. But some of the runners on those teams were the hardest workers he had ever coached. They loved to run just to run and gave their best even though they finished far back. But this year's team had both talent and motivation, and even a little luck in getting the rare ninth-grader who could run in the top five. All of the pieces were in place, Mr. Renner thought. They just had to finish it out and get the reward at the end for all of their hard work. He thought carefully about each workout, trying to find the right balance between under-coaching and over-coaching. Even though he had coached teams that had been to the state meet, he felt uncharacteristically nervous about this team. He just didn't want to blow it. It meant a lot to him and he knew it meant a lot to them. He could tell they had put their trust in him and he wanted to make sure he came through for them. He kept an even keel so as not to betray his nervousness to the team. But neither did he want them to get complacent, thinking they had done enough. After the Midland Invitational he told them, "You can't rest on your laurels. No one's going to give it to you. If you want it, you have to work for it right to the end." He took advantage of small opportunities at practice to speak a few quiet words to Mark or Kent off to the side, and they in turn, provided leadership and encouragement to the rest of the team. The team continued to gain fitness and confidence as their workout times improved in the cooler October days.

Len ran to his clearing now in the morning two or three days a week, and all the way to the river on Sundays. He stayed up with Mark and Kent more often in the longer workouts, separating himself from Phil and Rich. This provided strong motivation for Phil, who worked hard in every practice to stay as close to Len as he could. Gradually, Phil began to separate himself from Rich. The top four became strong and consistent. Rich was still doing well, but now Rob ran with him more often, placing six runners in the space where earlier there had been five.

The team practiced running as a pack in more workouts and in the dual meets. There were duals they knew they would win, so they ran them with assurance. Mark and Kent slowed their first mile a little and encouraged the rest to keep the top seven intact. The pack usually broke up in the second mile, but the meets were still won easily, with no more than one or two guys from the other teams breaking into the Central pack.

The bus picked Len up at the junior high for these meets. The rest of the team was already on the bus. In one of the meets, the team decided to all wear caps as a tribute to Dave Wottle. Len wore a blue and white striped railroad conductor's cap. The others ranged from military caps to Twins caps. The atmosphere was loose and fun on the warm-up. When the gun went off, Central's top seven went to the front, and after the first few minutes, had separated from the rest of the field. They ran together easily through the first mile, feeling and looking more like a team than ever before in their caps. Mark and Kent set the pace. Phil and Len ran right behind, then Rich and Rob. Wayne was the caboose. The pack hit the mile in 5:25.

"Good job guys," said Mark.

"Keep it going," said Kent.

Wayne dropped back halfway through the second mile, and shortly after, Rich and Rob began to fall off.

"Stay together," urged Kent.

"Get tough guys," said Mark.

Rich and Rob held on until close to the two mile mark, then a gap began to open behind Len. Phil was now beside him beginning to struggle. It was an unseasonably hot day, and despite a dry throat, Len felt good and knew he could finish at this pace. Mark and Kent kept a steady pace as they turned toward the finish. Phil now dropped back a few yards.

As they approached the finish, Kent looked over his shoulder at Len, then waved his arm and said, "Get up here Lenny!" Len came up beside him and they crossed the finish line three abreast. Phil followed six seconds later. Then came Rich eight seconds later and Rob another eight seconds later. Wayne out-kicked the other team's first runner, completing a sweep of the top seven spots. Len felt great coming across the line with Mark and Kent!

# 56

# A Well Led Team

Saturday morning, the week before the conference meet, Len rode his bike to the school for practice. The team ran over to Como Park to do three times a mile on the conference course for the last time.

"Run the first mile the same as you would in a race," said Mr. Renner. "You should feel like you're going quick, but there's more there. The second mile, you have to be aggressive. Don't settle in. Find your best pace. The third mile, you have to dig deep and bring it home like the last mile of a race. If you run it right, your mile times should be fairly even. You just have to put a little more into each mile to maintain the same pace, and by the end, you've used it all up."

Mark and Kent led a pack of six through the first mile in 5:15. Len could tell by looking at Mark and Kent that this had been for the benefit of the team, but that the pace was about to drop. It was now every man for himself.

The second mile was fast from the start, putting Rich and Rob off the back before the first turn. Phil was working hard from the get go and dropped back at the half mile. Len held on all the way but was unsure if he could do it again. The second mile had been run in 5:11, the fastest mile Len had ever run on this course.

The recovery was two minutes for this workout, whereas it had been three minutes the previous times they had done it. No one was talking now as they moved slowly around the start, waiting to lay it on the line again. The team took off for the last one. A quarter mile in, a gap began to open in front of Len.

"Come on Lenny!" yelled Kent.

Len struggled to maintain the distance, but the best he could do was to gradually lose ground. He was giving it everything he had and still felt himself slowing and his ability to move his legs waning. He came over the final rise and saw Mr. Renner standing at the finish with his stop watch. Kent had not stayed with Mark either. Len was wheezing as he finished in 5:16. He was disappointed in slowing down, but it was still the best he had ever done in this workout. The rest of the team had also run the workout well and the mood was upbeat and confident as they jogged back to the school.

"If that didn't get us ready for conference, nothing will," said Rich.

"Yeah, that was a ball buster," said Bodine.

"We ran tough," said Mark.

"You were flying on that last one," said Kent to Mark.

"Yeah, I felt good today," said Mark.

Len had come to look up to Mark for his steady leadership and unwavering optimism. He was not a senior or a captain but was a natural leader. Kent and Phil were the elected captains but felt no uneasiness or resentment toward Mark because he never tried to be more than a good teammate. He never said he was a leader, he just was. His hard work in the off-season and during the season, and his encouragement of teammates gave him credibility. He was the rock solid center of the team when courage was needed in a tough workout or race. Between the two senior captain's camaraderie with the team and Mark's consistent strength, the team was well led.

Autumn was at its brilliant peak as Len went out for his long run the next day. Red, yellow and orange blazed in a dazzling sun. Leaves were falling like snowflakes from some trees. Cars drove slowly along the River Road, their occupants oohing and aahing and pointing at the most radiant trees as if they were fireworks. Len slipped down onto his path and kept running all the way to the water, then turned and started back up. He stopped at the clearing to give his legs a break from the climb and to stretch. The crab apples that had fallen had softened in the sun and a sweet fragrance filled the clearing. The sumac had turned bright red, the cottonwoods bright yellow. The water rode higher after the fall rain and was dotted by innumerable leaves that had fallen into it from Itasca down to St. Paul. An earthy, musty smell permeated the valley as it had since the river was created, and would as long as it existed.

That week, the team felt fit and positive as they neared the conference meet. They had won all of their dual meets since the opening loss to South.

"We've improved a lot," said Mark one day.

"We've improved more than South," said Kent. "They were better at the start of the season, so they don't have as much room for improvement."

"They'll still be tough," said Mark.

"Yeah, but if we run the way I think we can, we can beat them," said Kent.

"Speak for yourself," piped in Bodine. "If I run the way I think I can, we're in trouble."

"Ha!" laughed Rich. "You have to run the way you think you can't."

"I know I can't run fast enough for us to beat South, so it's up to you guys," said Bodine.

"We can do it," said Mark.

# 57

# All-Conference

The team arrived at Como Park for the St. Paul City Conference meet on a resplendent, sunny Friday afternoon. Yellow school buses were already dispensing some of the teams in the parking lot. Other teams were searching out the best spot to set up their camp. Spectators were beginning to wander onto the course, peering around to find the start and finish area. Central hauled out their tarp and headed for the same clump of trees where they always stretched when working out here. They laid the tarp out, dropped their spikes on top and began the warm-up jog. They ran the first mile and part of the last mile of the course. They finished jogging and stationed themselves on and around the tarp to stretch.

Some of Len's junior high cross country friends had come to watch, including Russell, Steve and Paul. They stood off to the side, away from the tarp, looking at the team. Len waved them over. They walked over but became quiet as they approached, not wanting to interrupt the team's concentration or say anything dumb in their presence. Next year this would be their team too, and Len was looking forward to it. He still hung out with them, but missed spending time with them at the enjoyable junior high cross country practices. They had continued to improve this year and were the leaders of the junior high team.

Del and a friend had come to watch too. They walked over to the tarp. Del was easy to pick out because he wore nearly the same thing everyday these days: sandals with no socks, bell-bottom jeans with the hem taken out so that the bottoms were fringed, and a t-shirt with some slogan or symbol. Today his shirt had a large peace sign on the front. He wore a thin, rawhide head band around his shoulder-length hair, and had begun to grow a mustache.

"Hey, good luck, Squirt," he said as he approached Len.

"Thanks," said Len.

"So this is your brother, the jock," said Del's friend, who dressed similar to Del, except that his headband was a bandana.

"Yeah, this is him," said Del, "He's cool."

"Far out," said Del's friend, "Go get 'em kid."

Len didn't know what to say.

"Alright, show 'em what you got," said Del.

"Alright," said Len.

As the team sat changing into their spikes, Len saw Tom standing a ways off, near the starting line. The team got up and jogged out in front of the line to do their final sprints. At the end of the sprints, Len jogged over near Tom.

"Are you ready to go?" asked Tom.

"Yeah," said Len.

"Good luck," said Tom.

"Thanks," said Len, "And thanks for coming."

"I had to see you run after all the bragging you've been doing," said Tom with a smile.

"I don't brag," protested Len.

"I know, I'm just kidding. Have a good race."

Len smiled and jogged back to the team. He looked at the South runners. They usually looked confident and loose before meets, but today looked more tense and business-like. Central had run better against them at the Midland Invitational than they had at their opening dual meet or for several years. Now South looked like they were here to show that they were still at the top of the city conference heap, that any aspirations Central had of overtaking them were nonsense.

"They look serious today," said Kent.

"They're nervous. They know we're getting good," said Mark.

The team settled into their starting box in the thick grass. The starter walked out to the middle of the small field and stopped about twenty yards in front of starting line. He blew a whistle, then raised his arms above his head, one hand holding a starter's pistol, the other a red flag. The teams tensed and waited. They heard a click as the flag was dropped, and all took off. The gun had not fired but the race was on.

The South pack asserted themselves in the front. Central knew what going out too hard on this course could mean, especially when the grass had not been mown in awhile. They knew that, in this condition, the course would add a lot to the effort and to the final times. They dropped in behind the South team. The pace at the front was pushed hard and Kent began to go with it, but Mark grabbed his arm to hold him back. Kent eased off and stayed beside Mark. Len ran right behind Mark. Phil was beside Len. Rich and Rob right behind. Five Highland runners had gone out with the lead, but already looked like they were running hard. Central had beaten them in a dual meet in which they had gone out hard and faded. Len knew the pace was quick but didn't feel he was putting too much effort into it yet. He could tell that Mark and Kent weren't either. Phil had a look of commitment on his face that Len knew meant that he was fully invested today.

The lead pack navigated a series of sharp turns, then climbed a long, gradual hill to the mile mark. The South pack looked strong, but started to break up beginning the second mile. South's top two kept the pressure on and opened a gap. Stretching out behind them was a string of South and Highland runners just waiting for Central to pick off. Coming out onto the open field at halfway, spectators crowded closely on both sides of the course. The South spectators were ecstatic!

"Yeah! You own this race!" Len heard a kid in a South letter-jacket yell as the top South runners passed up ahead of him.

The voices of the Central fans, and those from the other schools, rose as Len came up to the crowd. The leaders entered the turns beginning the second half of the race. With each turn now, Central accelerated ahead of another of the faltering line of quick starters. But their pack was stringing out as well. The outcome would come down to which team could hang on the best. Len felt better now than he had at this point in the mile repeats the week before. He was moving up through the pack and determined to pass as many as he could. Phil was grimacing but hanging tough. Mark and Kent were still together, also moving up. They were right behind South's third and fourth runners. Phil and Len were with South's fifth and sixth runners. Highland's top two were hanging tough near Mark and Kent, but the rest of their team was fading.

Into the last mile, the two South runners were clear of the field and would take first and second. Mark and Kent were still battling South's third and fourth runners. The two Highland runners were still between Len and Kent, but Len had pushed out in front of the fifth South runner. Coming down the small rise onto the field for the finish, Len could see that the two South runners were done. Mark was sprinting into third place, Kent would get a close sixth. Then came the two Highland runners. Len poured it on for ninth. Just after crossing the finish line, he felt two hands on his back. He turned to see Phil in tenth. He had out-kicked the fifth and sixth South runners. Then came another Highland runner and a couple guys from other teams followed by Rich.

The team gathered back at the tarp, changed their shoes and went back onto the course for a cool down.

"That's my fastest time ever on this course," said Kent.

"Yeah, mine too," said Mark.

"We still didn't get South," said Kent.

"But that's who we have to race," said Mark. "If we race them, we won't have to worry about anyone else."

When they got back, Mr. Renner said they had taken second by ten points. Central had matched South with four All-Conference runners. Highland had the other two. At the awards, Len got a big cheer from the team and his friends when his name was announced. He was the top freshman in the race. Phil was ecstatic at getting the last All-Conference place. A photo was taken of the All-Conference runners and Len thought the South runners seemed perturbed at having their picture taken with so many Central runners. But when he looked over at Mr. Renner, he looked as happy as Len had ever seen him.

As the All-Conference runners were being positioned for their photo, Len saw Tom walking away alone far across the field. He had been surprised that Tom had come to watch. But in their brief greeting before the race Tom had seemed happy to be there and excited for his race. Len thought for the first time that maybe Tom was lonely. He had stayed away from other people down by the river, but he seemed to like Len's company and talking about running. Len wondered what he would do, how he would live, now that it was getting colder.

# 58

# On Top of the World

Len showered at the high school, then got a ride from Rich to the last junior high football game of the year. He had not been to any this season. The sun was setting and had laid a gauzy, orange apron over the wide western sky. A faint, gray half-moon hovered in the east. The field lights had come on and glared white onto the gridiron. The teams had finished their warm-ups for the second half and were massed on the sidelines, waiting for the game to begin again. Coach Shipp prowled the near sideline scowling at his minions, barking and braying his final instructions while spittle collected in the corners of his mouth. The smallest players were already taking their seats on the bench. Their body language said they had given up. The teams trotted onto the field and Len made his way to the stands to meet up with his buddies.

Settling in the stands, Len surveyed the crowd. As he looked to one side, he saw that Jan was sitting about twenty feet away, looking at him. She smiled, leaned toward him in a very feminine way, he thought, and called brightly, "How did you do today?"

Len didn't want to yell back, so he made his way over to her. Her friends surrounded her on both sides so he sat down in the row behind. The scent of her hair floated over him on a gentle breeze. He looked down at her, impressed that she even knew he had raced today. She looked up at him expectantly.

"I did good," said Len. "I was ninth and the team got second."

"Wow!" she said excitedly, "congratulations!"

He had a feeling she would have said the same thing no matter what he said.

"Thanks," said Len.

"You must be really happy!"

"Yeah, I am."

Just then one of her friends said, "Hey, Jan!"

The friend closest to her said, "She's busy flirting."

Jan blushed beautifully, Len thought, then gave her friend a funny look, and looked back up at Len and smiled. He stayed there for a few more minutes but neither one of them said anything, so Len said, "I'm going to go back and sit with them," nodding his head toward his friends. She looked at him, and he added quickly, "Not that I don't want to sit here, it's just."

"Yeah, I know," she said with a smile, "It's okay."

As the game finished, people began filtering out of the stands, groups began to disperse, and Len saw Jan part with her friends and walk alone behind the bleachers to a gate leading to the street. Len walked with his friends out of the stands, then said, "I'll catch up to you," and followed Jan. His friends looked after him with puzzled looks until Paul pointed to where Jan was standing. "We'll be at the A & W," he called.

As Len walked through the gate, Jan said, "I'm getting picked up."

"Want some company while you wait?" Len found himself asking.

"Sure," she said.

She looked over at his friends, who were now crossing the football field to a far gate.

"You can go ahead with them if you want, my mom will be here any minute," she said.

"That's ok, I'll wait with you," said Len.

The harsh glare of the field lights was pacified here by the bleachers and a row of trees lining the athletic field fence, creating a soft, shadowy glow. When Jan turned toward Len to say something, he thought she looked like one of those starlets in old movies whose close-ups were always done in a flattering light with cheese cloth over the lens. Her beautiful brown eyes widened and poured over him like chocolate syrup. He melted like a scoop of vanilla under her gaze. She looked more beautiful than he could almost stand. He saw headlights coming from the end of the block. Jan looked at the lights, then back at Len.

"That's probably my mom," she said. "She's always on time or early."

As she said this, Len's brain registered nothing to say. Then, in the awkward silence, as if drawn by a magnetic force out of his control, he leaned slowly forward. As his face came closer to hers, her eyes opened wider but she didn't move. Then she closed her eyes and lifted her chin slightly. Len closed his eyes and touched his lips gently to hers. They felt so soft, like a hint. Her fragrance enveloped him and some kind of current traveled through his entire body. He leaned slowly back. She was smiling slightly, with a dreamy, far away look on her face. He took a step further back into the shadows as the car approached.

"Bye," she said softly.

"Bye," said Len.

She turned quickly and walked out to the curb. Len turned and began to follow in the direction of his friends. He heard the car door close and the car drive away. He took in a long, deep breath. A rush of oxygen filled his body and mind. He exhaled slowly and felt on top of the world.

Once across the football field, Len broke into a run and caught up with his friends just as they reached the A&W. He was ravenous. He ordered a teen burger, fries and a root beer float, and when it came, devoured it as if he hadn't eaten in days.

At the end of the night, as he lay in bed, it seemed like he had lived a lifetime in just one day. All of the events of that thrilling, triumphant, tender day ran through his head, punctuated by the ethereal kiss. As his mind drifted through everything that had happened, the weight of the day came down onto his eyelids and he fell sound asleep, and slept for a long time.

# 59

# Making It

When Len opened his eyes in the morning, the events of the previous day were still there. He lay in bed for some minutes, feeling older, more worldly and experienced. He went for an easy run to the river and down onto his path. It was a cool, sunny morning and Tom was sitting in the clearing with a large blanket wrapped around him.

"You ran a good race yesterday," he said.

"Yeah, I got All-Conference. And there was a guy from South that beat me last year in junior high when he was at Johnson but I beat him. He's a year older than me."

"You were mentally strong. You had Sisu."

"When it gets hard in a race I think about Prefontaine when he said he could push harder and take more pain than anyone, and try to do that."

"That's when you know you've given it your best."

"Our coach says we're peaking at the right time."

"That's what counts. Are you doing a long run today?"

"No, I'm going short today. I'm tired. I'll go longer tomorrow."

"Remember when this used to be your long run?"

"Yeah, I'm in a lot better shape now."

"You're getting good."

The next day, Len felt good on his long run. The leaves were all down now, creating a leafy mat along the path, obscuring some of the roots and rocks. He was familiar with the contours of the path, but ran easy anyway down to the water. There was a turtle the size of a dinner plate sunning itself on the sand bar next to the water. Further along the bank, stood a couple of blue herons in a small, shallow inlet spearing at minnows with their long beaks.

On the way back up the path, Len glanced over at Tom's tarp on the limestone cliff and wondered if he was inside. As he ran home he thought more about Tom. When he got home his dad was in the kitchen. Len stood by the sink with a glass of water as he did after most of his runs.

"Are there any jobs at your work for people who haven't gone to college?" Len asked.

"You need some money?" his dad asked.

"It's not for me."

"Sometimes there are openings on the loading dock."

"Do you think there are any now?"

"I don't know. Do you have someone in mind?"

"There's a guy I know that might need a job."

"How do you know this guy?"

Len told him about Tom. At first his dad was alarmed, then skeptical. But as Len talked, his dad could see that this was important to Len and would have to be dealt with directly.

"I'll check and see if there's anything that might be a good fit for him," said his dad, "They might like to help out a guy like this."

Len ran easily Monday morning but took Tuesday morning off. That afternoon the team ran meat grinders, but only six instead of twelve. They finished feeling invigorated rather than exhausted.

Wednesday, Janet was working at the A&W, so the team ran there and called, "Hi Janet!" as they passed. Business was slow so Janet waved while her coworkers looked on.

Thursday the team ran six times 220 on the grass behind the school and Friday they jogged the perimeter of the practice fields.

The bus left for the region meet early Saturday morning. The race was on a wide open golf course on the far fringe of the metropolitan area. A gentle breeze blew from the west across the predominant north-south fairways. The leafless trees provided no wind block. The course ran up and down the long north-south fairways and made broad turns at the ends. There were not any tight turns or areas where runners would be crowded. There were no hills to speak of, but the course was slightly higher on the south end so that going north there was a long, very gradual downhill and going south a long, very gradual uphill. The clubhouse was on the south end and had a good view of most of the course from there. That's where the start and finish was and where the team laid their tarp.

They jogged out onto the course for their warm-up. This time when they saw the South team, they were back to their loose, confident demeanor. The team returned to the tarp to stretch and change into spikes.

"Don't get too excited at the start," said Mark, "it's a long race."

"Come on guys," said Kent.

"Let's go Lenny," said Rich to Len as they jogged out onto the course.

There were double the number of teams than the St. Paul City Conference, but only the top seven from each team would race. The starter walked out onto the course. The teams ended their final sprints and took their places behind the starting line. A whistle blew. The runners became still and there was silence out across the vast course. The runners crouched slightly as the flag went up, and sprang off the line at the sound of the gun.

The pace felt fast to Len right away. "Relax guys," said Mark. Runners from both sides closed in quickly on Central. They were further back in the pack than they had talked about, but even before the mile had began moving up through the field. Before the race Mr. Renner had said, "You can't win the race in the first mile, but you can lose it if you run it too fast." Approaching the mile, Mark and Kent had kept the team controlled and together. Now Len had to decide if he would try to stay with them or let them go as they pushed into the second mile. Even though they had checked themselves during the first mile, the pace was fast and Len was unsure if he could hold it. Phil and Rich had already made their decision and were now ten yards back. Len rounded a turn and took a quick look back. Rob was right behind Phil and Rich. Len didn't see Wayne.

Len turned to the front and pressed into the breeze. Somehow around the turn, he had lost five yards on Mark and Kent. He knew that his, and the team's, race depended on staying as close together as they could. He focused on them. Mr Renner had said, "To run as a team you don't have to be in physical contact but you have to stay in mental contact. Focus on your teammates in front of you and they will pull you along." Len had learned this was true, not only of teammates but of anyone in front of him. The two Johnson runners had pulled him along in the mile the previous spring, and the two guys at the Midland Invitational had pulled him along. He also knew that the opposite was true. In one of the dual meets when he wasn't feeling his best, he had fallen behind Phil. Instead of focusing on staying with Phil, his thoughts turned to not letting runners behind catch him. But the more he thought of them, the closer they got, and in the end he was out-kicked by two of them. He knew that his focus had to be on what he wanted, not what he did not want. He focused on Mark and Kent in front of him and thought, "Stay with them!" He thought no further ahead than that. He had come to understand that when Mr. Renner had talked about doing his best and being proud of his effort, these were the moments he was talking about. In the days following a race, it was these tough moments that were in his mind, that defined his effort, that told him if he had truly given his best. Sometimes he thought he had, but other times he knew he could have given more and resolved to do so next time.

At the end of the second mile, there was a broad turn and Len could see the entire race in front of him. South was running well, and barring a disastrous third mile, would win. After that, he could not tell. Mark was now by himself in around fifth place. Kent was around tenth. Len was around twentieth, but not that far behind Kent, with a pack of five or six in front of him. He didn't know if he could get them all, but thought he could get at least a couple if the pack broke up. He was on the long, gradual downhill section of the course and remembered what Mr. Renner had said about running downhill. He leaned slightly forward and took shorter, quicker strides, letting gravity do some of the work. He began to slowly reel in the pack.

Beginning the third mile, he looked at the pack in front of him and thought, "That's your race! C'mon, get 'em! You can do it! C'mon! C'mon!" He knew from the hardest workouts that if he talked to himself like this, urged himself on, cheered for himself, it intensified his focus and kept negative thoughts at bay. The last mile seemed to go on forever as Len's fatigue grew deeper. But he kept talking to himself, and had caught the back end of the pack as it started to break up. There was still a half mile to go and heads were rolling from side to side, arms were pumping, eyes were squinting, faces grimacing, sweat and spit were flying as they battled for precious team points. Mark had said before the race to get every runner you could because going to state could come down to just one or two points. Len tried to lift his legs faster but could not. He put his head down and pumped his arms quicker. His legs began to follow. One by one he picked off the remnants of the pack.

In the last hundred yards, Len came out the front of the pack, looked up and saw Kent not far in front of him. He saw the banner above the finish line and drove hard for it with everything he had left. He crossed the line and nearly fell over. He gasped for air. He teetered on wobbly legs. The familiar refrain of "Keep moving, keep moving" rang in his ears as he was guided through the chute. He steadied himself by putting his hands on the shoulders of the runner in front of him, as nearly all of the runners in front of him were also doing, and he felt the runner behind him doing.

Len took card fourteen at the end of the chute and walked out to find Mark and Kent waiting.

"How'd you do?" Mark asked.

"Fourteen," said Len.

"Way to go!" said Mark.

"You almost got me," said Kent, holding up his card with eleven on it.

"What were you?" Len asked Mark.

"Third," he said.

"Wow," said Len.

Just then, Phil joined them. He handed his card to Mark and bent over, hands on his knees. His card was twenty-two.

"Great job," said Mark, putting his hand on Phil's back.

Rich walked up with a worried look, then a grin spread across his face. He held up his card with twenty-eight on it. They walked back to the tarp and sat down to change shoes.

"I think we peaked at the right time," said Mark.

"Yeah, but that was a tough race," said Rich. "I felt like I was just hanging on for dear life the first two miles. Then all the sudden, in the last mile I was passing guys ... and I was slowing down!"

"I think a lot of guys went out way too fast and died in the last mile," said Kent. "I was dying in the last mile, but so was everyone around me."

"There was a pack in front of me with a mile to go and I passed them all," said Len.

"After you caught them, I started catching them," said Phil.

"I couldn't go with you," said Rob.

"We had a good race," said Mark. "I hope it's enough."

The team jogged out for their cool down. As they got back to the tarp, they saw Mr. Renner walking toward them from the scorer's table. They waited. He was walking at his usual slow pace.

"He doesn't look too excited," said Kent.

Mr. Renner walked up and seemed to notice the team for the first time.

"We got second," he said. "We're going to state!"

"Yes!" yelled Kent.

"Way to go guys!" said Mark.

"Does this mean you're going to take us out for dinner?" Rich asked Mr. Renner.

"We'll go out for dinner the night before the state meet," said Mr. Renner.

"All right, I love McDonald's!" said Kent.

"Ha!" laughed Rich, "I wish we hadn't made it!"

"No, we'll go out for a nice dinner downtown," said Mr. Renner.

"Do we have to dress up?" asked Rob.

"I think ties would be appropriate," said Mr. Renner.

"The chicks downtown don't know what they're in for," said Rich with a smile.

The team went to the awards ceremony. The team captains were called to come up and get the trophy, but Mark and Kent waved everyone along. The team marched joyously forward, thrust the trophy high and cheered for themselves. As they walked back to the tarp, Mark handed the trophy to Mr. Renner, who had a big smile on his face.

"I'm proud of you boys," he said.

# 60

# Cafe di Napoli and Pools of Water

Len woke up just after dawn to go out for his long run. A cold front had moved in overnight. It was the coldest morning of the year so far. Len could see his breath rise through the orange sunrise. A light frost had been laid across the front yard. His thick, cotton sweats were warm enough but the low crotch of the pants was slightly inhibiting and chafed the inside of his legs if he wore them for more than a couple of miles. Bodine had come up with a solution for this. He had taken the drawstring out of the pants and attached a pair of suspenders. That lifted the crotch up to his actual crotch but then the top of the pants rose to his rib cage. Nonetheless, Len thought it was a good solution and looked cool. He decided he would do the same when he had a chance.

Len didn't stop in the clearing but continued down to the water and back. He didn't see Tom that day. He guessed he was trying to stay warm in his cave. It wasn't a hard run but he felt tired at the end from the race and his heavy sweats.

It felt great all week to Len to be on a team that was going to state. The mood on the team was buoyant. Monday the team ran four times 440, but ran them together rather than as meat grinders. All seven runners stayed together. Tuesday they ran around the A&W and when they yelled, "Hi Janet!" she came running out with a camera held up high over her head in one hand, yelling, "Wait! Wait! I want to get a picture!" The team went over and posed around an outside picnic table and she took a picture. It was a sunny day and they all squinted into the camera in front of the orange facade. She got her boss to tape the picture up inside the A&W and write "Good

Luck At State!" over it. Wednesday they ran four times 220 behind the school.

"That's it," said Kent, "the last workout of the year."

"Thank god," said Rich.

"No more meat grinders until next year," said Len.

"You don't like meat grinders?" asked Mark.

"Yeah, he loves meat grinders," said Rich, and punched Len in the arm.

Thursday the team jogged around the practice fields.

Friday they got out of school early and took a bus to the state meet course at the University of Minnesota golf course under a low sky of dark, thick clouds. It had been raining all day, sometimes hard. Mr. Renner had on a pair of army-green rubber waders that came up to his chest, and a matching jacket, that he used for foul weather hunting and fishing.

"Renner's got his duck suit on today," said Rich.

"Quack," said Wayne.

"Is there a duck in here?" asked Rich.

"Quack, quack," said Wayne, louder.

"Yeah, I think so," said Kent.

"It sounds like a big one," said Rich.

"Quack!" said Wayne, louder still.

Everyone was laughing now, except Mr. Renner, who was blithely talking to the bus driver.

The team could see the large finishing banner as they pulled into the parking lot. There were a lot of other school buses already there, dispensing teams out onto the course. The ground was saturated and they sunk into the turf a little with each step, forcing out some water around the imprint of their shoes. They jogged the first two miles of the course, then stretched and did some wind sprints out of their starting box. The course had some tough hills, and some of the low spots had gotten swampy. It was already getting dark by the time they boarded the bus to go back to the school.

"It's gonna be a tough race tomorrow," said Kent.

"Yeah, it's pretty sloppy," said Mark.

"We need to get out the meat hooks," said Rich, referring to the longest spikes in their spike kit. They hadn't worn them all year, but the course was already muddy from all of the teams jogging on it. Kent was closest to the front of the bus and called, "Hey Coach, should we put in longer spikes. It's pretty sloppy out there."

"We'll get them when we get back," said Mr. Renner.

The team showered at the school while Mr. Renner got out the meat hooks, then got back on the bus to go to dinner. They all had on ties and Mr. Renner had on a sports coat as well. It had started raining again and was coming down steadily. He took the team to the Cafe di Napoli in downtown Minneapolis. It was a famous old Italian restaurant with dark wooden booths and a big mural of Naples, Italy on the wall. It was a good-sized restaurant but was filling up quickly. Mr. Renner had made a reservation, so the team got right in to a table in the middle of the room. They could tell that there was no other place in the world Mr. Renner would rather be than with his cross country team the night before the state meet.

It rained all night. It was still raining when Len got dropped off at the bus in the morning. By the time the team got to the course, the rain had slowed to an intermittent mist, but the course was inundated. Where the low spots had been swampy the day before, there were now ponds. The white chalk line laid down along the entire route was totally submerged in places, disappearing into dark pools, how deep was hard to tell. There was no wind and it had turned unseasonably muggy. The team put their tarp off to the side, dropped their spikes on top and began the warm-up.

They jogged over near the starting area, then headed out onto the course. They came over a rise half-a-mile in, down into a valley filled with water. They turned around before entering the pond, retraced their steps, then jogged part of the second mile. Even the higher parts of the course were muddy. There were ponds throughout the course, but eventually, they patched together enough running to complete the warm-up. As they returned to the tarp, Len noticed a familiar raincoat nearby. It was Tom. Standing next to him in galoshes and holding a bright floral umbrella was Lawrence. Len jogged over to them.

"Hey, you came to watch!" exclaimed Len.

"Yeah, I saw that you made it," said Tom.

"I thought you didn't follow sports," Len said to Lawrence.

"I don't, but I follow you," said Lawrence with a smile.

"I talked him in to giving me a ride out here so I wouldn't have to take the bus," said Tom.

"This is exciting," said Lawrence. "I've never been to a cross country race before."

Len smiled. "It's really muddy and there's some parts under water," said Len.

"It's the same for everybody," said Tom, then added with a smile, "If it's a pure guts race, you're the only one who can win."

"Okay," said Len, smiling.

"Good luck," said Lawrence.

"Thanks, I'll see you after the race," said Len. Then looking at Tom, he said, "There's someone I want you to meet."

Len jogged back to the tarp. The team pinned on their numbers, put on their spikes and jogged out onto the course in front of their starting box. Their legs were already streaked with mud, their shirts wet against their backs. As they did their final wind sprints, a whistle sounded, calling them to the starting line. The teams crowded into their boxes. The starter walked onto the course, farther out than in any other meet. The aggregation of the state's best high school runners, from the north woods to the southern corn fields, became still. The starter raised his red flag and starting pistol into the gray mist. Len took in a deep breath and waited. A muffled-sounding shot was fired into the air and the Central boys sprang forward into the middle of the mass of runners.

There were nineteen teams of seven and another twenty-four individual qualifiers for a total of 157 runners, all sprinting up a gradual incline to a spot fifteen yards wide a couple of hundred yards out. With each step the pressure of the pack tightened around the Central team, until it held them snugly within the driving herd.

Flecks of mud and water hurtled into the air from the back kicks of the runners in front of them, striking the fronts of their shirts and their blinking faces. Their shirts and shorts became plastered against their muculent skin.

They crested the first rise and descended into a valley of water on the other side. What was left of the white, chalk line marking the course disappeared into a turbid pond at the bottom of the hill, then reemerged fifty yards later going up the next hill. Len struggled to raise his stride high enough to get his feet out of the water. He caught sight of the backs of Mark and Kent as they rose up out of the pond on the far hill. They were about twenty runners ahead. Len pumped his arms hard when he got to the hill, hoping to stay close to them, but by the time he got to the top of the hill, he had lost sight of them.

Len felt like he was in the midst of a fast moving rapids in a winding river, carried along with the current, able to go no faster and no slower no matter how hard he tried. He rose and fell, turned left or right, with the contours of the course at a pace determined by the current of runners. He pushed to the front of those around him going up the hills, only to have them coalesce back around him coming down the other side. He was running hard just to keep his place.

His arms pumped, his quads burned coming up the last hill. At the top, he looked down the gradual slope to the finish banner through watery slits. A runner came by on his right, his quicker cadence propelling him past Len and onto others ahead. Len tried to meet the challenge but could not, and neither could the mud-caked, wheezing, sweat-drenched, grimacing, near-spent battery of runners around him. They fought each other fiercely every inch of the final straight to gain one more precious place. Len crossed the line and felt his legs begin to buckle. A large hand grabbed his arm and pulled him forward. A harsh, baritone voice barked, "Keep moving!" Runners staggered into and through the chute with more hands reaching in from the side to apply gentle, but persistent pressure to their shoulders to keep the bedraggled line moving.

Len made his way slowly through the cluster of disheveled runners back to the tarp. A wry smile came over Kent's face when he saw him.

"Have fun out there?" Kent asked.

Len opened his mouth to respond but only a hoarse croak came out. Kent smiled bigger. Len coughed and said, "Yeah, how about you?"

"Yeah, I had a lot of fun."

"What place did you get?"

"Thirty-fifth," said Kent.

"Wow, good job!"

"What place were you?" asked Kent.

Len showed him his card with sixty-seven on it.

"Nice run!" said Kent, "There probably weren't too many ninth-graders ahead of you."

Mark was there but had not said anything. "Where were you?" Len asked Mark.

"Forty-eighth," said Mark glumly.

"Good job," said Len, but knew this wouldn't cheer him up.

Phil and Rich came back together. They had finished eighty-fifth and ninety-fourth. Then came Wayne and Rob, who both finished in the low one-hundreds.

"That was crazy," said Rich, "I didn't know if you were going to get up again," he said to Phil.

Phil shook his head and looked down at his mud-smeared shirt.

"I came over a hill and saw all these guys jumping out of the way," said Rich. "Then I saw Phil on his stomach at the bottom. I caught up to him and said, 'Let's go!' but he didn't go. So I kept going, and on the last hill I heard this grunting and spitting and moaning next to me, and I look over and it's Phil getting ready to out-kick me. And I was like 'Come on, go with him!' and I did for a little while."

"Are you okay?" Kent asked Phil.

"Yeah, I don't even know what I tripped on," said Phil, "All the sudden I hit my stomach hard and was sliding down the hill. A bunch of guys passed me, but I got a lot of them back."

"I felt like I was running in a dream the whole way," said Rob, "The harder I ran, the slower it felt. Then Wayne blew by me at the end."

Just then Mr. Renner walked up, gathered the finish cards and headed to the scorer's tent.

"How do you think we did," asked Kent.

"I think we did fine," he said, "I was just watching us and South and I think we might have beat them. A couple of their top guys had bad races. It'll be close."

"It would be so great to beat South," said Kent.

"Bartley was behind me," said Mark.

"Whoa! I bet we did beat them then," said Kent, "he was All-State last year."

"Anyone feel like cooling down?" asked Mark.

There was a chorus of nahs and Mark said, "Me neither," so the team relaxed on the tarp and waited to get the results from Mr. Renner. When he hadn't come back after awhile, Rich said, "He flew south for the winter with the other ducks."

Len took the opportunity to look for Tom. He spotted Lawrence's umbrella and then Tom's rain coat not far off and went over to them.

"That looked tough," said Tom.

"Yeah, it was, but it was fun too," said Len.

"You did really well!" said Lawrence.

"Thanks," said Len.

"You've come a long way since summer when I first saw you lying on the path," said Tom.

"That seems like so long ago," said Len.

"It seems like just yesterday to me," said Tom.

"I want you to meet my dad," said Len.

This took Tom by surprise and he said, "I don't know if that's such a good idea."

"It'll be okay," said Len, "Come on."

Len brought Tom over near the tarp where parents and friends had gathered.

"Dad, this is Tom," said Len.

"Nice to meet you Tom," said his dad, and held out his hand.

Tom shook his hand and said, "Nice to meet you."

"I told my dad about you and he is going to see if there are any jobs at his work," said Len.

Tom looked at Len but didn't say anything. As much as he had enjoyed living by the river during the summer, it had gotten more difficult as the nights dipped below freezing. He also knew he needed to get a job. He had been to the Jobs Center but did not have anything yet.

"I think we can find something for you if you want it," said his dad.

"I do," said Tom.

"Can you come over to 3M Monday morning?"

"Yeah, I can do that."

"Come to building twelve and ask for Murray."

Tom looked at Len and smiled, then at his dad and said, "Okay, I'll see you Monday morning."

Len felt good and was proud of his dad.

Just then, Mr. Renner came back to the tarp with a sheet of paper in his hand.

"We got fourteenth," he said. "South was fifteenth."

"All right!" said Kent.

"Way to go guys," said Mark.

"They had a bad day, but we still beat them," said Kent.

There was an announcement that the awards ceremony would start in five minutes. The team pushed themselves up off the tarp and shuffled toward the awards stand. They listened as the team standings were announced, starting at nineteen and finishing with the champion. Then the top twenty-five runners were called to the stand, beginning at twenty-fifth. These were the All-State runners. There was a podium for the top ten, and as Len watched those runners step up into their positions, an ambition rose in him to also gain a spot on the podium. After the Olympics, just the word podium held a special meaning to him.

After the ceremony, the team shook the mud and water off of the tarp and got onto the bus. Len had come to enjoy the feeling of riding on the bus after a meet, letting the tiredness set in as the bus gently rocked along. When there was a lull in the talking, his mind usually drifted back to the race and all of the moments during it that had passed in a blur but that now made him wonder, cringe or smile. His last three races had been, as Bobby Fischer said about chess, war. He had walked away from the finish lines satisfied with his effort and the outcomes, but knew he wanted to be closer to the front of the pack by next year. He wasn't sure he could match Fischer's ruthless investment or Dan Gable's intensity, but he was excited about running and was looking forward to running more. As the bus neared the school, Len thought of Tom and hoped it would work out for him to get a job at 3M and a warm place to live.

# 61

## New Bends in the Road

Len didn't run for a couple of weeks after the state meet, during which he felt like he had too much time on his hands. He went home after school instead of to the high school. He called Wayne and borrowed Bodine's copy of *Welcome To The Monkey House*. He had never read short stories before, but it turned out to be the perfect diversion to fill his non-running time. It was bite-sized reading that he didn't have to think too hard about. The stories fit with his first impression of Vonnegut from *Slaughterhouse-Five*. They were a little crazy, a little funny, and often revealed some aspect of human nature. Each story inhabited his imagination for days afterward. He imagined himself and Jan in the roles of Newt and Catharine in "Long Walk To Forever."

He had gotten up through "Tom Edison's Shaggy Dog" by Thanksgiving, and began to feel the urge to run again. He decided Thanksgiving morning would be the day for his first run back. He had second thoughts when he woke up to a thin covering of snow over everything as he looked out the window. But he knew this would not have stopped Van or Buddy or Ron, so he got dressed and went out the door.

There was enough snow to cover the ground but not enough for anyone to shovel. It crunched under his feet as he ran toward the river. His muscles warmed under the thick sweats after a few blocks and it felt refreshing cutting through the wintery air. He turned onto the River Road into an altered landscape, devoid of all of the fading remnants of autumn that were present the last time he had run here. When he got to his path, he saw that there was one set of footprints coming up from the from the river, but none going down. Tom had been working on the loading dock at 3M for a couple of weeks. His supervisor told Len's dad that he was doing a good job. So when Tom got his first paycheck, Len's dad had filled out a reference so he could get an apartment.

Len jogged down to his clearing. The vast river valley spread out before him like never before. Without the lush flora growing and overgrowing along the banks, the view took in a wide swath of the river north and south, and across to the west. The brown water snaked between the white bluffs under a gray sky, with the dark, barren trees in relief against the frosted banks. The air seemed fresher and cleaner than ever. Smooth, thin sheets of ice covered parts of the river, interspersed with equal-sized areas of open water. A large flock of Canada geese was on the river, their clamorous honking echoing through the valley. A huge flock of cawing crows answered in the trees along the bank. Len had never heard such a racket here.

He jogged back up the path, slipping a little with each step on the smooth leaves beneath the snow, and ran easily back to his house feeling a light stiffness growing in his legs. He had decided to begin running as he had during the summer, a few times a week as he felt the desire. He had also decided to run farther on some days, pushing up into Van's high school range of seven to ten miles. He thought of Van running in temperatures way below zero and in a couple of feet of snow. He wasn't sure he would do that, but he would wait for that time to come before deciding.

There had been a couple of snowfalls that stayed on the ground by late December, so Len's runs were along shoveled sidewalks with growing piles of snow on either side. He started his runs after getting home from school as the sun touched the horizon. He often witnessed brief but stunning sunsets that displayed gorgeous parts of the color spectrum that defied naming. Sometimes it touched something poignant inside him, like a minor chord in a sad song. As the sky darkened, he felt the familiarity of the same penumbral winter evenings in which he had delivered newspapers. The same lights came on in the same houses, the same people settled in to watch the evening news or prepare their dinner. Even as he whisked silently past without their knowledge, he felt comfort from the warm glow of their windows.

He had not run on the River Road recently because the snow pushed aside by the street plow was piled up on the dirt path. Nor was the path to his clearing runnable. But he wanted to see what it looked like in the snow, so one day during Christmas break he ran to the river and along the River Road to the top of his path. He walked unsteadily down the path, his feet sinking into the smooth crystalline snow a few inches with each step. At the clearing, he stopped and looked out onto the wide, hoary valley. The entire river was now covered with ice except for a few dots of open water. The far side of the river was an intricate silhouette of dark, barren trees against the snowy bank. He continued slowly down to the bottom of the limestone cliffs, that now had ice deposits hanging from them where water had seeped through the cracks. He walked to the river. It looked like he could walk all the way to the other side across the ice but he knew this was probably deceptive. He felt cold. He turned back onto the path and started to trudge up to the River Road. He glanced over toward Tom's cave and was glad that Tom was not living there anymore. His feet were covered with snow and his toes had begun to get numb. When he reached the top he stamped the snow off his feet and started running slowly for home. He felt uncoordinated as he began to run, but gradually warmed as he went.

Len began to extend his Sunday runs farther out along the River Road. It was his only run during the week done entirely in the daylight, and he had discovered it was a day when there was little traffic on the road. As much as he had begun to enjoy his evening runs through the neighborhood, he looked forward to these long runs along the river. As he ran farther to parts of the river he had never been, each new bend in the road lured him on to see what was beyond it. He felt a part of a running lineage of all those who had run along it before him. A lineage that began with Buddy Edelen and continued through Ron Daws and Van Nelson to him.

In early January, a big snow storm hit and Len ran through large falling flakes as they piled up on the sidewalk. People were just getting home from work but hadn't shoveled yet so he ran through six inches of new snow, thinking of Van. The storm was followed by a biting shot of cold Arctic air. The sidewalks were cleared of the storms remnants, so he decided to run in the twenty below zero temperature just to see how it felt. He put on a pair of long underwear, with his thick sweats over that. On top, he put a t-shirt, long sleeve turtle neck and his thick sweatshirt that hung down over the top of the sweatpants, which were now held up by suspenders, creating a double thick layer across his mid-section. Over this he put a wind breaker. Finally, he put on his thick stocking hat rolled up into a double layer on the bottom over his ears and wool mittens and went out the door.

He started right out at a good clip and felt the cold for the first few minutes, but then began to generate enough heat to create a layer of warmer air next to his skin under the loose clothing. It was a great run! His legs felt good and he moved along at a steady pace. He felt satisfied when he finished, knowing that most of those he would compete against in the spring had not run this day.

As the cold streak eased and the temperature rose above zero for the first time in three days, Len went out for his long Sunday run. Where zero had previously felt cold, it now felt warm. He felt good as he turned onto the River Road under a blue sky made gray by hazy muslin clouds. He had not decided how far he would run, just that he wanted to run very long. The air felt fresh and invigorating on his face. He didn't push the pace but ran steady. He got to the farthest point he had ever been and decided to go farther, out around a big bend in the river. There were no houses on this bend, only a park on one side of the road and the river, far below the bluff on the other. As he ran further around the bend, the river widened and the tip of an island came into view. He continued running to see if he could see the other end of the island. It came in another several minutes. It looked like the island was about a mile long, reposed in the middle of the river like a sleeping giant. He saw the river merge together again even wider on the far side of the island, gaining momentum and strength as it cut its way across the continent. There was a scenic overlook on the side of the road and he stopped for a minute to stretch. He had been running for almost an hour.

He started home and was able to keep the same pace for about half the way back before his legs started to stiffen and his energy began to wane. Even as his pace slowed, Len pushed on, driven by the thought of Buddy and Ron doing runs of up to thirty miles and making themselves into Olympians. His growing fatigue was of a different kind than what he experienced during cross country training and racing. But it felt good to him, like he was taking his body somewhere it had never been. He got back to his house in a little over two hours. Later that day and for the remainder of the day, his legs felt warm, like there was more blood in them than before. The next morning, he was stiff getting out of bed and moving around throughout the day. But the day after, as the stiffness eased, his legs felt stronger than they had before the long run, and he understood the importance of what he had done.

# 62

# Running Long

Over the years, it was this stretch of the River Road where Len developed his ability to run long and fast. For the rest of high school and throughout his collegiate running at the university and after, in all seasons and weather, nearly all of his long runs were done here. He enjoyed the runs when he brought teammates along, but also the times he ran alone. It was those times when he went the longest and pushed the hardest. He ran out past the island, and beyond. His favorite runs were those done in a fresh dawn or hazy twilight as the sky reflected light, shadow and mood onto the water. On his longest runs it felt like the road would go on forever, tracing the iconic river into some romantic American infinity. On most runs, he went at a comfortable pace on the way out but gradually dropped the pace on the return so that the second half was several minutes faster than the first. Sometimes on the way back, his pace increased easily, with little effort, his body running as if it were made just for this. He discovered a couple more trails down the bluff to the river further out and explored them. He rarely saw other people on them so, like his path, it was a mystery to him how they came to be. They looked like they had been there a long time. Every year, off one of the trails somewhere along the river, he saw a tent or tarp or line strung between two trees that indicated someone was living there, at least temporarily. He never approached any of them or discovered who any of the people were. He assumed most were there due to some unfortunate life circumstance, but knew that some may have been drawn there by a desire to rekindle a remote and latent connection to the river that has bound innumerable souls to it and to one another.

# 63

## Tom's Ashes

Len began to get chilled as the sun lowered in the purple western sky across the river. He was glad he had come to his path and the clearing to run. It was the best place to remember Tom, and what Tom had meant to him, from the day they had met on the path until now. After Tom's funeral, Len would come back to spread his ashes down below the limestone cliff as Tom had asked. Even though Tom had moved out of the cave when he got the job at 3M, he still came back and camped here a few weekends each summer. And sometimes, over the years, Len and Tom had come here to run together.

Len worked his legs up into a jog going back up to the River Road and along the paved path to his car. He stretched for a few minutes in the soft, mauve twilight. As he got in the car, a boy ran out from the neighborhood and crossed the River Road onto the path. The boy was coltish with floppy hair and a t-shirt he would have to grow into. "I wonder if he knows that Olympians and near-Olympians have run here?" thought Len. "Will he be the next great Minnesota runner?" The boy ran in the direction of Len's path and Len wondered if he would ever venture off the paved path down into the enduring Mississippi River valley. Would he discover the clearing and the gnarly old crab apple tree? Or the path down through the limestone cliff to the water, and the sandy shore? Or the cave in which Tom had lived?

Len slowly drove back through the neighborhood, along his old running route past his parents house and the Corner Market. As he drove, he thought of Tom, the river and running, and all the things that had happened since he met Tom on the path so long ago. He had not run in the Olympics, but he had been close. He ran in the Olympic Trials and at Hayward Field in front of the great crowd. He had also run in Munich and Tokyo. He ran several marathons through spectator-lined streets and understood even more what Buddy and Ron had felt. Tom had been with him at the Olympic Trials and at Hayward Field. He was a part of the clapping, stomping crowd as Len ran his fastest 10,000 meter race ever. He had been with Len at high school and college meets and seen him step up onto the podium at state and NCAA meets. They had gone to see Billy Mills together when he came to St. Paul to talk. They went up and talked to him afterward and Billy remembered Tom from the prison. Billy said he was proud of Tom for turning his life around and was glad that he was still running. They met Buddy Edelen when he was inducted into the Minnesota Distance Running Hall of Fame. They laughed afterward about how excited Buddy still was about running, even though he did not run very far or fast anymore. They went to hear Ron Daws speak about his Olympic experience, training and Lydiard's influence. At the talk, Daws displayed several of his water-color paintings of famous runners. Several years later, Len was surprised to learn that a friend's daughter attended the school where Van Nelson was a teacher. Len contacted him, and he and Tom spent an enjoyable afternoon with Van, listening to stories of his training and racing that enriched what they already knew.

Even though Len had not become an Olympian, he had watched as other Minnesota distance runners who ran on the River Road had: Garry Bjorklund, Steve Plasencia, Janis Klecker, Bob Kempainen and Carrie Tollefson. He had become friends with several of them. But it was Tom who was his best and oldest running friend, who had helped him become a runner in 1972, and he was going to miss him.

Made in United States
Orlando, FL
03 April 2022